Grammar Sense 2

TEACHER'S BOOK

Cheryl Pavlik

OXFORD

UNIVERSITY PRESS

OXFORD

UNIVERSITY PRESS

198 Madison Avenue
New York, NY 10016 USA

Great Clarendon Street
Oxford OX2 6DP England

Oxford New York

Auckland Bangkok Buenos Aires Cape Town Chennai Dar es Salaam
Delhi Hong Kong Istanbul Karachi Kolkata Kuala Lumpur Madrid
Melbourne Mexico City Mumbai Nairobi São Paulo Shanghai Taipei
Tokyo Toronto

OXFORD is a trademark of Oxford University Press

ISBN 0-19-436574-3

Editorial Manager: Janet Aitchison
Senior Editor: Stephanie Karras
Editor: Jeff Holt
Art Director: Lynn Luchetti
Design Project Manager: Mary Chandler
Designer (cover): Lee Anne Dollison
Production Manager: Shanta Persaud
Production Controller: Eve Wong
Composition: Lyndall Culbertson

Cover image: Kevin Schafer/Peter Arnold, Inc.

Printing (last digit): 10 9 8 7 6 5 4 3 2 1

Printed in Hong Kong

Contents

Series Introduction

Series Director: Susan Kesner Bland

Grammar Sense: A Discourse-Based Approach

Grammar Sense is a comprehensive three-level grammar series based on the authentic use of English grammar in discourse. The grammar is systematically organized, explained, and practiced in a communicative, learner-centered environment, making it easily teachable and learnable.

Many people ask, why learn grammar? The answer is simple: meaningful communication depends on our ability to connect form and meaning appropriately. In order to do so, we must consider such factors as intention, attitude, and social relationships, in addition to the contexts of time and place. All of these factors make up a discourse setting. For example, we use the present continuous not only to describe an activity in progress *(He's working.)*, but also to complain *(He's always working.)*, to describe a planned event in the future *(He's working tomorrow.)*, and to describe temporary or unusual behavior *(He's being lazy at work.)*. It is only through examination of the discourse setting that the different meanings and uses of the present continuous can be distinguished from one another. A discourse-based approach provides students with the tools for making sense of the grammar of natural language by systematically explaining *who, what, where, when, why,* and *how* for each grammatical form.

SYSTEMATICALLY ORGANIZED SYLLABUS

Learning grammar is a developmental process that occurs gradually. In *Grammar Sense* the careful sequencing, systematic repetition, recycling, review, and expansion promote grammatical awareness and fluency.

Level 1 (basic level) focuses on building an elementary understanding of form, meaning, and use as students develop basic oral language skills in short conversations and discussions. Level 1 also targets the grammar skills involved in writing short paragraphs, using basic cohesive devices such as conjunctions and pronouns.

At **Level 2 (intermediate level)** the focus turns to expanding the basic understanding of form, meaning, and use in longer and more varied discourse settings and with more complex grammatical structures and academic themes. Level 2 emphasizes grammar skills beyond the sentence level, as students begin to initiate and sustain conversations and discussions, and progress toward longer types of writing.

Finally, at **Level 3 (high intermediate to advanced level)** the focus moves to spoken and written grammar in academic discourse settings, often in contexts that are conceptually more challenging and abstract. Level 3 emphasizes consistent and appropriate language use, especially of those aspects of grammar needed in extended conversations and discussions, and in longer academic and personal writing.

INTRODUCTION OF FORM BEFORE MEANING AND USE

Form is introduced and practiced in a separate section before meaning and use. This ensures that students understand what the form looks like and sounds like at the sentence level, before engaging in more challenging and open-ended activities that concentrate on meaning and use.

FOCUS ON NATURAL LANGUAGE USE

Grammar Sense uses authentic reading texts and examples that are based on or quoted verbatim from actual English language sources to provide a true picture of natural language use. To avoid unnatural language, the themes of the introductory reading texts are only subtly touched upon throughout a chapter. The focus thus remains on typical examples of the most common meanings and uses.

Exposure to authentic language helps students bridge the gap between the classroom and the outside world by encouraging awareness of the "grammar" all around them in daily life: in magazines, newspapers, package instructions, television shows, signs, and so on. Becoming language-aware is an important step in the language learning process: Students generalize from the examples they find and apply their understanding to their independent language use in daily living, at work, or as they further their education.

SPECIAL SECTIONS TO EXTEND GRAMMATICAL KNOWLEDGE

Understanding grammar as a system entails understanding how different parts of the language support and interact with the target structure. *Grammar Sense* features special sections at strategic points throughout the text to highlight relevant lexical and discourse issues.

- **Beyond the Sentence** sections focus on the structure as it is used in extended discourse to help improve students' writing skills. These sections highlight such issues as how grammatical forms are used to avoid redundancy, and how to change or maintain focus.

- **Informally Speaking** sections highlight the differences between written and spoken language. This understanding is crucial for achieving second language fluency. Reduced forms, omissions, and pronunciation changes are explained in order to improve aural comprehension.

- **Vocabulary Notes** provide succinct presentations of words and phrases that are commonly used with the target structure, such as time expressions associated with the simple past, or the use of *say, tell*, and *ask* in reported speech.

- **Pronunciation Notes** show students how to pronounce selected forms of the target language, such as the regular simple past ending *-ed*.

STUDENT-CENTERED PRESENTATION AND PRACTICE

Student-centered presentation and practice allow learners at all levels to discover the grammar in pairs, groups, and individually, in both the Form and in the Meaning and Use sections of each chapter. Numerous inductive activities encourage students to use their problem-solving abilities to gain the skills, experience, and confidence to use English outside of class and to continue learning on their own.

FLEXIBILITY TO SUIT ANY CLASSROOM SITUATION

Grammar Sense offers teachers great flexibility with hundreds of intellectually engaging exercises to choose from. Teachers may choose to skip chapters or sections within chapters, or teach them in a different order, depending on student needs and time constraints. Each Student Book is self-contained so teachers may choose to use only one book, or the full series, if they wish.

Components at Each Level

- The **Student Book** is intended for classroom use and offers concise charts, level-appropriate explanations, and thorough four-skills practice exercises. Each Student Book is also a useful reference resource with extensive Appendices, a helpful Glossary of Grammar Terms, and a detailed Index.

- The **Audio Cassettes** and **CDs** feature listening exercises that provide practice discriminating form, understanding meaning and use, and interpreting non-standard forms.

- The **Workbook** has a wealth of additional exercises to supplement those in the Student Book. It is ideal for homework, independent practice, or review. The Answer Key, on easily removable perforated pages, is provided at the back of the book.

- The **Teacher's Book** has many practical ideas and techniques for presenting the Form and the Meaning and Use charts. It also includes troubleshooting advice, cultural notes, and suggestions for additional activities. The Answer Key for the Student Book and the complete Tapescript are also provided.

- **TOEFL®-Style Tests** and Answer Keys, along with advice on conducting the tests and interpreting the results, are available for teachers to download from the Internet. (See www.oup.com/elt/teacher/grammarsense)

Tour of a Student Book Chapter

Each chapter in *Grammar Sense* follows this format:

The **Grammar in Discourse** section introduces the target structure in its natural context via a high-interest authentic reading text.

• Authentic reading texts show how language is really used.

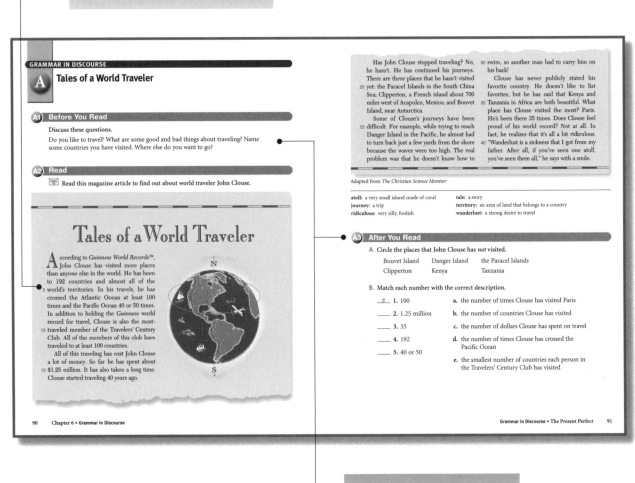

GRAMMAR IN DISCOURSE

A Tales of a World Traveler

A1 Before You Read

Discuss these questions.

Do you like to travel? What are some good and bad things about traveling? Name some countries you have visited. Where else do you want to go?

A2 Read

Read this magazine article to find out about world traveler John Clouse.

Tales of a World Traveler

According to *Guinness World Records™*, John Clouse has visited more places than anyone else in the world. He has been to 192 countries and almost all of the world's territories. In his travels, he has crossed the Atlantic Ocean at least 100 times and the Pacific Ocean 40 or 50 times. In addition to holding the *Guinness* world record for travel, Clouse is also the most-traveled member of the Travelers' Century Club. All of the members of this club have traveled to at least 100 countries.

All of this traveling has cost John Clouse a lot of money. So far he has spent about $1.25 million. It has also taken a long time. Clouse started traveling 40 years ago.

Has John Clouse stopped traveling? No, he hasn't. He has continued his journeys. There are three places that he hasn't visited yet: the Paracel Islands in the South China Sea; Clipperton, a French island about 700 miles west of Acapulco, Mexico; and Bouvet Island, near Antarctica.

Some of Clouse's journeys have been difficult. For example, while trying to reach Danger Island in the Pacific, he almost had to turn back just a few yards from the shore because the waves were too high. The real problem was that he doesn't know how to swim, so another man had to carry him on his back!

Clouse has never publicly stated his favorite country. He doesn't like to list favorites, but he has said that Kenya and Tanzania in Africa are both beautiful. What place has Clouse visited the most? Paris. He's been there 35 times. Does Clouse feel proud of his world record? Not at all. In fact, he realizes that it's all a bit ridiculous. "Wanderlust is a sickness that I got from my father. After all, if you've seen one atoll, you've seen them all," he says with a smile.

Adapted from *The Christian Science Monitor*

atoll: a very small island made of coral
journey: a trip
ridiculous: very silly, foolish
tale: a story
territory: an area of land that belongs to a country
wanderlust: a strong desire to travel

A3 After You Read

A. Circle the places that John Clouse has *not* visited.

| Bouvet Island | Danger Island | the Paracel Islands |
| Clipperton | Kenya | Tanzania |

B. Match each number with the correct description.

__e__ 1. 100   a. the number of times Clouse has visited Paris

____ 2. 1.25 million   b. the number of countries Clouse has visited

____ 3. 35   c. the number of dollars Clouse has spent on travel

____ 4. 192   d. the number of times Clouse has crossed the Pacific Ocean

____ 5. 40 or 50   e. the smallest number of countries each person in the Travelers' Century Club has visited

• Structured reading tasks help students read and understand the text.

The **Form** section(s) provides clear presentation of the target structure, detailed notes, and thorough practice exercises.

• *Inductive **Examining Form** exercises encourage students to think about how to form the target structure.*

FORM

B   The Present Perfect

Examining Form

Look at the sentences and complete the tasks below. Then discuss your answers and read the Form charts to check them.

1a. He has crossed the Atlantic many times.
1b. He crossed the Atlantic in 1999.

2a. They flew to Paris last night.
2b. They have flown to Paris many times.

1. Which two sentences are in the simple past? Which two sentences are in the present perfect? How many words are necessary to form the present perfect?

2. Underline the verb forms that follow *has* and *have*. These are past participles. Which form resembles the simple past? Which form is irregular?

3. Look back at the article on page 90. Find five examples of the present perfect.

Affirmative Statements

SUBJECT	HAVE/HAS	PAST PARTICIPLE	
I	have		
You			
He She It	has	traveled flown	to Paris.
We	have		
You			
They			

CONTRACTIONS			
I've			
She's		traveled	to Paris.
They've			

Negative Statements

SUBJECT	HAVE/HAS	NOT	PAST PARTICIPLE	
I	have			
You				
He She It	has	not	traveled flown	to Paris.
We	have			
You				
They				

CONTRACTIONS			
I	haven't		
She	hasn't	traveled	to Paris.
They	haven't		

Yes/No Questions

HAVE/HAS	SUBJECT	PAST PARTICIPLE	
Have	you		
Has	it	traveled flown	to Paris?
Have	they		

Short Answers

YES	SUBJECT	HAVE/HAS	NO	SUBJECT	HAVE/HAS + NOT
	I	have.		I	haven't.
Yes,	he	has.	No,	he	hasn't.
	they	have.		they	haven't.

Information Questions

WH- WORD	HAVE/HAS	SUBJECT	PAST PARTICIPLE	
Who	have	you	seen?	
What				
Why	has	she		
How long	have	they	been	in the hospital?

WH- WORD (SUBJECT)	HAS		PAST PARTICIPLE	
Who	has		traveled	to Paris?
What			happened?	

• The past participle of a regular verb has the same form as the simple past (verb + -d/-ed). See Appendices 4 and 5 for the spelling and pronunciation of verbs ending in -ed.
• Irregular verbs have special past participle forms. See Appendix 6 for a list of irregular verbs and their past participles.

B4) Completing Conversations with the Present Perfect

A. Complete these conversations with the words in parentheses and the present perfect. Use contractions where possible.

Conversation 1

Silvio: How long _____ have _____ you _____ lived _____ (live) here?
                        1   2

Victor: Five years. _____ you _____ (be) here long?
                              3   4

Silvio: No, I _____ (not). I _____ only
                      5   6

_____ (be) here for six months.
     7

Conversation 2

Gina: Hi, Julie. I _____ (not/see) you for a long time.
                        1

Julie: Hi, Gina. I think it _____ (be) almost three years since we last
                                  2

met. How _____ your family _____ (be)?
            3   4

Gina: Oh, there _____ (be) a lot of changes. My older brother, Chris,
                      5

_____ (get) married, and Tony and his wife, Marta,
       6

_____ (have) two children.
       7

B. Practice the conversations in part A with a partner.

B5) Building Sentences

A. Build eight logical sentences: four in the present perfect and four in the simple past. Punctuate your sentences correctly.

Present Perfect: *She has been a good friend.*   Simple Past: *She went to a restaurant.*

		been	for a long time
she	have	waited	to a restaurant
they	has	learned	a good friend
		went	English

B. Rewrite your sentences as negative statements.

• *Clear and detailed **Form Charts** make learning the grammar easy.*

• *A wealth of exercises provide practice in manipulating the form.*

The **Meaning and Use** section(s) offers clear and comprehensive explanations of how the target structure is used, and exercises to practice using it appropriately.

• *Inductive **Examining Meaning and Use** exercises encourage students to analyze how we use the target structure.*

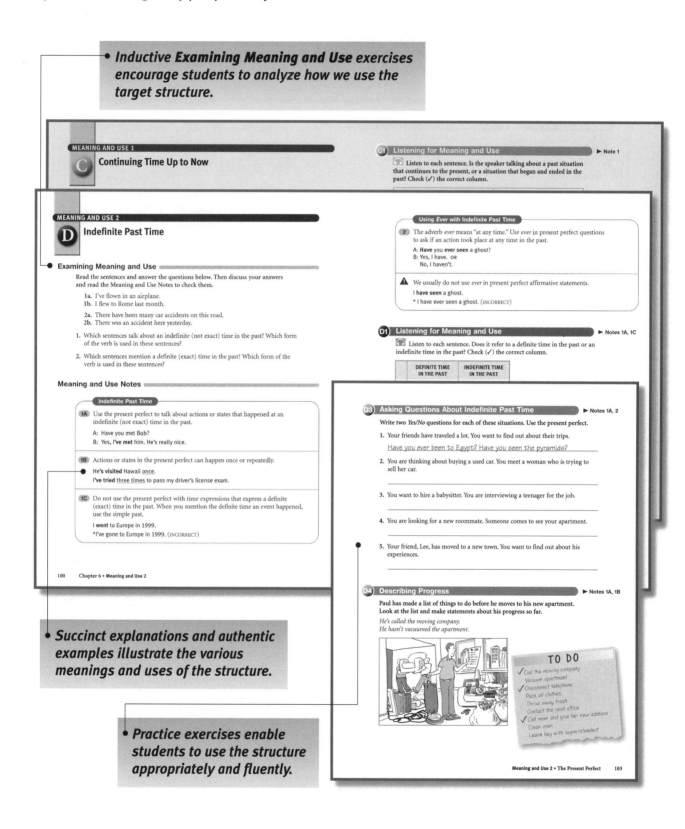

MEANING AND USE 1

C **Continuing Time Up to Now**

C1 **Listening for Meaning and Use** ► Note 1

🔊 Listen to each sentence. Is the speaker talking about a past situation that continues to the present, or a situation that began and ended in the past? Check (✓) the correct column.

MEANING AND USE 2

D **Indefinite Past Time**

Examining Meaning and Use

Read the sentences and answer the questions below. Then discuss your answers and read the Meaning and Use Notes to check them.

1a. I've flown in an airplane.
1b. I flew to Rome last month.

2a. There have been many car accidents on this road.
2b. There was an accident here yesterday.

1. Which sentences talk about an indefinite (not exact) time in the past? Which form of the verb is used in these sentences?

2. Which sentences mention a definite (exact) time in the past? Which form of the verb is used in these sentences?

Meaning and Use Notes

Indefinite Past Time

1A Use the present perfect to talk about actions or states that happened at an indefinite (not exact) time in the past.
A: Have you met Bob?
B: Yes, I've met him. He's really nice.

1B Actions or states in the present perfect can happen once or repeatedly.
• He's visited Hawaii once.
I've tried three times to pass my driver's license exam.

1C Do not use the present perfect with time expressions that express a definite (exact) time in the past. When you mention the definite time an event happened, use the simple past.
I went to Europe in 1999.
*I've gone to Europe in 1999. (INCORRECT)

100   Chapter 6 • Meaning and Use 2

Using *Ever* with Indefinite Past Time

2 The adverb *ever* means "at any time." Use *ever* in present perfect questions to ask if an action took place at any time in the past.
A: **Have** you **ever seen** a ghost?
B: Yes, I have. OR
No, I haven't.

⚠ We usually do not use *ever* in present perfect affirmative statements.
I **have seen** a ghost.
* I **have ever seen** a ghost. (INCORRECT)

D1 **Listening for Meaning and Use** ► Notes 1A, 1C

🔊 Listen to each sentence. Does it refer to a definite time in the past or an indefinite time in the past? Check (✓) the correct column.

DEFINITE TIME IN THE PAST	INDEFINITE TIME IN THE PAST

D3 **Asking Questions About Indefinite Past Time** ► Notes 1A, 2

Write two *Yes/No* questions for each of these situations. Use the present perfect.

1. Your friends have traveled a lot. You want to find out about their trips.
   Have you ever been to Egypt? Have you seen the pyramids?

2. You are thinking about buying a used car. You meet a woman who is trying to sell her car.
   _____

3. You want to hire a babysitter. You are interviewing a teenager for the job.
   _____

4. You are looking for a new roommate. Someone comes to see your apartment.
   _____

5. Your friend, Lee, has moved to a new town. You want to find out about his experiences.
   _____

D4 **Describing Progress** ► Notes 1A, 1B

Paul has made a list of things to do before he moves to his new apartment. Look at the list and make statements about his progress so far.
He's called the moving company.
He hasn't vacuumed the apartment.

TO DO
✓ Call the moving company
Vacuum apartment
✓ Disconnect telephone
Pack all clothes
Throw away trash
Contact the post office
✓ Call mom and give her new address
Clean oven
Leave key with superintendent

Meaning and Use 2 • The Present Perfect   103

• *Succinct explanations and authentic examples illustrate the various meanings and uses of the structure.*

• *Practice exercises enable students to use the structure appropriately and fluently.*

The **Review** section allows students to demonstrate their mastery of all aspects of the structure. It can be used for further practice or as a test.

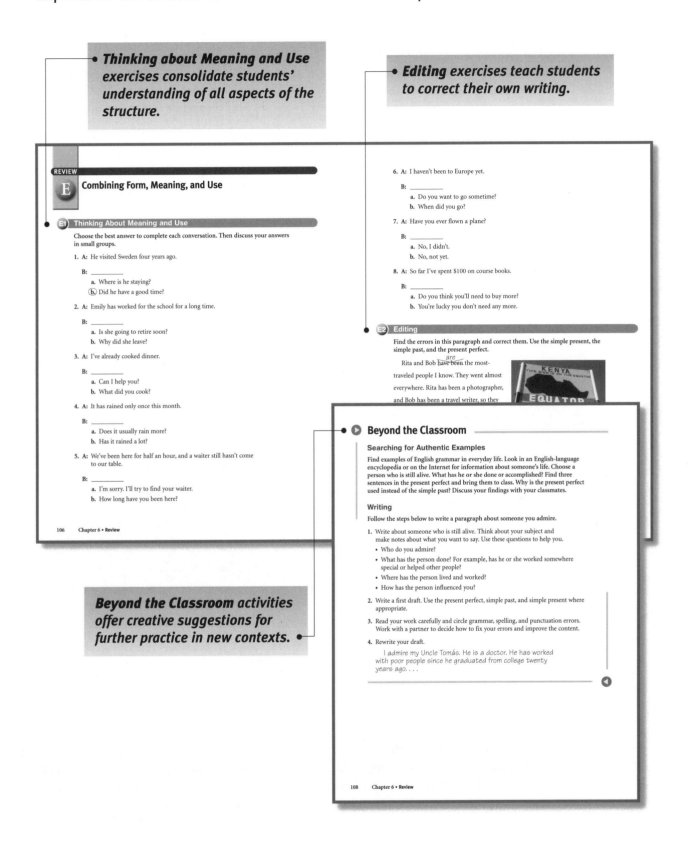

• Thinking about Meaning and Use exercises consolidate students' understanding of all aspects of the structure.

• Editing exercises teach students to correct their own writing.

Beyond the Classroom activities offer creative suggestions for further practice in new contexts. •

E Combining Form, Meaning, and Use

E1 Thinking About Meaning and Use

Choose the best answer to complete each conversation. Then discuss your answers in small groups.

1. **A:** He visited Sweden four years ago.

   B: _____
      a. Where is he staying?
      ⓑ Did he have a good time?

2. **A:** Emily has worked for the school for a long time.

   B: _____
      a. Is she going to retire soon?
      b. Why did she leave?

3. **A:** I've already cooked dinner.

   B: _____
      a. Can I help you?
      b. What did you cook?

4. **A:** It has rained only once this month.

   B: _____
      a. Does it usually rain more?
      b. Has it rained a lot?

5. **A:** We've been here for half an hour, and a waiter still hasn't come to our table.

   B: _____
      a. I'm sorry. I'll try to find your waiter.
      b. How long have you been here?

6. **A:** I haven't been to Europe yet.

   B: _____
      a. Do you want to go sometime?
      b. When did you go?

7. **A:** Have you ever flown a plane?

   B: _____
      a. No, I didn't.
      b. No, not yet.

8. **A:** So far I've spent $100 on course books.

   B: _____
      a. Do you think you'll need to buy more?
      b. You're lucky you don't need any more.

E2 Editing

Find the errors in this paragraph and correct them. Use the simple present, the simple past, and the present perfect.

   Rita and Bob have been the most-
traveled people I know. They went almost
everywhere. Rita has been a photographer,
and Bob has been a travel writer, so they

▶ Beyond the Classroom

Searching for Authentic Examples

Find examples of English grammar in everyday life. Look in an English-language encyclopedia or on the Internet for information about someone's life. Choose a person who is still alive. What has he or she done or accomplished? Find three sentences in the present perfect and bring them to class. Why is the present perfect used instead of the simple past? Discuss your findings with your classmates.

Writing

Follow the steps below to write a paragraph about someone you admire.

1. Write about someone who is still alive. Think about your subject and make notes about what you want to say. Use these questions to help you.
   • Who do you admire?
   • What has the person done? For example, has he or she worked somewhere special or helped other people?
   • Where has the person lived and worked?
   • How has the person influenced you?

2. Write a first draft. Use the present perfect, simple past, and simple present where appropriate.

3. Read your work carefully and circle grammar, spelling, and punctuation errors. Work with a partner to decide how to fix your errors and improve the content.

4. Rewrite your draft.

   I admire my Uncle Tomás. He is a doctor. He has worked
with poor people since he graduated from college twenty
years ago. . . .

Special Sections appear throughout the chapters, with clear explanations, authentic examples, and follow-up exercises.

• Pronunciation Notes *show students how to pronounce selected forms of the target language.*

• Beyond the Sentence *sections show how structures function differently in extended discourse.*

• Pronunciation Notes

Pronunciation of Verbs Ending in *-ed*

The regular simple past ending *-ed* is pronounced in three different ways, depending on the final sound of the base form of the verb.

1. The *-ed* is pronounced /t/ if the verb ends with the sound /p/, /k/, /tʃ/, /f/, /s/, /ʃ/, or /ks/.
   work – worked /wɔrkt/   wash – washed /wɑʃt/   watch – watched /wɑtʃt/
2. The *-ed* is pronounced /d/ if the verb ends with the sound /b/, /g/, /dʒ/, /v/, /ð/, /z/, /ʒ/, /m/, /n/, /ŋ/, /l/, or /r/.
   plan – planned /plænd/   judge – judged /dʒʌdʒd/   bang – banged /bæŋd/
   bathe – bathed /beɪðd/   massage – massaged /məsɑʒd/   rub – rubbed /rʌbd/
3. The *-ed* is also pronounced /d/ if the verb ends with a vowel sound.
   play – played /pleɪd/   sigh – sighed /saɪd/   row – rowed /roʊd/
   bow – bowed /baʊd/   sue – sued /sud/   free – freed /frid/
4. The *-ed* is pronounced as an extra syllable, /ɪd/, if the verb ends with the sound /d/ or /t/.
   guide – guided /ˈgaɪdɪd/   remind – reminded /rɪˈmaɪndɪd/
   rent – rented /ˈrɛntɪd/   invite – invited /ˌɪnˈvaɪtɪd/

B3 Pronouncing Verbs Ending in *-ed*

🎧 Listen to the pronunciation of each verb. Which ending do you hear? Check (✓) the correct column.

	/t/	/d/	/ɪd/

• Vocabulary Notes

More Adverbs with the Present Perfect

Never means "not ever" or "not at any time." We can use *never* instead of *not* in negative statements. Do not use *never* with *not*. *Never* comes before the past participle.
   She has **never** been to Greece.

Already means "at some time before now." Use *already* with questions and affirmative statements. It comes before the past participle or at the end of a sentence.
   She has **already** left.   Have they **already** eaten?   What has he **already** done?
   She has left **already**.   Have they eaten **already**?   What has he done **already**?

Yet means "up to now." Use *yet* with negative statements and *Yes/No* questions. It comes at the end of a sentence.
   They haven't arrived **yet**.   Have you met him **yet**?

Still also means "up to now." It has a similar meaning to *yet*, but with the present perfect is used only in negative statements. It comes before *have* or *has*.
   She **still** hasn't called. (= She hasn't called yet.)

So far means "at any time up to now." Use *so far* in affirmative and negative statements and in questions. It comes at the beginning or end of a sentence.
   So far he's spent $500.   How much money have you spent **so far**?
   So far I haven't had a good time.   Have you had a good time **so far**?

D5 Using Adverbs with the Present Perfect

A. Rewrite these sentences. Place the word or words in parentheses in an appropriate position in each sentence. Use contractions where possible.

Conversation 1

A: Have you asked Sara to help you (yet)?
   Have you asked Sara to help you yet?

B: No, I haven't asked her (still).
   _____
                                  2

Conversation 2

A: Have you played golf (ever)?
   _____
                                  1

B: No, I've played golf (never).
   _____
                                  2

104   Chapter 6 • Meaning and Use 2

• Beyond the Sentence

Introducing Background Information with the Past Continuous

The past continuous and simple past often occur together in the same story. The past continuous is used at the beginning of a story to describe background activities that are happening at the same time as the main events of the story. The simple past is used for main events.

   Yesterday <u>was</u> beautiful. The sun **was shining**, the birds **were singing**, and I **was walking** in a valley. Suddenly, a UFO <u>landed</u> on the ground. Three small green men <u>appeared</u>. They <u>took</u> my hand and <u>said</u>, "Come with us."

C4 Introducing Background Information with the Past Continuous

A. Work with a partner. Imagine that each sentence is the beginning of a story. Write two sentences in the past continuous to give background information.

1. The beach was gorgeous. <u>The sun was shining on the water. The waves</u>
   <u>were moving quickly.</u>

2. The bank was full of customers. _____
   _____

3. The students were late to class. _____

4. My boss was very angry. _____

• Informally Speaking

Reduced Forms of *Have* and *Has*

🎧 Look at the cartoon and listen to the conversation. How is the underlined form in the cartoon different from what you hear?

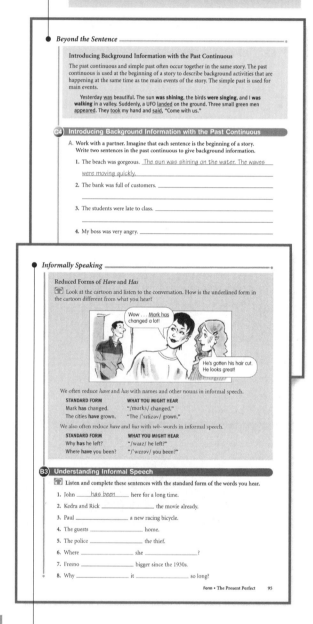

We often reduce *have* and *has* with names and other nouns in informal speech.

STANDARD FORM	WHAT YOU MIGHT HEAR
Mark **has** changed.	"/mɑrks/ changed."
The cities **have** grown.	"The /ˈsɪtizəv/ grown."

We also often reduce *have* and *has* with *wh-* words in informal speech.

STANDARD FORM	WHAT YOU MIGHT HEAR
Why **has** he left?	"/waɪz/ he left?"
Where **have** you been?	"/ˈwɛrəv/ you been?"

B3 Understanding Informal Speech

🎧 Listen and complete these sentences with the standard form of the words you hear.

1. John ___has been___ here for a long time.
2. Kedra and Rick _____ the movie already.
3. Paul _____ a new racing bicycle.
4. The guests _____ home.
5. The police _____ the thief.
6. Where _____ she _____?
7. Fresno _____ bigger since the 1930s.
8. Why _____ it _____ so long?

Form • The Present Perfect   95

• Vocabulary Notes *highlight the important connection between key vocabulary and grammatical structures.*

• Informally Speaking *sections show the differences between written and spoken language.*

Teacher's Book Introduction

Susan Iannuzzi

About the Teacher's Book

THE CHAPTERS

- **Overview:** Each chapter of the Teacher's Book begins with an overview of the grammar presented in the Student Book chapter. It enables the teacher to focus on the main points covered in the chapter, and highlights difficulties students may have with the structures.

- **Grammar in Discourse:** This section provides directions to help the teacher effectively teach the Before You Read, Read, and After You Read activities in the Student Book. It suggests creative ways to activate background knowledge, offers innovative reading strategies, and gives tips on checking comprehension.

- **Form:** This section offers two alternative ways to teach the inductive Examining Form exercises: Method 1 for students who are unfamiliar with the structure and may need extra support, and Method 2 for students who are already familiar with the structure and may be able to work more independently. The section also contains step-by-step instructions for presenting the Form Charts, and directions for utilizing the Special Sections such as Informally Speaking.

- **Meaning and Use:** This section offers advice on teaching the inductive Examining Meaning and Use exercises. It also provides step-by-step instructions for presenting the Meaning and Use Notes and directions for using the Special Sections such as Vocabulary Notes and Beyond the Sentence.

- **Trouble Spots:** These notes, placed at strategic points throughout the Teacher's Book, alert the teacher to problems that students may have with the grammar. They suggest how to address these problems effectively, and, where relevant, direct the teacher to parts of the Student Book that clarify or offer practice of the grammar point.

- **Cultural Notes:** These occasional notes give background about American culture that students typically do not know, and that may help their understanding of the topic in the Student Book. The teacher can relay this information to students as appropriate.

- **Additional Activities:** The Student Book provides extensive practice of each grammatical structure. However, for teachers who want to give further practice, each Teacher's Book chapter contains at least one additional writing or speaking activity. In most chapters there is also an activity called Returning to Grammar in Discourse, which has students return to the Grammar in Discourse reading at the beginning of each chapter and demonstrate their understanding of key meanings and uses of the target structures in the chapter.

AT THE BACK OF THE BOOK

- **Student Book Tapescript:** A complete tapescript is available for every listening activity in the Student Book.

- **Student Book Answer Key:** The Teacher's Book contains the answers to all the Student Book exercises. (The answers are not available in the Student Book.)

Teaching Techniques for the Grammar Classroom

TEACHING STUDENTS AT THE INTERMEDIATE LEVEL

Students at this level probably will have been exposed to the form, as well as the meaning and use, of most grammar structures presented in the Student Book. Although they may have good control of the form of many of these structures, they will need additional practice of the key structures, such as continuous and perfect verb forms. Students at this level may find that the meaning and use rules that they were taught do not always hold true, which can cause frustration and anxiety. *Grammar Sense 2* can help students at this level work through these issues because it focuses on appropriate meaning and use in specific contexts and provides a wealth of exercises to expand their grammar knowledge.

PRESENTING THE FORM SECTIONS

Examining Form Exercises

One of the most challenging aspects of teaching grammar is finding clear and concise ways to present new forms to students. The Examining Form exercise in each chapter is a series of inductive tasks in which students work on *identifying* the target structure and its most important structural features. In these exercises, students are asked to return to the reading text in the Grammar in Discourse section of the chapter, and follow the steps to recognize or systematically analyze key aspects of the form (such as the number of different parts in a structure, the addition of suffixes, word order, agreement, and so on). This serves as an introduction to the structural features illustrated and explained in the Form Charts, which students may then consult to check their answers.

Form Charts

In chapters with particularly challenging structures, you may need to help students work through and internalize the information in the Form Charts before they start on the form exercises. The following is a compilation of some of the most successful techniques for guiding students through this section. Choose appropriate techniques based on your teaching style, class size, class level, and students' previous experience with the grammar point. Most importantly, vary the techniques you use to accommodate the different learning styles of your students—some students may prefer to read and discuss every example in the chart before moving on to the exercises, while others may need to study the material less intensively.

Whole Class Techniques

1. After students have finished the Examining Form exercise, ask them to close their books. Elicit examples of the target grammar from the reading text by asking questions that will produce the target grammar. When possible, personalize your questions. For example, to elicit possessive pronouns, hold up a book and ask, *Whose book is this?* with the aim of eliciting responses such as *It's his. It's mine.* When students answer, write their responses on the board. If a student gives an incorrect response (e.g., *It is her.*), you should still write it on the board. Incorrect answers are as valuable as correct ones, because they can be used to focus students' attention on the structure. Likewise, if a student answers correctly but uses a different structure than the one you wish to focus on (e.g., *It's her book.*), write this answer on the board and ask if anyone knows an alternative response (e.g., *It's hers.*). Write students' responses on the board, then have them open their books to the Form Charts and find sentences that use the same structures as those on the board.

2. To focus more closely on the various parts of a structure, copy the chart headings onto the board, or construct other types of contrastive charts (e.g., *-s/-es/-ies*, or singular/plural, etc.). Elicit examples from the reading text to illustrate each point, or ask students to create their own examples. Have individual students come to the board and fill in the charts.

Then ask the rest of the class to decide if their examples are correct or not, and to explain why.

3. After students have finished the Examining Form exercise, ask them to silently review the Form Charts for a few minutes. Assess their understanding of the charts by asking questions about the form. For example, for *Yes/No* questions in the present tense, you might ask *Where is the subject? What word does the question begin with? How many* Yes/No *question forms are there?* In this way, you will be able to judge whether students have fully understood the form of the target grammar.

Pair or Group Work Techniques

1. Divide students into pairs or small groups. Assign each group a Form Chart and ask them to read and study the information. Then ask each group in turn to present the form in their chart to the rest of the class. Students can use their own example sentences to aid their presentation, in addition to those provided in the book.

2. Divide students into pairs or small groups. Write two correct sentences and one incorrect sentence on the board. (Make sure the error is one of *form*, not meaning and use.) Tell students that one sentence is incorrect. Ask them to work together to identify the incorrect sentence by looking at the Form Charts. Some students may know the answer without using the charts, but ask them to point to the information or example in the chart that shows why it is incorrect. This insures that they know how to interpret the charts.

PRESENTING THE MEANING AND USE SECTIONS

Examining Meaning and Use Exercises

Once students have grasped the form of a given structure, the next challenge is to find creative and engaging ways to help them understand the meaning and use. The Examining Meaning and Use exercises do just this by offering carefully constructed examples, often in the form of minimal pairs, and asking students to use contextual cues to draw inferences about key aspects of meaning and use. These inductive tasks serve as an introduction to the features of meaning and use that are further elucidated in the Notes that follow.

Meaning and Use Notes

Students need to read and absorb the Meaning and Use Notes before starting the exercises. What follows are some techniques for helping students work through the Meaning and Use Notes. Regardless of the technique you choose, it is important that you have a clear understanding of the scope of the Meaning and Use Notes before you present them. In some instances, a particular structure may have multiple meanings and uses, but the chapter will not address all of them. In Levels 1 and 2, certain meanings and uses of structures are omitted to avoid overwhelming the students with too much information, while in Level 3, basic meanings and uses may be de-emphasized in order to focus on more complex issues.

Whole Class Techniques

1. Give students an opportunity to read and ask questions about the Meaning and Use Notes. Check their understanding by writing several original sentences on the board and asking them to match the meaning and use in each sentence to the Meaning and Use Notes. With more advanced students you can include a few incorrect sentences among the examples and have students identify correct and incorrect meanings and uses. Before you do this, be sure you have a firm grasp of the meaning and use you are focusing on so you can clearly explain why the examples you provided are correct or incorrect.

2. If there are several Meaning and Use Notes, or if you think students will find the content challenging, have them read and demonstrate their understanding of one Note at a time. Once they have read the Note, elicit sentences that demonstrate the meaning and use of the Note they just read. For example, to elicit sentences with *used to* when talking about a

situation that was true in the past but is not true now (Student Book 2, page 65, Note 1A), have students talk about something they did when they were younger but don't do today. This should elicit sentences such as *I used to eat a lot of candy. I used to play baseball every summer.*

Pair or Group Work Techniques

1. Divide students into pairs or small groups. Assign each pair or group a Note and ask students to study it. Then ask each pair or group to present their Note to the rest of the class. Students can create their own example sentences to aid their presentation, in addition to those provided in the book. Again, be sure you fully understand the meaning and use in question so you can tell students whether their examples are correct or incorrect and, most importantly, *why* they are correct or incorrect.

2. Divide students into pairs or small groups. Have each pair or group read one Note and create two example sentences to illustrate the information presented in the Note. Ask each pair or group to come to the front of the class to explain the Note and write their example sentences on the board. Ask the class if the sentences are correct examples of the information in the Note. If not, call on individual students to suggest alternate correct sentences.

General Teaching Techniques

Grammar Sense contains a wealth of exercises covering all four skills areas: reading, writing, listening, and speaking. Depending on your students, curriculum, and time frame, these exercises can be taught in many ways. Successful grammar teaching requires skillful classroom management and teaching techniques, especially in the areas of elicitation (drawing information from students), grouping procedures (groups, pairs, or individuals), time management (lengthening or shortening exercises), and error correction (peer or teacher correction, correction of spoken or written errors).

ELICITATION

Elicitation is one of the most useful teaching techniques in the grammar classroom. In essence, elicitation draws information out of the students through the use of leading questions. This helps students to discover, on their own, information about grammar forms as well as meanings and uses. For example, to elicit the difference in meaning between a gerund and an infinitive when used after the verb *stop*, write the following sentences on the board: *Alan stopped to smoke. Alan stopped smoking.* Then, in order to elicit the difference in meaning between the two sentences, ask questions such as, *In which sentence are we talking about a smoker? Which sentence is about a reformed (or ex-) smoker?* These questions require students to analyze what they know about the grammar and make inferences about meaning.

Knowing when to elicit information can be difficult. Too much elicitation can slow the class and too little elicitation puts students in a passive position. Avoid asking students to judge whether something sounds natural or acceptable to them because, as non-native speakers, they will not have the same intuitions about English as native speakers.

GROUPING STUDENTS

Group work is a valuable part of language learning. It takes away the focus from the teacher as the provider of information and centers on the students, giving them the opportunity to work together and rely on each other for language acquisition. Shyer students who may be less likely to speak out in class have an opportunity to share answers or ideas. Your class level will inform how you approach group work. Be sure to circulate among groups to monitor the progress of an activity, particularly at lower levels, and to answer any questions students cannot resolve on their own. Although students at the higher levels are more independent and can often manage their own groups, be attentive to the activities at hand, ready to offer feedback and keep everyone on-task. In classes where the level of students is uneven, try varying the composition of the groups to make the learning process interesting for everybody. Sometimes you can pair up a higher-level student with a lower-level student to give him or her an opportunity to help another classmate. However, other times you may want to group all the higher-level students together and offer them additional, more challenging activities. It is useful, especially in discussion activities, to conclude with a culminating task in which one or more students report back something (results, a summary) to the rest of the class using the target structure. This helps to refocus the class on the structure and provide a conclusion to the activity.

TIME MANAGEMENT

Some exercises are divided into steps, making it possible to shorten an activity by assigning part of it for homework or by dividing the class into two groups and assigning half the items to each group. Similarly, exercises can be lengthened. Many of the exercises in *Grammar Sense* require students to ask for or offer real-life information. You can ask students to create additional sentences within these activities, or have them do an activity again with a different partner. If your class does an activity well, ask them to focus on other aspects of the form, for example, transforming their affirmative sentences into negative ones, and vice-versa.

CHECKING EXERCISES

How you check exercises with students will depend on the level you are teaching. Having students check their answers in pairs or groups can be an effective technique, because it makes students revisit their work and resolve with other students the mistakes they have made. With lower levels, this requires careful teacher supervision. It is also possible at all levels to check exercises as a class, elicit corrections from students, and offer necessary feedback. It is often useful, especially for correcting editing exercises, to use an overhead projector. Be careful not to single out students when correcting work. Aim instead to create a supportive atmosphere whereby the class learns through a group effort.

CORRECTING ERRORS

Students can often communicate effectively without perfect grammar. However, in order to succeed in higher education or the business world, they need to demonstrate a high level of grammatical accuracy, and to understand that even a small change in form can sometimes result in a significant change in meaning. As students become aware of this, they expect to be corrected. However, their expectations as to how and when correction should be offered will vary. Many teachers have difficulty finding the optimal amount of correction—enough to focus students on monitoring errors, but not so much as to demoralize or discourage them. It is important to target specific types of errors when correcting students, rather than aiming to correct everything they say or write. The focus of the current lesson and your knowledge of your students' strengths and weaknesses will dictate whether you focus on form, pronunciation, meaning, or appropriate use. Discuss error correction with your students and determine how *they* would like to be corrected. Aim to combine or vary your correction techniques depending on the focus of the lesson and the needs of your students.

Spoken Errors

There are a variety of ways to correct spoken errors. If a student makes an error repeatedly, stop him or her and encourage self-correction by repeating the error with a questioning (rising) tone, or by gesturing. Develop a set of gestures that you use consistently so students know exactly what you are pointing out. For example, problems with the past tense can be indicated by pointing backwards over your shoulder, future time can be indicated by pointing your hand ahead of you, and third person can be shown by holding up three fingers. (Be careful not to choose gestures that are considered offensive by some cultures.) If your students feel comfortable being corrected by their peers, encourage them to help each other when they hear mistakes. Another option is to keep track of spoken errors during an activity, and then at the end elicit corrections from the class by writing the incorrect sentences you heard on the board. This way, students are not singled out for their mistakes, but get the feedback they need.

Written Errors

It is important to encourage students to monitor their written errors and learn strategies to self-correct their writing. Establish a standard set of symbols to use when marking students' work. For example, *pl* for *plural, agr* for *agreement, s* for *subject, v* for *verb*. When you find an error, do not correct it, but instead mark it with a symbol. Students will have to work out the exact nature of their error and correct it themselves. This will reduce your correction time and encourage students to learn for themselves by reflecting on their errors. Peer correction is another useful technique by which students can provide feedback on a partner's work. In order for it to be effective, give students clear and limited objectives and do not expect them to identify all the errors in their classmate's work. Note that students may be resistant to peer correction at first, and nervous about learning others' mistakes. But once they develop a trust in one another, they will be surprised at how much they can learn from their classmates.

1 The Simple Present

Overview

The simple present is most commonly used to talk about repeated activities such as habits, routines, and scheduled events (e.g., *I always take the bus to school. She never eats breakfast. Class starts at 9:00 A.M.*). For repeated activities, frequency is often expressed with adverbs such as *always, sometimes,* and *never.* The simple present is also used to describe general truths, scientific facts, and definitions (e.g., *Housing in New York City is expensive. Stars emit light in many colors.* Climate *means "typical weather conditions in a place."*). It is also used with stative verbs to talk about states or conditions such as physical descriptions and feelings (e.g., *Dinner smells good. I hate the cold weather.*).

Form: The key challenges are remembering

- the final *-s* for third-person singular (*he, she,* and *it*).
- the *do/does* auxiliary in negative statements and in *Yes/No* and information questions.

A GRAMMAR IN DISCOURSE

Mysterious Island

A1: Before You Read

- Write the word *island* on the board. Elicit its meaning (land smaller than a continent completely surrounded by water). Explain that the class will be reading about an unusual island.

- Put students into pairs and have them discuss the questions. Explain that there are no right or wrong answers, and encourage them to give their opinions.

- Bring the class together and have each pair write the names of countries they listed on the board. Leave the lists on the board for future reference.

A2: Read

- If students are using the *Grammar Sense* series for the first time, write the word *glossary* on the board. Elicit or explain that the glossary gives the meanings of important words in the quiz and that these words may be new to them. Encourage students to use the glossary before turning to a bilingual dictionary.

- Call on individuals to read one point in the geography quiz aloud.

- Have students work in pairs to discuss the questions in the quiz. Tell them to check their answers on page 5.

A3: After You Read

- Give students a few minutes to answer the true/false questions on their own. Tell them to underline the sentences (in the quiz and in the answer key to the quiz) that gave them the answer.

- Have students compare their answers with a partner's. If any of their answers do not match, remind them to return to the text and underline the sentence that gave them the answer.

- Call on individuals to read a true/false statement aloud and give their answer. If a student needs help, ask for volunteers from the class.

- For a follow-up activity, put students into pairs with books closed. Ask them to write down as much information about Iceland as they can remember. Finally, share the information as a class to see who remembered the most.

The Simple Present

EXAMINING FORM

Method 1

(For students not familiar with the structure)

- **Question 1:** Call on individuals to read sentences 1a–1c aloud. Write the verbs on the board. *(sell, sells)* Ask *What is different about the verb in 1b?* (It ends with an *s*.) Ask which verb is singular and which is plural, and have students identify the subject of each verb to help reveal the answer. *(I sell, He sells, We sell)*

- **Question 2:** Point out that sentences 2a–2c are negative. Call on different students to read them aloud. Ask *What is different about the verb in 2b?* (It has a different form, *doesn't.*) Ask which verb is singular and which is plural, and have students identify the subject of each verb to help reveal the answer. *(You don't buy, She doesn't buy, They don't buy)*

- **Question 3:** Put students in pairs to find two more examples each of affirmative and negative sentences in the geography quiz on page 4. Elicit examples from different pairs.

- **Question 4:** Ask students which question would get a *yes* or *no* answer. (a; Explain that this type of question is called a *Yes/No* question.) Then ask students which question asks for specific information. (b; Explain that this type of question is called an information question.) Have students study the form of the two questions and describe how they are different. (The information question begins with a *Wh-* question word.)

  - Have students refer to the charts to check their answers and study the new structures.

Method 2

(For students familiar with the structure)

- Have students work in pairs to answer the questions.

- Give students a few minutes to refer to the charts to check their answers and review the structures.

- Call on students to go over the exercise. Discuss any disagreements and have students make any necessary corrections.

FORM CHARTS

- Copy the following chart on the board:

ORIGINAL SENTENCE	CREATE
He eats ice cream	*Yes/No* question
	Negative short answer
	Affirmative short answer
They go to school.	Information question (with *where*)
	Information question (with *who*)

- Have students work in pairs to change the sentences as directed. Tell them to write their work on a piece of paper.

- Have them exchange papers with another pair and check their answers. Then have them swap back.

- Discuss any disagreements and have students refer to the charts to check their answers and make any necessary corrections.

Pronunciation Notes: Pronunciation of Verbs Ending in -s or -es (p. 9)

- Play the recording.

- Read the pairs of verb forms in number 1. *(stop – stops, like – likes, laugh – laughs)* Then read them again and have students repeat after you. Elicit or explain that in these words the *-s* ending sounds like an /s/. Write the verbs *eat, walk, sit, cook,* and *sleep* on the board. Call on students to read individual words and then say the third-person singular forms.

- Read the pairs of verb forms in number 2. *(leave – leaves, run – runs, go – goes)* Then read them again and have students repeat after you. Elicit or explain that in these words the *-s* ending sounds like a /z/. Write the verbs *go, send, hug, dream,* and *buy* on the board. Call on students to read individual words and then say the third-person singular forms.

- Read the pairs of verb forms in number 3. *(notice – notices, buzz – buzzes, watch – watches)* Then say them again and have students repeat after you. Elicit or explain that in these words the *-es* ending sounds like /iz/. Emphasize that for these words we are adding an extra syllable. Have students tap their desks as they pronounce two syllables for each verb. Write the verbs *wash, match, kiss, mix,* and *exercise* on the board. Call on students to read individual words and then say the third-person singular forms.

C MEANING AND USE

The Simple Present

EXAMINING MEANING AND USE

- Have students work in pairs to answer the questions. (1. c; 2. a; 3. b)
- Give students a few minutes to refer to the Notes to check their answers.
- Call on students to read the questions and answers aloud. Discuss any disagreements and have students make any necessary corrections.

MEANING AND USE NOTES

- There are four Notes in this section. Divide the class into four groups (or four pairs, if possible) and assign each group a Note. Explain that each group will teach the class about one of the Notes by explaining the information and reading the example sentences aloud.
- Have each group read their Note and write three new example sentences collectively. Circulate, helping as necessary.
- When they are finished, have one student from each group write their new sentences on the board, and have another group member read them aloud. Ask the class if the sentences use the simple present correctly. Discuss any disagreements and make any necessary corrections.

ADDITIONAL ACTIVITIES

Writing and Speaking: What Makes You Different?

In this activity students will have the opportunity to use the simple present to write and speak about themselves.

- Tell students to write five unique things they do that they think their classmates do not do. Remind them to use the simple present.

For example:
> *I sew clothes for my family.*
> *I drive my father to work.*
> *I don't eat meat.*
> *I cook gourmet meals.*
> *I study English six hours every day.*

- Have students walk around the class and ask other students if they do or don't do these things. For example, *I sew clothes for my family. Do you? Yes, I do. / No, I don't.*
- Tell students that if they find someone who does what they do, they must cross it off their list.
- Have students compare their results. Ask students if anyone did not cross off any item or if anyone crossed off all items on their list.

Writing: Imaginary People

The purpose of this activity is for students to practice using the simple present while writing a paragraph about an imaginary person.

- Bring in (or ask students to bring in) pictures of ordinary (not famous) people from magazines.
- Let each student choose a picture and write a paragraph about that person. The paragraph should answer questions such as these:
  > What is her or his name?
  > Where is she or he from?
  > Where does she or he live?
  > What does she or he do?
  > What does she or he like to do?
  > Who does she or he look like?
  > Is she or he married?
- You may wish to add more questions or have the class brainstorm questions to answer. Remind students not to include the questions in their paragraphs.
- Call on volunteers to read their paragraphs aloud.
- Review students' papers to correct any errors in form, meaning, or use, especially of the simple present.

Returning to Grammar in Discourse

The purpose of this activity is to check students' understanding of key meanings and uses of the target structures in the chapter by having them return to the quiz at the beginning of the chapter and apply what they have learned.

- Write the following extracts from the quiz on the board (or type them up and photocopy them before class). Have students work in pairs to find them in the quiz. Make sure they read the complete sentences that these extracts come from.

  1. *The interior of this island nation contains incredible contrasts.*
  2. *Icelanders eat fresh fruit and vegetables all year, . . .*
  3. *In the summer the sun doesn't go down . . .*

- Now write the following items on the board:
  a. *a repeated activity*
  b. *a scientific fact*
  c. *a state or condition*

- Have students think about the use of the simple present in each extract and match each one to the letter of the item above that best describes it. (1. c; 2. a; 3. b)

- Bring the class together. Call on pairs to give their answers, and have them offer explanations. If students still have problems, revisit the Meaning and Use Notes.

2 Imperatives

Overview

Imperatives are used for commands, advice, requests, directions, instructions, warnings, and offers. When used for commands, they usually signal authority of the speaker over the listener. Adding *please* softens a command and is often a good idea if students are not sure (e.g., *It's hot in here. Please open a window.*). The subject *you* is rarely used, though it is understood to be the subject. If the speaker is addressing a specific person, *you* can be used after the person's name (e.g., *Dan, you do the dishes and I'll cook dinner.*).

Form: The form of the imperative is not usually difficult. Some students may have problems with the negative imperative (e.g., *Don't be angry.*); they may use *not* without *do,* particularly when the negative imperative verb is *be* (e.g., **Be not angry.*).

A GRAMMAR IN DISCOURSE

Do's and Don'ts with Bears

A1: Before You Read

- Write the phrase *Do's and Don'ts* on the board. Elicit or explain the meaning (a list of things to do and not to do in a particular situation). Brainstorm examples of situations that you might find such a list about (e.g., *learning English, sailing a boat, giving a speech*).

- Put students into small groups and give them a few minutes to discuss the questions.

- Call on several students to share their experiences with the class, especially those who have encountered bears.

A2: Read

- Tell students to read the leaflet to find out about the do's and don'ts with bears. Ask *Are there more do's or don'ts?*

- Elicit from the students the do's and don'ts and write them on the board in two columns. Your list will look like this:

DO'S	DON'TS
Make noise.	Hike at night.
Stay in your car.	Run.
Burn food waste.	Fight.
	Climb a tree.
	Keep food in your tent.

A3: After You Read

- Have students do this exercise individually and then compare their answers with a partner. Remind them to note the places in the article where they found their answers.

- Go over any difficult or problematic items with the whole class.

- For a round-up activity, ask the class *Was this article helpful? Are you more or less eager to hike in the woods?*

B FORM

Imperatives

EXAMINING FORM

Method 1
(For students not familiar with the structure)

- **Question 1:** Have four students write one sentence each (a, b, c, or d) on the board and underline the verb in the sentence *(are; do not climb; do not attack; lie, be)*. Ask the class if the correct words have been underlined and make corrections if necessary. Have the same students circle the subjects of the sentences *(bears, most bears)*. Focus on the two sentences without subjects (b and d) and ask *Why are there no subjects?* (These are imperative sentences. The subject is *you*, but we don't usually say it.)

- **Question 2:** Have students work individually to underline five imperative sentences in the leaflet. Call on students to read the sentences aloud to check that everyone has identified the imperative sentences.

- Have students refer to the charts to check their answers and familiarize themselves with the new structures.

Method 2
(For students familiar with the structure)

- Have students do the exercise in pairs.

- Give students a few minutes to refer to the charts to check their answers and review the structures.

- Call on students to go over the exercise. Discuss any disagreements and have students make any necessary corrections.

FORM CHARTS

- Write the word *run* on the board. Ask students for an affirmative imperative sentence and a negative imperative sentence (e.g., *Run to the store and buy some milk. Don't run in the house!*). Focus on form and explain that the subject in the sentences is *you* even though it is not used.

- Write these verbs on the board:

  | read | enter | listen | wash | go |
  | eat | be | send | move | guess |

- Put students into pairs and have them write five affirmative imperative sentences and five negative imperative sentences using the verbs above.

- Call on different pairs to read their sentence for a particular verb. Correct form where necessary. When helpful, write problematic sentences on the board and elicit corrections. Answer any questions.

C) MEANING AND USE

Imperatives

EXAMINING MEANING AND USE

- Have students work in pairs to answer the questions. (1. d; 2. c; 3. a; 4. b)

- Give students a few minutes to refer to the Notes to check their answers.

- Call on students to read the sentences and answers aloud. Discuss any disagreements and have students make any necessary corrections.

MEANING AND USE NOTES

- For Note 1, write these words on the board:
  1. *command*
  2. *advice*
  3. *request*
  4. *directions*
  5. *instructions*
  6. *warning*
  7. *offer*

- If you think your students can do this, put them in pairs and have them write the definitions of the words. Then bring the class together and have students write the definitions on the board. Provide meanings for words students cannot define.

- Have students work in pairs to create sample sentences for the different meanings of imperatives. Refer them to Note 1 to check their answers.

- Bring the class together and call on different pairs to share their examples of specific types of imperatives. Discuss any problem areas and have students make necessary corrections. Sample answers:
  1. *Command: ordering someone to do something (Leave the house now!)*
  2. *Advice: telling someone what is good to do (Study hard.)*
  3. *Request: politely asking someone to do something (Please open the door.)*
  4. *Directions: telling someone how to get somewhere (Turn left.)*

5. *Instructions: telling someone how to do something (Push the power button on.)*

6. *Warning: telling someone to be careful or something bad may happen (Watch out! A car is coming.)*

7. *Offer: asking someone if they need or want something (Have some more pie.)*

- Write these imperatives on the board: *Be afraid. Leave now.* Ask two students to write the negative form next to each imperative. *(Don't be afraid. Don't leave now.)*

- For Note 2A, ask two other students to come to the board and add the word *please* next to each negative imperative:

  Please don't be afraid. OR *Don't be afraid, please.*

  Please don't leave now. OR *Don't leave now, please.*

- Point out that when *please* is at the end of a sentence, it is separated with a comma, which is represented by a slight pause in speaking. Point to the two sentences on the board with *please* at the end and have students repeat after you.

- Tell the class that they are going to do a similar activity, but instead of writing the imperative forms, they are going to say them aloud. Begin by saying an imperative sentence. *(Go to sleep.)* Call on a student to say the negative imperative form. *(Don't go to sleep.)* Finally, call on another student to say the negative imperative form with *please*. *(Please don't go to sleep.* OR *Don't go to sleep, please.)*

- Repeat these steps, using different imperatives (e.g., *Open the door. Have some tea. Eat your vegetables.*).

ADDITIONAL ACTIVITIES

Speaking: Giving Directions

The purpose of this activity is to have students practice using imperatives to give directions.

- Tell students that they are going to give directions using imperatives. Have them draw a simple map of their neighborhood, including street names and local landmarks, and tell them to mark one place on the map that will be the starting point.

- Put students in pairs and have them swap maps with their partner. Explain that each student will both give and receive directions. Have pairs decide who will give directions first.

- Instruct them to begin at the starting point and give directions to three places in the neighborhood (e.g., *Turn left at the corner of Oak and High Streets. There is a large school there. Walk past the school. . . .*). As one student gives directions, the other listens and marks the route on the map, finally identifying the destination.

- Listen to the students give directions, and make sure they use the imperative form and not the modals *have to* or *should*.

- When both students have had a turn to give and receive directions, ask them to look at the maps and see if they are correct.

Writing: Giving Advice

The purpose of this activity is to have students practice giving advice using the imperative form.

- Tell students to imagine that someone they know is moving to their town. Have them write this person a list of suggestions about where to live, where to shop, what school to go to, and so on. They should justify their advice. For example:

  Don't live on Chase Street because it's very noisy.

  Buy your groceries at Super Food. It's not expensive.

- As they work, remind students to use the imperative form and not modals, which are also used for giving advice.

- Have students read their advice aloud. If any students live in the same town or city, have them compare the advice to see if they agree.

3

The Present Continuous

Overview

The present continuous is used to describe an action happening at the exact moment the speaker is talking (e.g., *I am talking on the phone right now.*) and an activity in progress but not necessarily at the moment of speaking (e.g., *I am reading* Romeo and Juliet *this semester.*). It is also used for a situation that is in the process of changing (e.g., *The weather is getting warmer.*). Students will probably be familiar with the "right now" use of the present continuous, but it is important for them to understand the other uses as well. All three are common in everyday speech.

Form: Students may have a problem with the concept of stative verbs. At this level, students should understand that many stative verbs cannot be used in the present continuous (e.g., *know, own, mean*) and that some stative verbs can be used in the present continuous, but their meanings are different from the simple present meanings (e.g., *She is looking for her keys. The food looks delicious.*).

(A) GRAMMAR IN DISCOURSE

Long-Distance Messenger

A1: Before You Read

- Take a quick survey of the class. Say *Raise your hand if you believe we will find life on other planets someday.* Then say *Raise your hand if you believe we won't ever find life on other planets.*

- Give students a few minutes to discuss the questions in small groups.

- Call on several students to share their opinions with the class. Be sure to select students with opposing opinions.

A2: Read

- Direct students' attention to the glossary. Elicit or explain that the glossary gives the meanings of important words in the article, which may be new to them. Encourage students to use the glossary before turning to a bilingual dictionary.

- Ask students to look at the picture in the article and tell you what it shows. (a spaceship, a spacecraft) Then have them scan the article to find the name of the spaceship *(Voyager I)*, when it left Earth (1977), and if it is carrying an astronaut (No). Then have students check their answers with a partner.

- Ask students to read the article to find out what *Voyager* is carrying. Meanwhile, write on the board *Voyager is carrying _____.*

- Have students go to the board and write one item that was mentioned in the article. (more than 100 pictures of life on Earth, greetings in over 50 languages, examples of animal sounds, different kinds of music, the sound of a mother kissing a baby, messages from world leaders, pictures of humans, or a map showing Earth's location) Leave the list on the board for later reference.

A3: After You Read

- Ask students to do this exercise individually and to note the places in the article where they found their answers. Then have students compare their answers with a partner. Go over any difficult items with the whole class and have students make necessary corrections.

- For a round-up activity, write these questions on the board:

  Why do you think scientists selected these items to send into space?

  What messages about Earth are scientists trying to send to other planets?

What other items would you suggest sending into space?

Which one do you think is most important?

- Tell students to look at the items that they listed on the board and discuss their ideas in pairs. Then have them share their ideas with the class.

B) FORM

The Present Continuous

EXAMINING FORM

Method 1

(For students not familiar with this structure)

- **Question 1:** Call on students to write sentences a and b on the board and have them underline the verbs. *(is, is carrying)* Ask the class if the correct words have been underlined and make corrections as necessary. Then ask *Which sentence uses the simple present form? Which uses the present continuous?* (Sentence a uses simple present; sentence b uses present continuous.)

- **Question 2:** Ask *How many words does the present continuous have?* (two: *be* and the verb) Ask *What ending is added to the base form of the verb?* (-*ing*)

- **Question 3:** Tell students to underline three examples of the present continuous in the article. Have them call out the examples they found and write them on the board until there is a total of five. If students include the adverbs *still* and *currently*, point out that these are not part of the verbs. Remind them that the present continuous form is *be* and verb + -*ing*. Finally, have students identify which verbs are singular and which are plural.

- Have students refer to the charts to check their answers and familiarize themselves with the new structures.

Method 2

(For students familiar with the structure)

- Have students do the exercise in pairs.

- Give them a few minutes to refer to the charts to check their answers and review the structures.

- Call on students to go over the exercise. Discuss any disagreements and have students make any necessary corrections.

FORM CHARTS

- Tell the class that they are going to practice the present continuous. Write the following lists of words on the board and to the right of them write a plus sign (+) and a minus sign (-).

I	sleep	
You	eat	
He	study	**+ −**
We	teach	
You	talk on the phone	
They	listen to me	

- Tell the class that you are going to point to words on the board, and they are going to create a sentence in the present continuous using those words. Explain that if you point to the plus sign, the sentence should be affirmative; if you point to the minus sign, the sentence should be negative. Demonstrate the activity by pointing to *I, teach,* and the plus sign, and then say *I am teaching.* Point to the minus sign to demonstrate the negative form, *I am not teaching.* Continue the activity, calling on students to say the sentences aloud.

- Write one sentence on the board (e.g., *I am sleeping.*) and ask students if there is a shorter way to say this. (*I'm sleeping.*) Elicit contractions with *be* for the entire list of pronouns. Then repeat the above activity pointing to words on the board and tell students to use contractions. Point out that negative contractions (with the exception of *I*) have two forms with the same meaning. (*You're not sleeping. You aren't sleeping.*) Both are equally acceptable.

- Have the class look at the *Yes/No* Questions, Short Answers, and Information Questions in the charts. Have students work in pairs using the words on the board to write three *Yes/No* questions and three information questions with original short answers.

C MEANING AND USE

The Present Continuous

EXAMINING MEANING AND USE

- Have students work in pairs to answer the questions. (1. b; 2. c; 3. a)

- Give students a few minutes to refer to the Notes to check their answers and review the uses of the present continuous.

- Call on students to read the questions and answers aloud. Discuss any disagreements and have students make any necessary corrections.

MEANING AND USE NOTES

- For Notes 1A–1C, draw the following chart on the board and write in the sample sentences as you proceed through the activity.

ACTIVITIES IN PROGRESS AT THIS MOMENT	ACTIVITIES IN PROGRESS, BUT NOT AT THIS MOMENT	SITUATIONS THAT ARE CHANGING
The students are working.	I'm taking four classes this term.	Our English is improving.

- Put students into small groups and have them write down as many sentences as they can to describe what is happening in the classroom at that moment. Provide a few examples and write one on the chart (e.g., *The students are working. Elena is playing with her hair. Stefan is scratching his head. The sun is shining outside.*). Tell students to look around the room and at their classmates to help them think of their sentences. Circulate, helping as necessary with vocabulary. When they finish, have each group read their sentences to the class and write one example on the chart. Monitor for correct usage and make necessary corrections.

- In the same groups, have students discuss what kinds of things they are doing these days but not necessarily at this minute (e.g., *I'm taking four classes this term. We are getting a lot of*

homework.). Write one example on the chart. Then have each group make a list and report back to the class, writing one example on the chart. Monitor for correct usage and make necessary corrections.

- Finally, have the groups discuss situations that are in the process of changing (e.g., *Our English is improving. The weather is getting colder.*). Again, have the groups write a few sentences and report back to the class, writing one example on the chart. Monitor for correct usage and make necessary corrections.

- Summarize by reviewing the three different uses of the present continuous on the chart and answer any questions. Refer students to Notes 1A, 1B, and 1C for more examples.

- For Notes 2A–2C: Write these verbs on the board:

know	*taste*	*think*
have	*feel*	*sound*

- Put students into pairs and have them write one sentence in the simple present for each of the listed verbs. Then have them write four new sentences in the present continuous. Point out that two of the verbs cannot be used in the present continuous.

- Combine the pairs into groups of four and have them compare their sentences. Write the following questions on the board and have the groups answer them:

  Which two verbs cannot occur in the present continuous? (know, sound)

  Why not? (These are stative verbs that cannot be used as action verbs.)

  Can you think of more examples of such stative verbs? (mean, believe, need, seem, own, mind)

  Compare the meanings of the verbs in the present continuous and the simple present sentences. Do they differ? (Yes)

- Refer students to Notes 2A, 2B, and 2C and to Appendix 7 to check their answers.

- As a class, go over the answers to the questions. Then call students to read their sentences for the different verbs and tenses. Note any problematic ones and write them on the board. A typical mistake might be *I am knowing you are right.* Try to elicit corrections from students. Answer any questions and discuss any disagreements. Have students make necessary corrections.

Vocabulary Notes: Adverbs and Time Expressions with the Present Continuous (p. 40)

- Have students read the Notes for *still* and the present continuous. Meanwhile, write these sentences on the board:

  He is still living with his parents. (He shouldn't be living with his parents now.)

  He still isn't living on his own. (He should be living on his own by now.)

- Explain that in an affirmative sentence, *still* expresses surprise that the activity hasn't ended. In a negative sentence, *still* expresses the expectation that the activity should have happened by now.

- Point out the placement of *still* in both sentences.

- Have students read the Notes for time expressions with the present continuous. Meanwhile, draw a calendar on the board to explain the meaning of *this week*. Circle today's date as a reference point and point to or elicit the appropriate dates as you say the expression. Your calendar should look something like this:

Sun.	Mon.	Tues.	Wed.	Thurs.	Fri.	Sat.
④	5	6	7	8	9	10

- Have students close their books. On the board write three sentences: one with *this month,* one with *this year,* and one with *nowadays.* Ask students to explain the meaning of each adverb.

- Put students into small groups and have them create sentences using the various adverbs. Circulate, helping as necessary.

- Call on students from each group to read one of their sentences aloud. Discuss and make corrections as necessary.

Speaking: Finding Out About Your Classmates

The purpose of this activity is to provide an opportunity for students to use the present continuous to ask and answer questions.

- Divide students into small groups and tell one student to ask a second classmate a present continuous question about a third classmate. If the student does not know the answer, he or she then asks the third classmate. Model this with two students. Write the questions and answers on the board as they are spoken:

  A: Where is Maria working these days?

  B: I don't know. Where are you working these days, Maria?

  C: I'm working at a shoe store.

- Have students follow the model and ask questions in groups. Circulate among the groups and listen to the language being used. Then bring the class together and elicit corrections to the errors—either on the board or reading the errors.

Writing and Speaking: Guessing the Activity

The purpose of this activity is for students to use the present continuous to write an activity and to guess the activity their classmates are miming.

- Ask each student to write an activity in the first-person singular using the present continuous on a piece of paper. It should be an activity that can be acted out (e.g., *I'm drinking hot coffee. I'm talking on the phone.*).

- Collect the papers, quickly glance at them to make sure the activities are written in the present continuous, and redistribute them.

- Divide the class into two teams and draw a chart with two columns on the board. Label the columns as *Team 1* and *Team 2.*

- Call on students to mime the activity they have written. The first team to guess the activity correctly gets one point. Then have the person who mimed write the sentence on the board in the appropriate column. Have students check the form of the written sentence. Make any necessary corrections. The team with the most points (and sentences) wins.

Returning to Grammar in Discourse

The purpose of this activity is to check students' understanding of key meanings and uses of the target structures in the chapter by having them return to the magazine article at the beginning of the chapter and apply what they have learned.

- Write the following extracts from the magazine article on the board (or type them up and photocopy them before class). Have students work in pairs to find them in the article. Make sure they read the complete sentences that these extracts come from.

   1. *They are still receiving messages from* Voyager *today.*

   2. *. . . these messages are still giving scientists important information . . .*

   3. *. . . it is carrying more than 100 pictures of life on Earth . . .*

   4. Voyager *is currently moving away from Earth at a speed of . . .*

- Now write the following items on the board:

   a. *an activity in progress at this exact moment*

   b. *an activity in progress, but it might not be happening at this exact moment*

- Have students think about the use of the present continuous in each extract and match each one to the letter of the item above that best describes it. (1. b; 2. b; 3. a; 4. a)

- Bring the class together. Call on pairs to give their answers, and have them offer explanations. If students still have problems, revisit the Meaning and Use Notes.

4 The Simple Past

Overview

The most common use of the simple past is to describe an action completed in the past. It is used for an action completed at a definite time in the past (e.g., *I met him yesterday.*) and it is used when the action clearly took place in the past even though the time is not mentioned (e.g., *I bought this camera in Japan.*). *Used to* describes a state in the past that has since changed (e.g., *He used to be shy.*). It also describes a habitual action in the past that no longer happens (e.g., *She used to visit her grandmother every Sunday.*).

Form: The key challenges are remembering

- the formation of irregular simple past verbs (e.g., *go – went*).
- the *did/didn't* auxiliary in questions and negatives.

A GRAMMAR IN DISCOURSE

The Decade That Made a Difference

A1: Before You Read

- If possible, bring to class old magazines or books with pictures from the 1960s. (*Life* magazine is a good source.) Show them to the class and discuss briefly.
- Divide the students into small groups and give them a few minutes to discuss the questions.
- Call on several students to share with the class their knowledge of the 1960s in the United States.

A2: Read

- Before students start reading, review the glossary and clarify the meanings of unfamiliar words.

- Write these questions on the board. Then ask students to scan the excerpt to find the answers.

   Who was president at the beginning of the 1960s?

   Who led the Civil Rights movement?

   What was the name of the famous music festival?

   How many days did it last?

   What did the hippies wear?

- Call on students for the answers. Then have them read the whole excerpt carefully.
- Ask students if any of these changes occurred in their home countries.

Cultural Notes

This excerpt has many references to people and events in the United States during the 1960s. Use the information below to answer students' questions or to give them historical background about this decade.

African Americans

African Americans are the people who were descended from the African slaves that were brought to North America in the 1700s and 1800s.

Beatles

A British singing group that was very popular all over the world especially from 1963–1969. The four members of the group were Paul McCartney, George Harrison, Ringo Starr, and John Lennon, who was killed by a fan in1980. Some of their most famous records were *A Hard Day's Night, Revolver,* and *Sgt. Pepper's Lonely Hearts Club Band.*

Civil Rights

The term *civil rights* refers to the rights that all citizens of a country enjoy. Unfortunately, before the 1960s, these rights were often denied to African Americans, particularly in the southern states. In the 1960s many people protested against these injustices. This movement ended the separation of whites and African Americans in housing, schools, restaurants, and other public places. It also made sure that everyone had a fair chance to register to vote.

Hippies

The hippies were young people who did not want to follow many of the social rules of the time. They dressed in unusual clothing and the men often wore long hair. They believed in peace and "free love"—that is, sexual relations outside of marriage. San Francisco was considered the home of the hippies, though they could be found in cities and on college campuses throughout the United States and many other countries.

John F. Kennedy

President of the United States from 1961–1963. He was assassinated on November 22, 1963. He and his wife, Jacqueline, were extremely popular both in the United States and around the world.

Vietnam War

The United States was involved in the civil war in Vietnam from 1965–1973. The United States was an ally of South Vietnam against communist North Vietnam. Many Americans disagreed with the government's involvement in the war and protested, sometimes violently. The war ended in 1973 when the South Vietnamese surrendered to the North.

Woodstock

Woodstock was a music festival held near the town of Woodstock, New York, in August 1969. Over 500,000 people attended. Many famous rock-and-roll stars performed at the festival, including Jimi Hendrix.

A3: After You Read

- Have students answer the true/false questions individually and compare their answers with a partner. Remind them to mark the places in the excerpt where they found the answers.
- Go over any difficult or problematic items with the whole class.
- For a round-up activity, ask students their opinion of the changes that occurred in the 1960s. Be sure to ask students with differing opinions.

B FORM 1

The Simple Past

EXAMINING FORM

Method 1
(For students not familiar with the structure)

- Write *Simple Past Verbs* on the board. Make two columns underneath and label them *Regular* and *Irregular*.
- **Question 1:** Tell students to underline the verb in each sentence. Call on individual students to say the verbs *(questioned, protested, believed)* aloud and write them on the board under *Regular*.
- **Question 2:** Have students work in pairs and ask them to circle three verbs in the excerpt in the past tense that end in *-ed*. List these verbs in the column labeled *Regular*.
- Ask students how the simple past tense of regular verbs is formed. (You add *-ed* to the base form of the verb.)
- **Question 3:** Have students find the simple past of the irregular verbs *make, lead, write,* and *go (made, led, wrote, went)* in the excerpt and list them in the column labeled *Irregular*.
- Ask students what *irregular* means. (It doesn't follow the rule for formation of the past tense.) Point out the word *was* in the excerpt and ask what the base form of this irregular verb is. *(be)*
- Have students work in pairs to circle regular and irregular verbs in the excerpt. Call on students to write the verbs in the appropriate columns on the board.
- Have students refer to the charts to check their answers and familiarize themselves with the new structures.

Method 2
(For students familiar with the structure)

- Ask students to work individually to circle regular and irregular past tense verbs in the excerpt.
- Put students in pairs to compare their answers. Tell them to put question marks next to any items they disagree on.

- Give students a few minutes to refer to the charts to check their answers and review the structures.
- Call on students to go over the exercise. Discuss any disagreements and have students make any necessary corrections.

FORM CHARTS

- Have students work in pairs to write four sentences in the simple past (two with regular verbs and two with irregular verbs). Tell them to include one negative sentence from each category. If necessary, refer them to Appendixes 4 and 6 for the spelling of regular and irregular simple past forms.
- Select individual students to write their sentences in the columns labeled *Regular* and *Irregular* on the board. Discuss any disagreements and correct as necessary.
- Ask students to read the *Yes/No* questions, short answers, and information questions in the charts.
- Call on individual students to change the simple past sentences on the board to *Yes/No* or information questions. Then call on other students to answer the questions.
- For homework, have them write ten true sentences using the simple past of regular and irregular vers and *be*, including affirmative and negative statements, *Yes/No* questions, short answers, and information questions.

Pronunciation Notes: Pronunciation of Verbs Ending in *-ed* (p. 53)

- Play the recording.
- Explain that the regular simple past ending is pronounced in three different ways. Write /t/, /d/, and /ɪd/ as column heads on the board. Say the words below aloud and write them in the correct column.

  worked   planned   started

- Go over the rules for each category on page 53. Emphasize that when the base verb ends in a /t/ or /d/ sound, an extra syllable is added.
- Say the following words aloud and ask students which column they belong in. Write them in the correct column.

wanted	(ɪd)
used	(d)
cooked	(t)
tasted	(ɪd)
laughed	(t)
played	(d)
washed	(t)
decided	(ɪd)
called	(d)
watched	(t)

- Ask students to think of other regular simple past verbs, and have them come to the board and write the verbs in the correct category. Discuss any disagreements.

Informally Speaking: Reduced Form of *Did You* (p. 56)

- Choose two students to read the text in the speech bubbles. Then tell the class you will play the recording and that they should listen to how the underlined form in the cartoon is different from what they hear. If needed, play the recording more than once.
- Have students point out the differences. (The cartoon reads "Did you," whereas on the recording this is pronounced "Didja.") Explain that the form on the recording is considered more informal English. Point out that the form in the cartoon is standard English and students should use this form when writing and speaking, although they may hear native speakers using the informal form.

C MEANING AND USE 1

The Simple Past

EXAMINING MEANING AND USE

- Have students work in pairs to answer the questions. (b and c; c; b; a)
- Give students a few minutes to refer to the Notes to check their answers.
- Call on students to read the questions and answers aloud. Discuss any disagreements and make any necessary corrections.

MEANING AND USE NOTES

- Select individual students to read one Note each (1A, 1B, 1C, or 1D) aloud.

- Divide students into small groups and have each group write four sentences, one for each meaning and use.

- Ask them to read their sentences to another group. Tell them to note if they disagree about the form or meaning and use.

- Call on the groups to read their sentences aloud. Write any problematic sentences on the board. Let the entire class decide on the correctness of these sentences. Guide them to the correct answer if necessary.

Vocabulary Notes: Time Expressions with the Simple Past (p. 60)

- If possible, use a large calendar to help explain the meanings of these time expressions.

- Have students close their books. On the board, write three sentences: one with *yesterday,* one with *this morning,* and one with *recently.* Ask students to explain the meaning of each adverb. (They can give the date relative to today, or they can use the calendar to show the meaning.)

- Tell students to open their books and read all seven sentences.

- Put students into small groups and have them create sentences using the various adverbs. Circulate, helping as necessary.

- Call on students from each group to read one of their sentences aloud. Discuss and make corrections as necessary.

Beyond the Sentence: Using Time Expressions with Tense Changes (p. 61)

This section is intended to give students practice with the meaning and use of grammar as it functions naturally in paragraphs and conversations.

- Explain that time expressions often tell you the verb tense, so using a time expression can make a sentence less confusing.

- Put students into pairs and have them talk about which paragraphs are less confusing and why. (The paragraphs with the time expressions are less confusing because the reader knows exactly when something happened.)

D FORM 2

Used To

EXAMINING FORM

- Have students do the exercise in pairs.

- Give them a few minutes to refer to the charts to check their answers and review the structures. (We use *used to* in affirmative statements; we use *use to* in negative statements and questions.)

- Call on students to go over the exercise. Discuss any disagreements and have students make any necessary corrections.

FORM CHARTS

- Write these sentences on the board:
  We walked.
  We didn't walk.
  Did we walk?

- Explain that these three sentences follow the rules for regular past tense verbs. Ask students to look at the charts and see if *used to* follows the same rules. (Yes, it does.)

- Put students in pairs to rewrite the sentences with the correct form of *used to.*

- Call on students to write the sentences on the board. Go over any difficult or problematic items with the whole class.

E MEANING AND USE 2

The Habitual Past with *Used To*

EXAMINING MEANING AND USE

- Call on individual students to read sentences 1a and 1b aloud.

- Ask students which sentence is about a repeated action in the past. (1a)

- Ask students to answer question 2 individually. (2a; 2b) Call on students to share their answers with the class.

MEANING AND USE NOTES

- Have students read the Notes and discuss them with a partner. Meanwhile, write these sentences on the board:

  People used to read books for relaxation. Now they watch TV.

  I didn't use to exercise at all, but now I exercise every day.

  He used to play soccer three times a week.

- Discuss these sentences and then ask students to write their own. Call on students to read their sentences aloud.

- Write these sentences on the board:

  Did you use to _____?

  Yes, I did.

  No, I didn't.

- Tell students to work with a partner to ask and answer three questions using these forms. Circulate as the pairs work, answering questions and pointing out any problems.

ADDITIONAL ACTIVITIES

Speaking About Past Events

The purpose of these activities is to have students use the simple past to discuss important events.

- Divide students into small groups and ask each student to think of a past event (historical, news-related, or personal) that they would like to talk about. Refer them to the book excerpt at the beginning of the chapter if necessary. Tell them that they will each have five minutes to speak.

- Circulate, helping out as necessary with vocabulary and grammar.

- As each student presents, have the class take notes so they can decide which events are the most interesting and why.

Guess Who

- Ask students to write on a sheet of paper a strange or unusual thing that happened to them or that they did in the past. Tell them that they must write about completed actions. They should not write their names on the papers.

- Collect the papers and redistribute them, making sure that no one gets his or her own paper.

- Tell students to find the person who wrote the paper by asking *Yes/No* questions (e.g., *Did you learn to swim when you were two? Were you born two months early?*).

- Have students walk around the classroom asking each other questions until they locate the right person.

Returning to Grammar in Discourse

The purpose of this activity is to check students' understanding of key meanings and uses of the target structures in the chapter by having them return to the book excerpt at the beginning of the chapter and apply what they have learned.

- Write the following extracts from the book excerpt on the board (or type them up and photocopy them before class). Have students work in pairs to find them in the excerpt. Make sure they read the complete sentences that these extracts come from.

  1. *Before the 1960s most Americans used to believe that the American way . . .*
  2. *John F. Kennedy became president; . . .*
  3. *Many young people were very angry with the government.*
  4. *The Beatles wrote their songs, . . .*
  5. *. . . many young Americans flocked to the famous . . .*

- Now write the following items on the board:

  a. *an action that happened once*
  b. *an action that happened repeatedly*
  c. *a state that lasted for a long time*

- Have students think about the use of the simple past in each extract and match each one to the letter of the item above that best describes it. (1. c; 2. a; 3. c; 4. b; 5. a)

- Bring the class together. Call on pairs to give their answers, and have them offer explanations. If students still have problems, revisit the Meaning and Use Notes.

5

The Past Continuous and Past Time Clauses

Overview

The past continuous is used to describe an action in progress at a specific time in the past (e.g., *She was living in Ecuador in 2000.*). It is also used to talk about several actions that were in progress at the same time in the past (e.g., *She was reading, he was watching TV, and the cat was sleeping.*). The past continuous also expresses a past action already in progress when another action interrupts it. In this case, *while* introduces the time clause with the past continuous action (e.g., *While they were cleaning, their guests arrived.*). *When* introduces the time clause with the simple past (e.g., *They were cleaning when their guests arrived.*).

Form: Students may try to use the past continuous when the simple past should be used to denote a completed action (e.g., **I was going to Ecuador last year.*).

A) GRAMMAR IN DISCOURSE

Galveston's Killer Hurricane

A1: Before You Read

- Write the word *hurricane* on the board. Elicit or explain its meaning (windstorm chiefly in the western Atlantic at speeds over 74 miles per hour, usually with heavy rain). Explain that the class will be reading about the worst hurricane in U.S. history.

- Put students in pairs and have them discuss the questions for five to ten minutes.

- Bring the class together. Call on several students to share their experiences with the class. List the different types of storms they describe on the board (e.g., thunderstorm, hailstorm, windstorm, sandstorm, snowstorm).

A2: Read

- Divide the class into small groups. Starting on one end of the classroom, assign each group one paragraph from the book excerpt, in the order they appear in the excerpt. Have students read the paragraph carefully and be prepared to retell it in their own words. Encourage students to use the glossary before turning to a bilingual dictionary.

- Bring the class together and ask a volunteer from each group to tell in their own words what happened in their paragraph. Discuss any disagreements.

A3: After You Read

- Ask students to do this exercise individually and note the places in the excerpt where they found their answers.

- Have them compare their answers in pairs.

- Circulate, note any problematic items, and go over them with the whole class.

- For a follow-up activity, ask *Besides building a seawall, what other things could people do to protect themselves from future killer storms?* (Have an evacuation plan in place. Have an early warning system.)

B) FORM 1

The Past Continuous

EXAMINING FORM

Method 1
(For students not familiar with the structure)

- **Question 1:** Tell students to find the underlined verb in the excerpt. *(were living)* Explain that the class will go through the excerpt together to find the other past continuous verbs.

- **Question 2:** Call on a student to explain how many parts the verb has. (two) Have students look at the underlined examples and tell you how they are formed. (*was/were* and the base form of the verb + -*ing*)
- Have students refer to the charts to check their answers and familiarize themselves with the new structures.

Method 2
(For students familiar with the structure)
- Have students do the exercise in pairs.
- Give them a few minutes to refer to the charts to check their answers and review the structures.
- Call on students to go over the exercise. Discuss any disagreements and have students make any necessary corrections.

FORM CHARTS
- Copy the following chart on the board:

ORIGINAL SENTENCE	CREATE
Susan was living in New York in 1998.	Negative statement
Steve and Josh were shopping.	Negative statement
Dan was working in the garden.	*Yes/No* question/ *Wh-* question with *where*
Their friends were studying together.	*Yes/No* question/ *Wh-* question with *when*

- Have students work in pairs to rewrite the statements. Tell them to record their work on a piece of paper.
- Have students swap papers with another pair and check their answers. Then have them swap back.
- Discuss any disagreements and have students refer to the charts to check their answers. Make any necessary corrections.

C MEANING AND USE 1

The Past Continuous

EXAMINING MEANING AND USE
- Have students work in pairs to answer the questions. (1. b; 2. a)

- Give students a few minutes to refer to the Notes to check their answers.
- Call on students to read the questions and answers aloud. Discuss any disagreements and make any necessary corrections.

MEANING AND USE NOTES
- Have students work in pairs to write three sentences using the past continuous to talk about actions that were in progress at a specific time in the past. Have pairs exchange and check each other's sentences.
- Put the pairs that exchanged papers into groups of four, and have them discuss any disagreements or problematic items. Circulate, answering any questions.
- Have members of each group write two of their sentences on the board. Discuss as a class and make corrections as necessary.
- Write these two sentences on the board: *I lived in Ecuador in 2002. I was living in Ecuador in 2000.* Ask *What is the difference in meaning?* (In the first sentence the action is completed. I am no longer living in Ecuador. In the second sentence I may still be living there after 2002 or perhaps not; it is not stated.)
- Put students in small groups and have them read Notes 2A and 2B. Ask each group to select a stative verb from Note 2B (*have, think, taste, weigh*), and have them write two sentences, one in the simple past and the other in the past continuous.
- Call on several students to write their sentences on the board. Discuss the different meanings of the past continuous and the simple past sentences.

Trouble Spots

Notes 2A and 2B can be difficult for some students. Most students have been taught that stative verbs express unchanging states or conditions and typically do not occur with the continuous. It is important to stress that some stative verbs can be used in the past continuous as action verbs. Used in this way, they have different meanings than if they were in the simple past.

Beyond the Sentence: Introducing Background Information with the Past Continuous (p. 79)

This section is intended to give students practice with the meaning and use of grammar as it functions naturally in paragraphs and conversations.

- Point out that the past continuous and the simple past often occur together in the same paragraph. The paragraph may begin with a sentence in the past continuous to describe the setting and the characters and then switch to the simple past to describe specific events that interrupt the setting. For example, *I was reading my book and listening to jazz. Suddenly a strong wind began to blow outside. . . .*

- Ask students to read the paragraph and pay close attention to the past continuous and simple past verbs. Talk about the tense change in the paragraph and why it occurs. (It starts with a description of the setting in the past continuous and then moves to the simple past to describe an action that interrupts the action in progress.) Go over any difficult or problematic items with the class.

D FORM 2

Past Time Clauses

EXAMINING FORM

Method 1
(For students not familiar with the structure)

- **Question 1:** Write the sentences on the board and read them aloud. Call on students to come to the board and underline the verbs. Discuss and make corrections as necessary. Ask *Which sentences have two verbs?* (b, *didn't worry* and *got;* and c, *ended* and *was*)

- **Question 2:** Explain that each verb in these sentences is in a clause. Say *A clause is a group of words that has a subject and a verb.* Number the clauses below the sentences:

  Cline didn't worry when he got the news.
      1   2

  After the storm ended, the city was in ruins.
          3   4

- Tell students that time clauses begin with a time word. Ask them the number of the time clauses (2 and 3) and the time word in each clause (*when* and *after*).

- Label the clauses on the board *Past Time Clause* (2 and 3) and *Main Clause* (1 and 4). Elicit or explain that time clauses are dependent in that they cannot stand alone as a sentence. Main clauses are independent and can stand alone as a sentence.

- Have students refer to the charts to check their answers and familiarize themselves with the new structures.

Method 2
(For students familiar with the structure)

- Have students do the exercise in pairs. Give them a few minutes to refer to the charts to check their answers and review the structures.

- Call on students to go over the exercise. Discuss any disagreements and have students make any necessary corrections.

FORM CHARTS

- Have students read the charts in pairs.

- Meanwhile, write these sentences on the board without commas:

  Before class started most of the students were laughing and talking.

  I was studying when the teacher walked into the room.

  After the test was over I was very happy.

- Ask students which sentences need commas. (1 and 3) Insert the commas after the initial time clauses in 1 and 3.

- Point out that when the sentence begins with a time clause, a comma is used to separate the clauses. However, a comma is not used when the time clause follows the main clause.

E MEANING AND USE 2

Past Time Clauses

EXAMINING MEANING AND USE

- Ask a student to write sentence a on the board. Have the student underline the action that happened first. *(I was taking a nap)* Ask the class if they agree. If not, put a question mark next to the sentence.

- Have another student write sentence b on the board and underline the action that happened first. *(I put on suntan lotion)* If the class doesn't agree, put a question mark next to the sentence. Do the same with sentence c. *(The two actions are happening at the same time.)*

- Put students in pairs to answer the questions. (1. c; 2. a; 3. b) Tell students to read the Meaning and Use Notes to check the answers.

- Go over any difficult or problematic items and answer any questions.

MEANING AND USE NOTES

- Write this sentence on the board: *[Name of student] was reading when [name of another student] walked into the room.* Call on the students you named to come up and act out the sentence before the class.

- Write this sentence on the board: *[Name of student] was reading while [name of other students] were sleeping.* Call on the students you named to come up and act out this sentence before the class.

- Divide the class into pairs. Tell half of them to write a sentence with *when* and the other half to write a sentence with *while*. Tell them that they must be able to act out their sentences. (If necessary, brainstorm verbs they could use: *read, write, sleep, eat, dance.*) Circulate to make sure students are writing sentences that can be acted out.

- Call on several pairs of students to act out their sentences. Tell the rest of the class to guess the sentence.

⬤ ADDITIONAL ACTIVITIES

Speaking: What Were You Doing When . . . ?

The purpose of this activity is to have students practice using the past continuous to talk about what they were doing when an important event occurred.

- Tell students to write a question about a past event. It should be an event not too far in the past unless it was so major that everyone will remember what they were doing when it occurred. For example:

   What were you doing when the president gave his speech last week?

   What were you doing when the hurricane hit?

- Let the students circulate "round robin," asking their question. They may wish to write down the answers to their question. Once everyone has asked and answered a question, call on a few students to report on the most interesting answers.

Returning to Grammar in Discourse

The purpose of this activity is to check students' understanding of key meanings and uses of the target structures in the chapter by having them return to the book excerpt at the beginning of the chapter and apply what they have learned.

- Write the following extracts from the book excerpt on the board (or type them up and photocopy them before class). Have students work in pairs to find them in the excerpt. Make sure they read the complete sentences that these extracts come from.

   1. *The tide was getting higher and higher when a four-foot wave went through . . .*

   2. *While the storm was going on, he was making careful notes . . .*

   3. *Cline didn't worry when the got the news.*

- Now write the following items on the board:

   a. *two events that were happening at the same time in the past*

   b. *a short event interrupting a longer event*

   c. *one completed event followed by another completed event*

- Have students think about the use of past time clauses with the past continuous and the simple past in each extract and match each one to the letter of the item above that best describes it. (1. b; 2. a; 3. c)

- Bring the class together. Call on pairs to give their answers, and have them offer explanations. If students still have problems, revisit the Meaning and Use Notes.

6

The Present Perfect

Overview

The present perfect expresses continuity between past and present time. It is used to describe an action that began in the past and continues up to or into the present (e.g., *I have lived here for ten years.*). It is also used for past actions when time is not mentioned because it is unimportant or unknown (e.g., *I have already eaten.*).

Form: The past participles of irregular verbs *(been, eaten, run)* are challenging for most students. Many irregular verbs express common everyday actions and their past participles need to be memorized. See Appendix 6 for a list of irregular verbs and their past participles.

A GRAMMAR IN DISCOURSE

Tales of a World Traveler

A1: Before You Read

- Write the term *world traveler* on the board. Ask *Who in the class is a world traveler? How many countries have you visited?*

- Put students in pairs and have them discuss the questions for five to ten minutes.

- Call on several students to share their answers with the class.

- For follow-up questions, ask *Have you visited other places in the United States or Canada? Which states/provinces/cities have you visited?*

A2: Read

- Ask students if they have heard of *Guinness World Records.* Explain that it is a book published every year that describes records that have been set. Some of these records are ordinary (e.g., the oldest living person in the

world), and some are very strange (e.g., the longest fingernails ever grown).

- Tell students to scan the article to answer these questions: *Why is John Clouse in* Guinness World Records? *What places has he visited?* Encourage students to use the glossary before turning to a bilingual dictionary.

- Call on students to answer the questions. Then have them read the entire magazine article.

A3: After You Read

- Give students a few minutes to answer the questions individually. Remind them to note the places in the article where they found their answers.

- Put students in pairs and give them five minutes to compare their answers and discuss what they found out about John Clouse. Have them share their answers with the class.

- For a follow-up activity, have students stay in pairs but with books closed. Ask them to write down as much information as they can remember. Finally, share the information as a class.

B FORM

The Present Perfect

EXAMINING FORM

Method 1

(For students not familiar with the structure)

- **Question 1:** Call on individuals to read the sentences aloud. Ask *Which two sentences are in the simple past?* (1b, 2a)

- Write these sentences on the board:

   1b. He crossed the Atlantic in 1999.

   1a. He has crossed the Atlantic many times.

- Underline *crossed* in sentence 1b. Tell students that 1a is a present perfect sentence. Underline *has crossed* and ask how many parts the verb has. (two) Ask *How do the two sentences differ?* (The simple past sentence has one verb and the present perfect has two.)

- **Question 2:** Write sentence 2b *(They have flown to Paris many times.)* on the board below 1a. Call a student to the board to underline the verb forms that follow *has* in 1a and *have* in 2b. *(crossed, flown)* Explain that these are past participles. Ask *Which form resembles the simple past? (crossed)* Point out that it is a regular past participle because it ends in -*ed*. Then ask *Which form is irregular? (flown)* Emphasize that the only way to learn irregular verbs is to memorize them.

- **Question 3:** Divide students into small groups and ask them to find and underline the other regular and irregular present perfect verbs in the article. Meanwhile, write *Regular Verbs* and *Irregular Verbs* on the board in two columns. Then have students call out the examples they found and write them on the board in the appropriate column. Point out again that the difference between regular and irregular verbs is that regular verbs have past participles ending in -*ed* and irregular verbs do not.

- Have students refer to the charts to check their answers and familiarize themselves with the new structures. You may also wish to refer students to Appendix 6 for a list of irregular verbs and their past participles.

Method 2
(For students familiar with the structure)

- Have students work in pairs to answer the questions.

- Give students a few minutes to refer to the charts to check their answers and review the structures.

- Call on students to go over the exercise. Discuss any disagreements and have students make any necessary corrections.

FORM CHARTS

- Have students read the Form charts individually.

- Ask them to work in pairs to write their own present perfect sentences: one affirmative, one negative, one *Yes/No* question and short answer, and one information question.

- Call on several students to write their sentences on the board. Go over each sentence and ask the class if the sentence is correct. If incorrect, ask a student to correct it. Discuss any disagreements or difficult items.

Informally Speaking: Reduced Forms of *Have* and *Has* (p. 95)

- Choose two students to read the text in the speech bubbles. Then tell the class you will play the recording and that they should listen to how the underlined form in the cartoon is different from what they hear. If needed, play the recording more than once.

- Have students point out the differences. (The cartoon reads "Mark has," whereas on the recording it is pronounced "Mark's.") Explain that the form on the recording is considered more informal English. Point out that the form in the cartoon is standard English and students should use this form when writing and speaking, although they may hear native speakers using the informal form.

C MEANING AND USE 1

Continuing Time Up to Now

EXAMINING MEANING AND USE

- Have students work in pairs to answer the questions. (1. 1b and 2b; 1a and 2a; 2. 1a and 2a; 1b and 2b)

- Give students a few minutes to look at the Notes to check their answers and review the structures.

- Call on students to read the questions and answers aloud. Discuss any disagreements and have students make any necessary corrections.

MEANING AND USE NOTES

- On the board, draw a time line like the one below. Make up a simple past sentence about yourself and write it on the board (e.g., *I went to school in Chicago from 1995 to 1998.*). Mark this on the line with the words *Begin* and *End* in the appropriate places.

Begin　End
1995　1998　2000　2001　Now

- Make up another sentence about yourself in the present perfect and write it on the board (e.g., *I have taught here since 1998.*).

- Ask *Which action started in the past?* (both of them) Then ask *Which one is finished and which is continuing to now?* Call on students to tell you which verb form is used for actions that are finished (simple past), and which is used for actions that started in the past and are continuing up to now (present perfect).

- Ask a student *When did you come to [your city]? How long have you lived in [your city]?* Put students in pairs and have them take turns asking and answering these questions.

- Call on a student to read the Notes on *for* and *since* aloud. Meanwhile, write these time phrases on the board and ask students if they are used with *for* or *since*:

1987	(since)
a short time	(for)
two hours	(for)
noon	(since)
I met her	(since)
five days	(for)

- Write these words and phrases on the board:
  driver's license
  married
  in this school
  job
  in this town/city
  English

- Ask students to work in pairs to write questions beginning with *How long*. Tell them to use the present perfect and the words on the board. Circulate to help as necessary.

- Have students ask their questions "round robin." Tell students to answer in complete sentences. Discuss any disagreements and make corrections as necessary.

D MEANING AND USE 2

Indefinite Past Time

EXAMINING MEANING AND USE

- Have students work in pairs to answer the questions. (1. 1a and 2a; present perfect; 2. 1b and 2b; simple past)

- Give students a few minutes to look at the Notes to check their answers and review the structures. Go over any difficult or problematic items.

MEANING AND USE NOTES

- Ask questions about past experiences that students have likely had, but do not have every day, and ask them to give a short answer. For example:

  Have you ever made a long-distance phone call? Yes, I have.

  Have you ever been on a train? Yes, I have.

  Have you ever eaten pizza? Yes, I have.

- Write their answers on the board as full sentences. (*Pedro has been on a train.*)

- Then ask questions that you think students will answer no to. For example:

  Have you ever visited Russia? No, I haven't.

  Have you ever seen Mt. Everest? No, I haven't.

- Write the negative answers on the board in full sentences. (*Reiko has never been to Russia.*)

- Point out that these sentences talk about actions that happened in the past, but the exact time is not mentioned.

Vocabulary Notes: More Adverbs with the Present Perfect (p. 104)

- Have students read the Notes in small groups. Assign each group an adverb and tell them to write at least three present perfect sentences using their adverb.

- Ask students to read their sentences aloud. Write any problem sentences on the board and ask students to look at the information in the Notes to correct them.

- Discuss any difficult or problematic items.

ADDITIONAL ACTIVITIES

Speaking: Find Someone Who . . .

The purpose of this activity is to have students practice asking and answering questions with the present perfect and *ever* and to report their findings to the class, using present perfect statements.

- Tell students to write a present perfect question that they would like to ask someone in the class (e.g., *Have you ever ridden a horse? Have you ever eaten snails?*).
- Circulate and check for grammar and vocabulary.
- Let students circulate for five to ten minutes to ask their question. Tell them to answer in the short form. (*Yes, I have.* OR *No, I haven't.*)
- When they are finished, ask students to report who answered *yes* to their question.

    Marta and Koji have ridden horses. Irina has eaten snails.

Returning to Grammar in Discourse

The purpose of this activity is to check students' understanding of key meanings and uses of the target structures in the chapter by having them return to the magazine article at the beginning of the chapter and apply what they have learned.

- Write the following extracts from the magazine article on the board (or type them up and photocopy them before class). Have students work in pairs to find them in the article. Make sure they read the complete sentences that these extracts come from.

    1. *Clouse started traveling 40 years ago.*
    2. *He has been to 192 countries . . .*
    3. *So far, he has spent about $1.25 million.*
    4. *Some of Clouse's journeys have been difficult.*
    5. *. . . he almost had to turn back just a few yards from the shore . . .*

- Now write the following items on the board:
    a. *indefinite past time*
    b. *definite past time*

- Have students think about the use of the present perfect or simple past in each extract and match each one to the letter of the item above that best describes it. (1. b; 2. a; 3. a; 4. a; 5. b)

- Bring the class together. Call on pairs to give their answers, and have them offer explanations. If students still have problems, revisit the Meaning and Use Notes.

7 Future Time: *Be Going To, Will,* and the Present Continuous

Overview

Future time is usually expressed in three ways: with *be going to, will,* or the present continuous. There are some differences, however, in meaning and use. *Be going to* and the present continuous are used to talk about intentions or future plans (e.g., *I'm going to study Russian next semester. We're dining out tonight.*). The present continuous usually refers to more definite plans than *be going to* (e.g., *I'm visiting my friends on Sunday* vs. *I'm going to visit my friends next month.*). *Will* or *be going to* is used to make predictions (e.g., *It is going to rain tomorrow. It will probably rain tomorrow.*). In the first person, *will* is used to express a promise (e.g., *I'll help you move.*).

Form: The challenge for many students will be choosing the correct form. They may find it confusing to use the present continuous for future time since they have already learned that it is used for present time. Another problem is the overuse of *will* (e.g., students may say *I will study tonight* rather than *I'm studying tonight.*).

A GRAMMAR IN DISCOURSE

The Election

A1: Before You Read

- Write the word *election* on the board. Elicit or explain its meaning. Ask for a show of hands in response to these questions: *How many of you have voted in an election? Who did you vote for?*

- Put students in small groups and have them discuss the questions.

- Then bring the class together and go over their ideas about politics and voting. For those students who aren't interested in politics or voting, ask why.

A2: Read

- Review the words in the glossary. Then ask students to read the article to find out what office the candidates are running for and what the main issues are.

- When students have finished reading, have them close their books. Elicit the office (governor) and the issues (helping poor people, raising/not raising taxes, improving education, bringing in more jobs, helping businesses) and write them on the board.

- Have students read the article again to find out which candidates are for which issues. Then elicit the names of the candidates and write them next to the issues on the board. (Greta Monroe: helping poor people, not raising taxes, improving education; Overmeyer: helping businesses, bringing in jobs; Kelly: raising taxes)

A3: After You Read

- Ask students to do this exercise individually and then compare their answers with a partner's. Remind them to note the places in the newspaper article where they found their answers.

- Call on individuals to read the question and answer it. Discuss any disagreements.

- For a round-up activity, ask students what they think the most important issues are for a mayor, governor, or president. Divide students into small groups to discuss the issues. Then call on a member of each group to give their group's consensus on the most important issue for each office. Write them on the board and discuss.

The Future with *Be Going To* and the Present Continuous

EXAMINING FORM

Method 1

(For students not familiar with the structure)

- Write the word *Future* on the board. Then draw two columns under it. Label one column *Be Going To* and the other *Present Continuous*.

- **Question 1:** Put students in pairs and have them find and underline three more affirmative examples of *be going to* + verb in the article (e.g., *is going to help, is going to win, I'm going to sit down*). Call on individual students to read an example aloud. Write each example in the appropriate column.

- **Question 2:** Call on students to answer question 2. *(are, is, am)* Have students look at the examples on the board and tell you how they are formed. *(am/is/are + going to + base form of the verb)*

- **Question 3:** Have students find and circle one more affirmative example of the present continuous as future (e.g., *I'm voting*). Write the example in the appropriate column and ask how it is formed. *(am/is/are + base form of the verb + -ing)*

- Point out the differences between the two forms.

- Have students refer to the charts to check their answers and familiarize themselves with the new structures.

Method 2

(For students familiar with the structure)

- Have students work individually or in pairs to underline examples of *be going to* and circle examples of the present continuous.

- Give students a few minutes to refer to the charts to check their answers and review the structures.

- Call on students to write the examples in the appropriate columns. Have them tell you how the examples are formed. Ask them to point out the differences between the two forms.

- Discuss any disagreements and have students make any necessary corrections.

FORM CHARTS

- Write these sentences in two columns on the board: *She is going to vote. We are going to leave tomorrow.*

- Ask students to go to the board and write the negative form of the sentences. *(She isn't going to vote. We aren't going to leave tomorrow.)* Do not make any corrections at this time.

- Have other students change the sentences to *Yes/No* questions. *(Is she going to vote? Are we going to leave tomorrow?)*

- Finally, ask students to change the sentences to information questions with *what, who,* and *when. (What is she going to do? Who is going to vote? When are we going to leave?)*

- Divide the class into groups and ask them to check the sentences against the information in the charts. When they are finished, ask them to come to the board to make any changes or additions. Make certain that both forms of the negative are on the board. *(she isn't, she's not)*

- Write these sentences on the board: *He is cooking dinner at Diane's house tonight. They are studying at the library tomorrow.*

- Put students into small groups. Tell them to write the negative forms including the contractions. *(He is not cooking dinner. He isn't cooking dinner. They are not studying. They aren't studying./They're not studying.)* Then have students change the sentences to *Yes/No* questions *(Is he cooking dinner? Are they studying?)* and information questions using *where, when,* and *what (Where is he cooking dinner? When is he cooking dinner? What are they studying?).*

- Have the groups check their work against the information in the charts.

- Review any difficult or problematic items.

Informally Speaking: Reduced Form of *Going To* (p. 118)

- Choose two students to read the text in the speech bubbles. Then tell the class you will play the recording and that they should listen to how the underlined forms in the cartoon are different from what they hear. If needed, play the recording more than once.

- Have students point out the differences. (The cartoon reads "going to," whereas on the recording this is pronounced "gonna.") Explain that the form on the recording is considered more informal English. Point out that the form in the cartoon is standard English and students should use this form when writing and speaking, although they may hear native speakers using the informal form.

C) MEANING AND USE 1

Be Going To and the Present Continuous as Future

EXAMINING MEANING AND USE

- Have students work in pairs to answer the questions. (1. a, c; 2. b)
- Give students a few minutes to refer to the Notes to check their answers.
- Call on students to read the questions and answers aloud. Discuss any disagreements and make any necessary corrections.

MEANING AND USE NOTES

- Select individual students to read a section of the Notes (1A, 1B, 1C, 2) aloud.
- Divide students into groups, and tell them to write four sentences, one for each Note.
- When the groups are finished, ask them to read their sentences to another group. Tell them to note if they disagree about the form or meaning and use.
- Call on the groups to read their sentences aloud. Write any problematic sentences on the board. Let the entire class decide on the correctness of these sentences. Guide them to the correct answer if necessary.

Vocabulary Notes: Future Time Expressions (p. 122)

- If possible, use a large calendar to help explain the meanings of these time expressions. Circle today's date as a reference point and point to

or elicit the appropriate date as you say an expression.

- Have students close their books. On the board write three sentences: one with *tomorrow*, one with *tomorrow morning*, and one with *next week*. Ask students to explain the meaning of each adverb. (They can give the date relative to today, or they can use the calendar to show the meaning.)
- Tell students to open their books and read all five sentences.
- Put students into small groups and have them create sentences using the various adverbs. Circulate, helping as necessary.
- Call on students from each group to read one of their sentences aloud. Discuss and make corrections as necessary.

D) FORM 2

The Future with *Will*

EXAMINING FORM

- Have students do the exercise in pairs.
- Give them a few minutes to refer to the charts to check their answers and review the structures.
- Call on students to answer the questions. (1. *will 'll decide, will raise, will vote, Will keep*; subjects: *I, He, They, Overmeyer*; 2. The form of *will* stays the same with different subjects. 3. In a question, *will* goes before the subject.) Discuss any disagreements and have students make any necessary corrections.

FORM CHARTS

- Write these sentences on the board: *She will go to the movies on Saturday night. They will drive to their friend's house in the morning.*
- Divide students into groups. Tell them to write the negative forms using the contractions. (*She won't go to the movies on Saturday night. They won't drive to their friend's house in the morning.*) Then have them change the sentences to *Yes/No* questions (*Will she go to the movies on Saturday night? Will they drive to their friend's house in the morning?*) and

information questions using *what, when, who,* and *where* (*What will she do on Saturday night? When will they go to their friend's house? Who will go to their house? Where will she go on Saturday night?*).

- Have the groups check their work against the information in the charts.
- Review any difficult or problematic items.

Informally Speaking: Reduced Form of *Will* (p. 129)

- Choose two students to read the text in the speech bubbles. Then tell the class you will play the recording and that they should listen to how the underlined forms in the cartoon are different from what they hear. If needed, play the recording more than once.
- Have students point out the differences. (The cartoon reads "Who will," whereas on the recording this is pronounced "Who'll"; the cartoon reads "boss will," but on the recording this is pronounced "boss'll.") Explain that the form on the recording is considered more informal English. Point out that the form in the cartoon is standard English and students should use this form when writing and speaking, although they may hear native speakers using the informal form.

E MEANING AND USE 2

Will vs. Be Going To

EXAMINING MEANING AND USE

- Have students read the conversations aloud in pairs.
- Read each question and call on students to give their answers. (1. c; 2. a; 3. b)
- Give students a few minutes to refer to the Notes to check their answers.
- Discuss any disagreements and make any necessary corrections.

MEANING AND USE NOTES

- Divide students into three groups and have members of each group read one Note aloud.

- Write the following chart on the board:

USE	WRITE A CONVERSATION USING THIS SENTENCE:
1. Predictions with *will* and *be going to*	I wonder what the world will be like in 2020.
2. Quick decisions with *will*	I can't find my pen.
3. Advance plans with *be going to*	What movie are you going to see tonight?
4. Promises with *will*	I'm tired of washing the dishes every night.

- Assign each group a use and have them write a two- to four-line conversation using the sentence that you provide. Tell the group to keep their assignment a secret.
- Ask each group to read their conversation aloud and have the other groups guess which use they are expressing.

ADDITIONAL ACTIVITIES

The purpose of these activities is to have students practice using appropriate future forms to make predictions about the future.

Speaking: What's Going to Happen?

- Find a television program that most students watch, or put the students into groups according to which television programs they watch. They must be programs with a continuing story line or cast of characters. Soap operas (daytime television dramas) work best, but any program that has the same set of characters interacting can also work.
- Lead a class discussion on what people think is going to happen in the program. If they are working in groups, assign someone to take notes. For example: *Is Gloria going to leave Mark and marry Victor? Are the police going to arrest Ana?*
- If you are leading a class discussion, write their ideas on the board. If they are working in small groups, have one person report the group's ideas to the class.

Writing: A Stranger's Future

- Put the students into pairs. Give each pair a magazine picture of one or more people. These pictures should have something about them that would enable students to guess what is going to happen. Tell the class that they will have to use their imagination. For example, if the picture is of a man holding a briefcase, *He is going to work. His boss is going to fire him today. He isn't going to be able to find a new job. He and his family are going to have to sell their house. In the end, he is going to win the lottery.*

- Tell students to think of three or four events that are going to happen to the person or people in the picture.

- Have each pair read their story to the class.

Writing: A Time Capsule

- Explain to the class that a time capsule is a special way to "talk" to people in the future. Many people make time capsules on special occasions (their wedding, when a child is born) and include photographs, objects, and often letters to look at in the future.

- Tell students to imagine that they are going to make a time capsule. Have them write a letter about the future. Read the following example aloud: *The future is going to be wonderful. Doctors are going to find a cure for cancer. No one will be hungry. . . .*

Returning to Grammar in Discourse

The purpose of this activity is to check students' understanding of key meanings and uses of the target structures in the chapter by having them return to the letter at the beginning of the chapter and apply what they have learned.

- Write the following extracts from the letter on the board (or type them up and photocopy them before class). Have students work in pairs to find them in the letter. Make sure they read the complete sentences that these extracts come from.

  1. *. . . we are going to have our first woman governor!*
  2. *I'm not voting for Monroe . . .*
  3. *. . . Overmeyer is going to win.*
  4. *All the business people will vote for him.*
  5. *I'm going to sit down this weekend . . .*

- Now write the following items on the board:
  a. *an intention or future plan*
  b. *a prediction*

- Have students think about the meaning of the present continuous or future with *going to* or *will* in each extract and match each one to the letter of the item above that best describes it. (1. b; 2. a; 3. b; 4. b; 5. a)

- Bring the class together. Call on pairs to give their answers, and have them offer explanations. If students still have problems, revisit the Meaning and Use Notes.

Future Time Clauses and *If* Clauses

Overview

Future time clauses begin with time words such as *after*, *before*, and *when*, and are used to express events in a sequence. These clauses are dependent clauses because they cannot stand alone. They must occur with a main clause. The verb in the dependent clause is usually in the simple present, and the verb in the main clause is usually in the future (e.g., *When he arrives, we'll go to the movies.*). Dependent clauses can also begin with *if*. The *if* clause expresses a probable condition or action, and the main clause states the result of that condition or action (e.g., *If the movie is bad, we'll leave right away.*).

Form: Students may want to use the future in both the dependent and main clauses (e.g., **When he will arrive, we will go to the movies. *If it will rain, I will stay home.*).

A GRAMMAR IN DISCOURSE

What Will Happen in the Future?

A1: Before You Read

- Write this question on the board: *What do you think will happen in the future?* Brainstorm a few ideas with the class (e.g., People will be identified with eye scanners. Climate will be controlled so there will be no rain or snow. People will have robots.).

- Elicit the names of the two robots pictured. (C3PO and R2D2 from *Star Wars*)

- Put students into small groups and give them a few minutes to discuss the questions.

- Bring the class together and call on each group to share their ideas with the class.

A2: Read

- Have the class read the article, and then call on students to describe what will happen by the years 2010, 2015, 2020, and 2025.

- For each prediction the students describe, write the corresponding *if* clause on the board.
  If robots find water on Mars, ___.
  If we live in smart houses, ___.
  If ordinary people travel on supersonic planes, ___.
  If we build a space station, ___.

- Call on several students to complete the sentences. It may be necessary to elicit the correct form (*will* + base verb). Write their answers on the board.

A3: After You Read

- Ask students to do this exercise individually and mark the places in the text where they found their answers.

- Tell students to compare their answers with a partner's. Circulate and note any problematic items.

- Call on individual students to read a prediction aloud and say if it is true according to the article.

- Discuss any disagreements or problematic items and have students make necessary corrections.

- For an optional follow-up activity, summarize the futuristic utopian society described by Lois Lowry in *The Giver* (Boston: Houghton Mifflin, 1993). You could also have students read excerpts from it. As a class, discuss their reactions to this society where weaker twins are "released" (killed) because two identical people are not allowed; climate is controlled; hills are flattened; color doesn't exist; the Committee of Elders decides your occupation for you; and the collective memories of citizens are retained by the Giver so the citizens do not have to suffer the memory of bad events such as war.

(Note: Though this book was written for middle school–aged children, its theme is adult, it is easy to read, and it is suitable to this context.)

B FORM

Future Time Clauses and *If* Clauses

EXAMINING FORM

Method 1
(For students not familiar with the structure)

- **Question 1:** Call on individual students to read a sentence each as you write them on the board. Ask students to come to the board and underline the main clauses. (*I'll see him, they're going to look for work, We're going to have dessert*) Ask what verb tense is used in the main clause. (future)

- **Question 2:** Have students circle the dependent clauses on the board (*before I leave, When they graduate, after we finish dinner*) and tell you what verb tense is used (simple present). Ask them which words introduce the dependent clauses. (*before, when, after*) Explain that *before, when,* and *after* introduce future time clauses.

- Point out that a dependent clause can come before or after a main clause, and the position does not change the meaning. If the dependent clause comes first, it is followed by a comma.

- **Question 3:** Call on a student to read the sentence with *if* while you write it on the board. Have a student come to the board and circle the dependent clause (*If I go to the store*). Ask what verb tense is used (simple present) and what word introduces the dependent clause (*if*). Explain that this is an *if* clause.

- **Question 4:** Have students look back at the article to find two future time clauses (*When the weather is cold, when the weather is hot*) and one *if* clause (*if a room is empty*). Call on individuals to read them aloud. Discuss any disagreements.

- Have students refer to the charts to check their answers and familiarize themselves with the new structures.

Method 2
(For students familiar with the structure)

- Have students work in pairs to answer the questions. Give students a few minutes to refer to the charts to check their answers and review the structures.

- Call on students to write the sentences on the board. Ask them to underline the main clause, circle the dependent clause, and identify the verb form in each clause.

- Discuss any disagreements and have students make any necessary corrections.

- Point out that the order of the clauses can be switched. Ask if changing the order changes the meaning of a sentence. (No) Ask what must be added to a sentence if the dependent clause comes before the main clause. (a comma)

FORM CHARTS

- Give students a few minutes to read the charts silently. Then, put students into small groups and have each group write four sentences using one of these words in each sentence: *after, before, when,* and *if.* Two of the sentences should begin with the main clause and two with the dependent clause followed by a comma.

- Have two members of each group write two of their sentences each on the board. Review them with the class. Have the class identify and correct errors. Make the corrections on the board.

C MEANING AND USE 1

Using Future Time Clauses for Events in a Sequence

EXAMINING MEANING AND USE

- Have students work in pairs to answer the questions. (a: we get the results; b: the teacher will review the homework; c: he comes home from the hospital; The time words *when, before,* and *after* tell the order of events.) Give students a few minutes to refer to the Notes to check their answers.

- Call on students to read the questions and answers aloud. Discuss any disagreements and have students make any necessary corrections.

MEANING AND USE NOTES

- Write these sentences on the board:

  Before I make dinner, I'll vacuum the carpet.
           2   1

  When she graduates, she'll get a job.
         1   2

  He'll write some letters before he goes to sleep.
        1   2

  After they watch the game, they'll play cards.
        1   2

  I'll take a nap when I finish studying.
    2   1

- Call on students to come to the board and circle the action that happens first. Have them label it *1*. Then have them underline the action that happens second and label it *2*.

- Discuss any difficult or problematic items.

D) MEANING AND USE 2

Expressing Future Possibility with *If* Clauses

EXAMINING MEANING AND USE

- Have students work in pairs to answer the questions. (1. 1a. *If you take some aspirin* is a possible situation; *you'll feel better* is a possible result; 1b. *if you help me with the housework* is a possible situation; *I'll take you out to dinner* is a possible result; 2. 1a gives advice; 1b makes a promise; 3. 2b) Give students a few minutes to refer to the Notes to check their answers.

- Call on students to read the questions and answers aloud. Discuss any disagreements and have students make any necessary corrections.

MEANING AND USE NOTES

- Write these sentences on the board, and in parentheses put the category that the students' corresponding sentence should describe:

  Eric wants to marry Rosa, but she's not sure about marrying him. (promise)

  She's going to the horse races. (prediction)

  There are many sharks in the ocean. (warning)

  He has a terrible toothache. (advice)

  I hope I get this job. (possibility)

- Put students in pairs and have them write a sentence about each situation using an *if* clause

and *be going to* or *will* in the main clause. For example, for the first sentence students should write a promise that Eric might make to Rosa: *If you marry me, I'll love you forever.*

- Call on the groups to read their sentences aloud. Discuss any difficult or problematic items and have students make necessary corrections.

ADDITIONAL ACTIVITIES

Writing: Making Promises

The purpose of these activities is to have students practice using *if* clauses to make promises, warnings, and predictions.

- Put students in pairs and explain that they will write promises that one person might make to another. Brainstorm some examples (e.g., *I'll never be late again. I'll be home by 11:00 P.M.*).

- Collect the promises and redistribute them to different pairs. Give each pair a few minutes to write a short conversation incorporating the promise.

- Ask pairs to read their conversations aloud.

- For an optional activity, you could have the class vote on the most creative conversation.

- You can do the same activity with warnings: *You'll get a cold. You'll lose a lot of money. Your teeth will fall out.*

Speaking: Superstitions

- Give students examples of two or three superstitions from English-speaking countries:

  If you break a mirror, you'll have seven years of bad luck.

  If you walk under a ladder, you'll have bad luck.

  You'll have bad luck if you see a black cat.

- Put students into small groups and have them talk about superstitions from their countries. Circulate to help them with vocabulary as needed.

- Bring the class together and have each group describe one of their superstitions.

9 Modals of Ability and Possibility

Overview

Many students find modals challenging because the same modal often has very different meanings. Modals can also express subtle shades of meaning. For example, *can* is used to express both present and future ability as well as possibility, but *could* is used for past ability. The false modal, *be able to,* also expresses present ability. In addition, *could, might,* and *may* express future possibility. Students should be encouraged to use the context to decide among the different possibilities of meaning.

Form: Modals are always followed by the base form of the verb. Students may want to use an infinitive after a modal (e.g., **I can to go tomorrow.*). Students also may find questions and negative statements challenging since modals do not use the auxiliary *do.*

A GRAMMAR IN DISCOURSE

A Real-Life Hero

A1: Before You Read

- Ask the class *Who is the most famous superhero?* (Superman) Then ask them to tell you why Superman is a hero. Ask *What are some of his characteristics?* (Superman can fly. He can hear sounds from far away. He can see through buildings.) List them on the board.

- Give students a few minutes to discuss the questions in small groups.

- Call on several students to share their opinions with the class. List the students' heroes on the board as they mention them.

A2: Read

- Ask students to look at the picture and tell you the name of the actor. (Christopher Reeve)

- Review the new vocabulary in the glossary and ask students to read the article individually.

- Put students in groups and have them summarize the article. Call on a member of each group to present their summaries.

A3: After You Read

- Ask students to do this exercise individually and mark the places in the text where they found their answers.

- Tell students to compare their answers with a partner's. Circulate and note any problematic items.

- Call on individual students to read a statement aloud and say if it is true or false.

- Discuss any disagreements or problematic items and have students make necessary corrections.

- For a round-up activity, ask *Is your hero like Christopher Reeve? Why or why not?*

B FORM 1

Modals of Ability: *Can* and *Could*; *Be Able To*

EXAMINING FORM

Method 1
(For students not familiar with the structure)

- **Question 1:** Draw a chart on the board like the one below. Go over the formation of the affirmative forms.

AFFIRMATIVE	NEGATIVE
can + base verb	*can not* + base verb
could + base verb	*could not* + base verb

- Call on a student to read the first paragraph of the article aloud.

- Write *can do* and *could fly* in the appropriate affirmative column.

- Ask *What form of the verb follows* can *and* could? (the base form)

- **Question 2:** Go over the formation of the negative forms in the chart above. Have students find negative forms of *can* or *could* + verb in the first two paragraphs (e.g., *can't do, could not defeat, couldn't jump, cannot write*). Call on students to write these verbs in the appropriate column. Ask what is unusual about the negative form of *can* + verb. (It is one word: *cannot*.) Have a student write the contracted negative forms of *can* and *could* in the chart on the board. Discuss any problems and correct as necessary.

- Have students refer to the charts to check their answers and familiarize themselves with the new structures.

Method 2
(For students familiar with the structure)

- Have students do the exercise in pairs.

- Give them a few minutes to refer to the charts to check their answers and review the structures.

- Call on students to go over the exercise. Discuss any disagreements and have students make any necessary corrections.

FORM CHARTS

- Add *be able to* in the affirmative column of the chart on the previous page and *be not able to* in the negative column. Point out that *to* is part of its form. Ask students to find one example of *be able to* + base verb (e.g., *is not able to move*).

- Put students into pairs and have them review and discuss the charts. Meanwhile, copy the following chart on the board:

ORIGINAL SENTENCE	CREATE
She can swim.	*Yes/No* question Affirmative short answer
He is able to move.	*Yes/No* question Negative short answer
We can go now.	Information question (with *when*)
Dan can go.	Information question (with *who*)
Ann can sing.	Information question (with *what*)

- Ask the pairs to rewrite the sentences according to the chart.

- Have them exchange papers with another pair and check their answers. Then have them swap back.

- Discuss any disagreements and have students refer to the charts to check their answers and make any necessary corrections.

C MEANING AND USE 1

Past, Present, and Future Ability

EXAMINING MEANING AND USE

- Have students work in pairs to answer the questions. (1. a; 2. c; 3. b)

- Give students a few minutes to refer to the Notes to check their answers and review the meanings and uses of *can, could,* and *be able to.*

- Call on students to read the questions and answers aloud. Discuss any disagreements and have students make any necessary corrections.

MEANING AND USE NOTES

- Write these words on the board as column headings: *Present, Future, Past.*

- Ask students to look at the Notes and decide which modals or phrases of ability belong in each column. Call on students to write the answers in the appropriate column.

Present	Future	Past
can	*will be able to*	*could*
		was able to

- Write these correct/incorrect sentences on the board. Do not write "correct" or "incorrect" yet; students will determine this.

  I couldn't run a mile yesterday. (correct)

  I wasn't able to run a mile yesterday. (correct)

  We can hear the music all last night. (incorrect—use *were able to* or *could*.)

  When I complete this class, I can speak English very well. (incorrect—use *will be able to*.)

  I'm studying now, but I can help you with your homework later. (correct)

  I'm studying now, but I will be able to help you with your homework later. (correct)

- Put students in groups. Have them identify and correct the incorrect sentences. Tell the groups to look at the Notes and check their answers.

- Have them read the sentences aloud. Discuss any problematic items and have students make necessary corrections.

Vocabulary Notes: *Know How To* (p. 166)

- Have students read the Notes in small groups. Then have each group write four sentences, one each with *can, can't, know how to,* and *doesn't/don't know how to.*

- Ask students to read their sentences aloud. Write any problem sentences on the board and ask students to look at the information in the Notes to correct them.

- Discuss any difficult or problematic items.

D) FORM 2

Modals of Future Possibility

EXAMINING FORM

- Have students work in pairs to answer the questions. (1. a: might; c: may; b; 2. a: He might not walk again. b: He doesn't have the strength of one hundred men. c: Researchers may not find a cure. Negative statements with modals use the modal + *not* + base form of the verb. Negative statements in the simple present use *do/does* + *not* + base form of the verb.)

- Give them a few minutes to refer to the charts to check their answers and review the structures.

- Call on students to go over the exercise. Remind them that these modals follow the same form as the others. Discuss any disagreements and have students make any necessary corrections.

FORM CHARTS

- Put students into pairs and have them review and discuss the charts. Meanwhile, copy the following chart on the board:

ORIGINAL SENTENCE	CREATE
She will be here on Saturday.	*Yes/No* question Affirmative short answer Negative short answer Information question (with *when*)
Josh might go.	Information question (with *who*)

- Have the pairs rewrite the sentences according to the chart.

- Have them exchange papers with another pair and check their answers. Then have them swap back.

- Discuss any disagreements and have students refer to the charts to check their answers and make any necessary corrections.

E) MEANING AND USE 2

Future Possibility

EXAMINING MEANING AND USE

- Have students work in pairs to answer the questions. (Sentence b is the most certain. Sentences a, c, d, and e are less certain.)

- Give students a few minutes to refer to the Notes to check their answers.

- Call on students to read the questions and answers aloud. For each sentence, ask *Which word in the sentence gives you information about the certainty of the event?* (the modal and the word *maybe* in sentence d)

- Discuss any disagreements and have students make any necessary corrections.

MEANING AND USE NOTES

- Divide students into four groups and assign one of the Notes to each group.

- Tell each group to read the Note and prepare to teach the information to the class. The groups should write two new sentences that clearly illustrate the meaning and use of the modals in their assigned Note.

- Circulate as the groups work, pointing out any problems in their example sentences.

- Ask each group to present, and have the rest of the class check if the example sentences are correct. If not, work together to improve them.

ADDITIONAL ACTIVITIES

Speaking: What Could You Do with a . . . ?

The purpose of these activities is to give students the opportunity to practice using the correct modals in correct contexts.

- Cut out magazine pictures of about 20 different common items. Make photocopies of the pictures so that you can give one set of pictures to each group. Choose some pictures that are easy to think of uses for and others that are more difficult.

- Put students into groups of three or four. Tell them that they are stuck on a desert island. Ask them to think of a way that they could use each item (e.g., *I could use a shovel to row a boat.*).

- When students have a use for each item, go to each group and ask them to give you one item and its use. If the sentence is correct and the use is logical, they get a point. No other group can get a point for that item unless they think of another use.

- Keep track of each team's points on the board. The team with the most points wins.

Speaking: How Amazing Are You?

- Ask everyone in the class to think of two things they can do that they think most other people in the class cannot do. For example:

  I can whistle very well.

  I can make bread.

  I can speak Russian.

  I can ride a unicycle.

- Have students circulate and ask at least three people each what they can do.

- Ask students to report what they found out about their classmates.

- Write the skills on the board as students report them. Have the class vote on which skill they think is the most amazing.

Returning to Grammar in Discourse

The purpose of this activity is to check students' understanding of key meanings and uses of the target structures in the chapter by having them return to the magazine article at the beginning of the chapter and apply what they have learned.

- Write the following extracts from the magazine article on the board (or type them up and photocopy them before class). Have students work in pairs to find them in the article. Make sure they read the complete sentences that these extracts come from.

  1. *He can do things . . .*
  2. *. . . might even walk again.*
  3. *. . . he is not able to move any part of his body . . .*
  4. *As Superman, Reeve could fly.*
  5. *He is able to talk, . . .*
  6. *His horse couldn't jump over a hurdle, . . .*

- Now write the following items on the board:

  a. *present ability*
  b. *past ability*
  c. *future possibility*

- Have students think about the meaning of *can, could, be able to,* or *might* in each extract and match each one to the letter of the item above that best describes it. (1. a; 2. c; 3. a; 4. b; 5. a; 6. b)

- Bring the class together. Call on pairs to give their answers, and have them offer explanations. If students still have problems, revisit the Meaning and Use Notes.

10 Modals and Phrases of Request, Permission, Desire, and Preference

Overview

By now most students will be very familiar with the form of one-word modals. In this chapter, however, they are also introduced to phrasal modals such as *would like*. Once again, it will be the overlapping uses of modals that present the most problems for students. In this chapter, most of the difference in meaning and use focuses on levels of formality. *Would like,* for example, is much more polite than *want,* and is especially appropriate in stores, offices, and restaurants.

Form: Be sure that students practice the question form of phrasal modals since it differs from that of one-word modals.

A GRAMMAR IN DISCOURSE

How *Not* to Ask for a Raise

A1: Before You Read

- If possible, bring in a *Dilbert* cartoon or other humorous comic strip about asking for a raise. Read it aloud and discuss. Pass it around the class.

- Write the phrase *ask for a raise* on the board. Take a survey of the class and ask for a show of hands for these questions: *How many people have a job now? How many have had a job in the past? How many have never worked? How many (of those who have worked) have ever asked for a raise? Did you get it?*

- If most of your students have not had jobs, brainstorm other kinds of things they have asked for (e.g., asking a parent for money, asking a teacher for permission to hand a

paper in late, or asking a neighbor for a favor). If your class is mixed, divide the students into groups based on their experiences.

- Put students into pairs or groups and give them a few minutes to discuss the questions.

- Bring the class together and call on several students to share their experiences with the class.

A2: Read

- Review the new vocabulary in the glossary, especially *performance review*. Then have students read the book excerpt silently.

- Divide them into groups and have them read the excerpt aloud. (One member of the group can read or they can take turns.)

- Have the groups identify and underline Bob's errors in asking for a raise.

- Call on students to read these sentences aloud and to explain the errors.

A3: After You Read

- Ask students to do this exercise individually and mark the places in the text where they found their answers.

- Tell students to compare their answers with a partner. Circulate and note any problematic items.

- Call on individual students to read a statement aloud and say if it is an error. Discuss any disagreements or problematic items and have students make necessary corrections.

- For a round-up activity, ask *What do you think is the best way to ask for a raise?*

Modals of Request; Modals of Permission; *Would Like, Would Prefer,* and *Would Rather*

EXAMINING FORM

Method 1

(For students not familiar with the structure)

- **Question 1:** Write this question on the board: *Could I speak to you?* Ask students to identify the modal *(Could)*, the subject *(I)*, and the base form of the verb *(speak)*. Write the form on the board: *modal + subject + base verb*.

- Put students in pairs to underline other examples in the article with *can, could,* and *would* (e.g., *Can we talk, Would you consider, Could we discuss, Can you please ask*).

- **Question 2:** Ask students to find the expressions *would rather* and *would like*.

- Have students compare the forms of these two expressions. How are they different? (*Would rather* is followed by the base form, but *would like* is followed by the infinitive form of the verb.) Write the forms on the board:

  would rather + base form

  would like + infinitive

Method 2

(For students familiar with the structure)

- Have students work in pairs to answer the questions.

- Give students a few minutes to refer to the charts to check their answers and review the structures.

- Call on students to go over the exercise. Discuss any disagreements and have students make any necessary corrections.

FORM CHARTS

- Write the following model conversation on the board. Then put students in pairs to create a conversation.

  A: I <u>would like to go</u> to the movies.

  B: I <u>would rather stay</u> home.

- Call on students to read their conversations aloud.

- Have students refer to the charts to check their answers and study the new structures.

- To review the question-and-answer form of one-word modals, copy the following chart on the board.

ORIGINAL SENTENCE	CREATE
He could buy some ice cream.	Affirmative short answer
You could help us.	Negative short answer
She can park the car here.	Negative short answer
I can study in the library.	Affirmative short answer
I could ask my friend for help.	Affirmative short answer

- Call on one student to change a sentence to a question. Then call on another student to reply with a short answer. Model the first sentence.

  I can smoke in this restaurant. (negative short answer)

  A: Can I smoke in this restaurant?

  B: No, you can't.

- Discuss any disagreements and have students refer to the charts to check their answers and make any necessary corrections.

C) MEANING AND USE 1

Modals of Request

EXAMINING MEANING AND USE

- Call on students to read the questions aloud. Then ask different students to act out each one. Encourage them to speak in a tone that corresponds with the level of politeness of the request.

- After the class has listened to the requests, ask them to underline the most polite (b) and circle the least polite (a).

- Discuss any disagreements and have students make any necessary corrections.

MEANING AND USE NOTES

- Write this conversation between friends on the board:

    A: *Will you give me a ride after school?*

    B: *No, I won't.* OR *No, I can't.* OR *I'm sorry, but I can't. I have to study.*

- Ask students which answer is most polite (the last one) and which is least polite (the first one). Ask *Why is the last answer the most polite?* (It gives a reason why the person cannot help.) Have students look at the Notes to check their answers.

D) MEANING AND USE 2

Modals of Permission

EXAMINING MEANING AND USE

- Put students in pairs to do question 1. Call on students to give their answers and write them on the board. (1a; 1b) Do not make corrections at this time. If there are any disagreements, put a question mark next to those answers.

- Tell the same pairs to do question 2 and put the answer on the board. (2a)

- Have students check the answers on the board with the information in the Meaning and Use Notes. Call on students to correct any answers on the board.

MEANING AND USE NOTES

- Assign the modals *can, could,* and *may* to different pairs of students. Tell them to write a mini-conversation using their modal to ask permission. Tell half the class to give permission and the other half to refuse permission. Students must tell the class who the speakers are (e.g., a mother and child, an employer and employee).

- Call on several pairs of students to role-play their conversations. Have the other students critique the conversations. Ask if the level of politeness is correct for the situation.

E) MEANING AND USE 3

Would Like, Would Prefer, and *Would Rather*

EXAMINING MEANING AND USE

- Ask four volunteers to read one sentence each. Do not let the class hear your instructions to the volunteers. Encourage the volunteers to say sentence 1a in a very informal manner and sentence 1b in a very formal manner, as if in an expensive restaurant.

- Ask the class to listen and compare the sentences. Then ask them questions 1 and 2. (1. 1b; 2. 2b, 2a)

- Give students a few minutes to refer to the Notes to check their answers.

- Call on students to read the questions and answers aloud. Discuss any disagreements and have students make any necessary corrections.

MEANING AND USE NOTES

- Write these pairs of sentences on the board. (Do not write the description in parentheses.) Tell students to look at the Meaning and Use Notes to find the difference between *a* and *b* in each pair.

    1. a. *I would like ice cream.* (request)

       b. *I like ice cream.* (expressing a like)

    2. a. *Would you like to dance?* (offer)

       b. *Do you like to dance?* (asking about a like)

    3. a. *Would you rather walk?* (asking about a preference)

       b. *Would you prefer to walk?* (asking about a preference)

    4. a. *I'd rather take the bus than the train.* (expressing a preference)

       b. *I like to take the bus.* (expressing a like)

- Call on students to give their answers. Write them on the board in parentheses.

class. Discuss any disagreements or problematic items.

- For a follow-up activity, put students into pairs or small groups and have them write their "rules" for finding the ideal mate. Then ask a member of each pair or group to read their rules to the class.

B FORM

Modals and Phrasal Modals of Advice, Necessity, and Prohibition

EXAMINING FORM

Method 1
(For students not familiar with the structure)

- **Question 1:** Tell students to reread the book review silently. Then put them in pairs to find another example of *must* and the verb that follows it. Meanwhile, draw two columns on the board and label them:

Affirmative	Negative
modal + base verb	modal + not + base verb

- Call on a student to read the sentence aloud, and have him or her write the modal and the verb that follows it in the appropriate column on the board. *(must play)* Ask *What form of the verb follows* must? (the base form)

- **Question 2:** Have students find an example of *should* and the verb that follows it. Call on a student to read the sentence aloud and write the modal and the verb that follows it in the appropriate column on the board. *(should stop)* Ask *What form of the verb follows* should? (the base form)

- **Question 3:** Have students find an example of the phrasal modals *have to, ought to,* and *had better.* Call on students to read the sentences aloud and have them write the modal forms and the verb that follows them in the appropriate column on the board. Ask *What form of the verb follows them?* (the base form)

- **Question 4:** Ask students to find the negative forms of *must, should,* and *have to.* Call on

students to read the sentences aloud and have them write the modal forms in the appropriate column on the board.

- Call on a student to explain the difference in the formation of the negative of *must* and *should* versus *have to.* (*must/should + not,* but *don't/doesn't have to*)

- Have students refer to the charts to check their answers and study the new structures.

Method 2
(For students familiar with the structure)

- Have students work in pairs to answer the questions.

- Give students a few minutes to refer to the charts to check their answers and review the new structures.

- Call on students to go over the exercise. Discuss any disagreements and have students make any necessary corrections.

FORM CHARTS

- Put students in groups and have them read the bulleted notes aloud.

- Ask each group to write
  - two affirmative sentences with modals of advice. (They can use either one-word or phrasal modals.)
  - one negative sentence with a modal of advice.
  - one affirmative sentence with a modal of necessity.
  - one negative sentence with a modal of prohibition.
  - one *Yes/No* question with *should* and an affirmative and negative short answer.
  - one information question with *should.*
  - one *Yes/No* question with *have to* and an affirmative and negative short answer.
  - one information question with *have to.*

- Have the groups exchange papers and review each other's sentences. Ask them to identify any sentences that are incorrect and write them on the board. Then have them swap back. Discuss these sentences with the class and correct as necessary.

Informally Speaking: Reduced Forms of *Ought To, Has To, Have To,* and *Have Got To* (p. 207)

- Choose two students to read the text in the speech bubbles. Then tell the class you will play the recording and that they should listen to how the underlined form in the cartoon is different from what they hear. If needed, play the recording more than once.

- Have students point out the differences. (The cartoon reads "ought to," whereas on the recording this is pronounced "otta"; the cartoon reads "have to," but on the recording this is pronounced "hafta.") Explain that the form on the recording is considered more informal English. Point out that the form in the cartoon is standard English and students should use this form when writing and speaking, although they may hear native speakers using the informal form.

C MEANING AND USE 1

Modals and Phrasal Modals of Advice

EXAMINING MEANING AND USE

- Ask students to find the two sentences that have the same meaning. (a and e) Ask what kind of idea these sentences express. (advice)

- Ask them which sentence expresses the strongest advice. (d)

- Write the words *suggestion* and *warning* on the board. Ask *Which is more serious?* (a warning)

- Tell them to look at the sentences again and find one with two suggestions. (b)

- Have students find the one that expresses a warning. (c) Ask them how they know. (It has a consequence.)

MEANING AND USE NOTES

- Write the following sentences on the board and have students complete them with different modals. Ask them to look at the Notes and decide which modals make the statement more or less serious.

You _____ call home when you are late.

You _____ read the directions before you set up the new computer.

- Draw a line on the board where *1* = not serious and *5* = very serious.

Not serious   Very serious

1 ——————————————————— 5

- Have students read their sentences and tell you what number the sentence is.

- Put students in pairs and ask them to write a mini-conversation with two answers using different modals. For example:

   A: *I'm worried about my English test.*

   B: *Well, you'd better study hard then.* OR *You could ask Ben for help.*

- Call on pairs to read both versions of their conversation. Have the class discuss the difference between them. Explain that *had better* is used between friends or members of a family or by a person in a position of authority such as an employer.

D MEANING AND USE 2

Modals of Necessity and Prohibition

EXAMINING MEANING AND USE

- Have students work in pairs to answer the questions. (1. 1a and 2a; 2. 1b and 2b)

- Give students a few minutes to refer to the Notes to check their answers.

- Call on students to read each pair of sentences and tell you the answers to the questions.

- Discuss any disagreements and make any necessary corrections.

MEANING AND USE NOTES

- Write this sentence on the board and ask students to complete it. Tell them to imagine that it is on a sign at the entrance of their school: *Visitors _____ sign in at the office.* (must)

- Now ask them to complete this sentence, telling another person about this rule: *When you go to the school, you _____ sign in at the office.* (have to)
- Ask them to refer to the Notes to check their answers, and then have them read their answers aloud.
- Discuss the difference between *mustn't* and *don't have to.* (prohibition versus lack of necessity) Next, write these sentences on the board and ask students to complete them with *must not* or *don't have to*:

  You have to be on the bus at eight. You _____ be late because the driver won't wait.

  You must have a ticket to get on the bus. You _____ take your lunch because we're going to stop at a restaurant.
- Call on students to read their sentences aloud.
- Ask students to give you other examples of things that they must not do and things that they do not have to do.

ADDITIONAL ACTIVITIES

The purpose of these activities is to give students practice in using several different modals in the correct context in writing and speaking.

Writing a Skit

- Explain to students that a skit is a very short play. Put students into pairs and have them write a skit about one of the following situations:
  - A parent is trying to give a son or daughter advice about choosing a husband or wife. The child does not agree with the parent's advice.
  - An teacher is explaining the school rules to new students. The students have a lot of questions.
- Call on students to perform the skits in front of the class.

"Dear Abby" (Giving Advice)

- Bring in a few advice columns from a newspaper. Choose different topics, especially ones that may seem humorous. Explain what

an advice column is and tell them that "Dear Abby" is the most popular advice column in the United States. Read one or two of them to the class. Ask students if they have advice columns in their native countries.
- Put students in pairs and have them write a letter to an advice column. Tell them that they do not have to be realistic; they can exaggerate as much as they want.
- Collect the letters and distribute them to new pairs. Ask each pair to write an answer.
- Call on students to read some of the letters and answers aloud. Have the class vote on the best answer.

Returning to Grammar in Discourse

The purpose of this activity is to check students' understanding of key meanings and uses of the target structures in the chapter by having them return to the book review at the beginning of the chapter and apply what they have learned.

- Write the following extracts from the book review on the board (or type them up and photocopy them before class). Have students work in pairs to find them in the review. Make sure they read the complete sentences that these extracts come from.
  1. *. . . women must play hard to get.*
  2. *. . . a woman must not call a man on the phone, . . .*
  3. *Women don't have to play games . . .*
  4. *. . . any woman who follows this advice had better buy a copy of the book for . . .*
  5. *. . . women should not follow the advice in this book . . .*
- Now write the following items on the board:
  a. *rules*
  b. *opinion*
  c. *warning*
- Have students think about the use of modals and phrasal modals in each extract and match each one to the letter of the item above that best describes it. (1. a; 2. a; 3. b; 4. c; 5. b)
- Bring the class together. Call on pairs to give their answers, and have them offer explanations. If students still have problems, revisit the Meaning and Use Notes.

12 Tag Questions

Overview

Tag questions are especially common in spoken English. They consist of a statement followed by a short question, called a tag. The meaning of the tag depends on the intonation. If someone is not sure of something, rising intonation is used on the tag because he or she is asking a question (e.g., *You like him, don't you?* This means "I don't know if you like him or not. Please tell me."). If someone is sure, falling intonation is used because he or she is simply asking for agreement or confirmation (e.g., *She doesn't speak German, does she?* This means "I am sure but I want confirmation."). After an affirmative statement, a negative tag is used (e.g., *Peter helped you, didn't he? Gina was at school, wasn't she?*). After a negative statement, an affirmative tag is used (e.g., *You can't swim, can you? That isn't Anita, is it?*).

Form: Students may have difficulty forming certain tags. For example, when *this* or *that* is the subject in the statement, *it* is used in the tag. (*This store is very big, isn't it?*) When *these* or *those* is the subject, *they* is used in the tag. (*These cookies are great, aren't they?*)

A GRAMMAR IN DISCOURSE

Women's Language and Men's Language

A1: Before You Read

- Write the title of the magazine article on the board: "Women's Language and Men's Language." Ask the class *Do you think women talk about different things among themselves than men do? Do they have different types of conversations?* Elicit a few different opinions.

- Divide the students into groups. Appoint a note taker for each group. Give them five to ten minutes to discuss the questions.

- Call on several note takers to report on their group's discussion. Note some of the key ideas on the board.

A2: Read

Note:

Although there were some early studies that seemed to show that women use tag questions more than men, recent work seems to contradict that theory. Current research seems to support the view that men and women use tag questions about equally, but women use the rising intonation more than men.

- Have students read the article individually.

- Put students in groups to discuss why they know the first conversation is between two men and the second is between two women.

- Bring the class together and ask students to share their ideas with the class. Discuss any disagreements.

A3: After You Read

- Ask students to do this exercise individually and note the places in the article where they found their answers.

- Have them compare their answers in pairs. Circulate, note any problematic items, and go over them with the whole class.

- Call on students to report their answers.

- For a follow-up activity, ask students to listen to conversations among men, women, and mixed groups for a day or two and note what differences they might hear. Discuss these at the beginning or end of a future class. Come prepared with a few of your own ideas to get the discussion started (e.g., Women use rising intonation in tag questions more than men.).

Tag Questions

EXAMINING FORM

Method 1
(For students not familiar with the structure)

- **Question 1:** Tell students to find the sentence with the underlined tag in the magazine article. (*It's a great day for tennis, isn't it?*) Write it on the board.

- Put students in pairs and have them go through the article to find three more tag questions. Call on students to come to the board and write the sentences with tag questions that they found. (*You aren't going to quit, are you? You're still looking for another job, aren't you? You didn't go to that awful restaurant again, did you?*)

- **Question 2:** Call on students to read the affirmative statements on the board. (*It's a great day for tennis, You're still looking for another job*) Ask what kind of tags they have. (negative)

- Call on students to read the negative statements on the board. (*You aren't going to quit, You didn't go to that awful restaurant again*) Ask what kind of tags they have. (affirmative)

- Have students refer to the charts to check their answers and familiarize themselves with the new structures.

Method 2
(For students familiar with the structure)

- Have students do the exercise in pairs. Give them a few minutes to refer to the charts to check their answers and review the structures.

- Call on students to go over the exercise. Discuss any disagreements and have students make any necessary corrections.

FORM CHARTS

- Put students in pairs to review the charts.

- Write these statements with blanks for tags on the board. Ask the pairs to complete them.

  You haven't finished, _____?
  _____, are they? (simple present or present continuous)

She saw him leave, _____?
_____, weren't we? (simple past or past continuous)
It'll be here tomorrow, _____?
_____, isn't it? (simple present or present continuous)

- Ask students to come to the board and complete the sentences. Discuss any problematic items.

- Write these statements on the board. Have students continue to work in their pairs to complete them.

  I'm here, _____?
  He never goes, _____?
  Someone gave you the answer, _____?

- Review the answers with the entire class. Discuss any disagreements and have students refer to the charts to check their answers. Make any necessary corrections.

Informally Speaking: Reduced Statements with Tag Questions (p. 230)

- Choose two students to read the text in the speech bubbles. Then tell the class you will play the recording and that they should listen to how the underlined form in the cartoon is different from what they hear. If needed, play the recording more than once.

- Have students point out the differences. (The cartoon reads "He's not very good, is he?" whereas on the recording the speaker says, "Not very good, is he?") Explain that the form on the recording is considered more informal English. Point out that the form in the cartoon is standard English and students should use this form when writing and speaking, although they may hear native speakers using the informal form.

C MEANING AND USE

Tag Questions

EXAMINING MEANING AND USE

- Read the pairs of sentences aloud.

- Put students in pairs to answer the questions. (1. 1b, 1a; 2. 2b, 2a)

- Give students a few minutes to refer to the Notes to check their answers.
- Call on students to read the questions and answers aloud. Discuss any disagreements.

MEANING AND USE NOTES

- Draw a rising arrow on the board: ↗ Remind the class that rising intonation expresses uncertainty. Point to the arrow and model the intonation with these sentences: *You went, didn't you? He's not in Paris, is he? They're hungry, aren't they?*
- Say the sentences again and have students repeat them after you.
- Draw a falling arrow on the board: ↙ Explain that falling intonation expresses certainty. Point to the arrow and model the falling intonation with the same sentences. Say the sentences again and have students repeat them.
- Write these tag questions on the board:

  Napoleon was French, wasn't he? (Yes, he was.)

  The sun doesn't rise in the west, does it? (No, it doesn't.)

  Astronauts have gone to Mars, haven't they? (No, they haven't.)

- Call on students to answer them. Discuss any difficult or problematic items.

Vocabulary Notes: Other Ways of Answering Tag Questions (p. 235)

- Read the information aloud and model the conversations with a student. Go over the various responses.
- Ask several students tag questions that you know they will agree with (e.g., *This is a great class, isn't it?*). Tell them to use one of the phrases to answer (e.g., *That's right.*).

Beyond the Sentence: Beginning Conversations Using Statements with Tag Questions (p. 236)

This section is intended to give students practice with the meaning and use of grammar as it functions naturally in paragraphs and conversations.

- Put students in pairs to read the two conversations.

- Ask them to read the tag questions aloud.
- Ask the class to think about the situation that the people are in (waiting for a train, in line in a cafeteria). Point out how the tag question is used to start a conversation or simply to pass time while waiting in line. Have the class share their ideas for other possible situations.

ADDITIONAL ACTIVITIES

The purpose of these activities is to have students practice using tag questions in natural speaking and writing situations.

Speaking: He's Bottecelli, Isn't He? (a Guessing Game)

This game is similar to Twenty Questions except that it uses tag questions instead of *Yes/No* questions.

- Put students in pairs. Tell each pair to think of two famous people, living or dead.
- Put two sets of pairs together. Tell them that each set of pairs is going to ask the other tag questions. The goal is to guess the famous person with as few questions as possible. The pair that guesses correctly with the fewest questions wins the game. For example:

  A: *It's a man, isn't it?*

  B: *Yes, it is.*

  A: *He makes movies, doesn't he?*

  B: *Yes, he does.*

  A: *It's Steven Spielberg, isn't it?*

  B: *Yes, it is.*

Writing a Conversation

- Divide the class into pairs and ask them to write a conversation about the following situation. Tell them to use tag questions, but remind them not to overuse tags or their conversations will sound very unnatural.

  Situation: Two students are studying for a geography or history test. They are trying to recall the facts that they need to know.

- Ask some pairs to perform their conversations in front of the class.

13 Additions with Conjunctions

Overview

Additions (attached statements) are common in spoken English. They are formed when the verb phrase of the second sentence is similar to the first sentence but is not repeated (e.g., *I like bagels, and my sister does too*). *And . . . too* is used with two affirmative statements; *and . . . either* is used with two negative statements (e.g., *I don't like spinach, and my brother doesn't either.*); and *but* is used to show a contrast between a negative and an affirmative statement (e.g., *I like bagels, but my mother doesn't.*). Responses (or rejoinders) are answers to statements (e.g., *A: I like bagels. B: I do, too.*).

Form: Most students will be familiar with the connectors *and, but,* and *too*. However, some students tend to use *too* even when they are connecting two negative ideas (e.g., **I don't like spinach, and Greg doesn't too.*). *Either* may be new to them. Students may find the reverse word order with *neither* and *so* challenging (e.g., *I don't like spinach, and neither does Greg. She likes bagels, and so does he.*).

A GRAMMAR IN DISCOURSE

Equal Rights for Apes?

A1: Before You Read

- Ask *Have you ever had a pet? Do you have one now?* Ask for a show of hands.

- Call on several students to talk about their pets. Ask *Is/was your pet treated like a member of the family? Does/did it live in the house or outside?*

- Put students in pairs to discuss the questions. Then bring the class together and be sure to call on students with opposing opinions.

A2: Read

- Have students read the letter individually.

- Divide them into small groups and have them discuss the letter. Write these questions on the board for the groups to discuss: *How are animals similar to humans? How are they different? Should animals have the right to be free? If so, which animals should have liberty rights? Apes? Dolphins? Parrots? Elephants? Dogs? Honeybees? Where do you draw the line?*

- Call on students from each group to share their ideas. Be sure to call on students with different opinions.

A3: After You Read

- Have students do this exercise individually and then compare their answers with a partner's. Remind them to note the places in the letter where they found their answers.

- Call on students to read the statements aloud and say if they think the writer would agree with them. If there are any disagreements, have them read the section that they underlined.

- Go over any difficult or problematic items with the whole class.

- For a round-up activity, ask the class *Do you think any animals will ever have "legal personhood," that is, the right to be a free person?*

B FORM 1

And . . . Too, And . . . Either, and But

EXAMINING FORM

Method 1
(For students not familiar with the structure)

- **Questions 1–4:** Put students in pairs to complete the tasks. Remind them to refer to the charts if they need help. While they are doing the exercise, draw the following chart on the board and save it for later reference.

FORM	FIRST SENTENCE	SECOND SENTENCE
A	Affirmative	Affirmative
B	Negative	Negative
C	Affirmative	Negative
D	Negative	Affirmative

- Call on students to read the answers aloud. (1. b, *and . . . too;* 2. c, *and . . . either;* 3. a, d, *but;* 4. *and, and, but;* They connect two affirmative clauses, two negative clauses, and an affirmative clause with a negative clause, respectively.)
- Ask students to tell you if the sentences match Form A, B, C or D from the chart on the board.

Method 2
(For students familiar with the structure)

- Have students do the exercise in pairs. While they are doing the exercise, draw the chart from Method 1 on the board.
- Give students a few minutes to refer to the charts to check their answers and review the structures.
- Call on students to read the answers aloud. Ask them to tell you if the sentences match Form A, B, C, or D from the chart on the board. Discuss any disagreements and have students make any necessary corrections.

FORM CHARTS

- Write these pairs of sentences on the board. Have students work individually to combine them by using *and . . . too, and . . . either,* or *but.*

  I can ski. Bob can ski. (I can ski, and Bob can too.)

  I can ski. Bob can't ski. (I can ski, but Bob can't.)

  I can't ski. Bob can't ski. (I can't ski, and Bob can't either.)

  My skis are old. His skis are new. (My skis are old, but his are new.)

Maria likes to ski. Bob likes to ski. (Maria likes to ski, and Bob does too.)

- Call on students to write the answers on the board. Discuss any disagreements and have students make any necessary corrections.
- Point out that a comma must be inserted before *and* or *but.*

C) FORM 2

Additions with *And So* and *And Neither*

EXAMINING FORM

- **Questions 1–3:** Put students in pairs to complete the tasks. As they are working, write the sentences on the board.
- Call on individual students to underline the subject and circle the verb in each addition. (1a. *are apes;* 1b. *apes are;* 2a. *are apes;* 2b. *apes aren't*) Then, call on other students to explain how the order is different. (In 1a and 1b the order is reversed; in 2a and 2b the order is reversed.) Finally, call on students to answer question 3. (*And so* connects two affirmative sentences; *and neither* connects two negative sentences.)
- Refer to the chart on the board from Form 1. Ask students to match each sentence with a form (A, B, C, or D).

FORM CHARTS

- Write these sentences on the board. Ask students to work individually to combine them with *so* or *neither.*

  Sara went to school, and Mike did too. (Sara went to school, and so did Mike.)

  We aren't working, and they aren't either. (We aren't working, and neither are they.)

  I enjoy reading, and Mike does too. (I enjoy reading, and so does Mike.)

  They didn't see that movie, and I didn't either. (They didn't see that movie, and neither did I.)

- Call on students to write the answers on the board. Discuss any disagreements and have students make any necessary corrections.

- Point out that a comma must be inserted before *and*.

D) MEANING AND USE

Expressing Similarities and Differences

EXAMINING MEANING AND USE

- Have students work in pairs to answer the questions. (Sentences a and c have the same meaning; sentences b and d have the same meaning. Each sentence expresses a similarity between the two subjects.)

- Give students a few minutes to refer to the Notes to check their answers and review the uses of additions.

- Call on students to read the questions and answers aloud. Discuss any disagreements and have students make any necessary corrections.

MEANING AND USE NOTES

- Write these cues on the board:
    1. *and . . . too*
    2. *and . . . either*
    3. *and so*
    4. *and neither*
    5. *but*

- Write these sentences on the board:
    I have two brothers. Lisa has two brothers. (I have two brothers, and so does Lisa / . . . , and Lisa does too.)
    She speaks German. He doesn't speak German. (She speaks German, but he doesn't.)
    Tony didn't go to school yesterday. I didn't go to school yesterday. (Tony didn't go to school yesterday, and neither did I / . . . , and I didn't either.)
    He went to Paris. His friend went to Paris. (He went to Paris, and so did his friend / . . . , and his friend did too.)

- Call on students to combine the sentences. Be sure to elicit two ways of combining each sentence (with the exception of sentences with *but*). Point to the appropriate cue on the board if they need help.

- Say the statements and the subjects that follow them below, and ask students to use the subject in a short response. Be sure to elicit both forms of the short response. Begin by modeling the exercise with volunteers:
    Instructor: I'm tired. I . . .
    Student 1: So am I.
    Student 2: I am too.
    I am hungry. I . . . (I am too. So am I.)
    John didn't do his homework. I . . . (I didn't either. Neither did I.)
    She runs every day. He . . . (He does too. So does he.)
    I didn't sleep well last night. Amy . . . (Amy didn't either. Neither did Amy.)
    She was late to class. He . . . (He was too. So was he.)

Informally Speaking: Pronouns in Short Responses (p. 252)

- Choose two students to read the text in the speech bubbles. Then tell the class you will play the recording and that they should listen to how the underlined form in the cartoon is different from what they hear. If needed, play the recording more than once.

- Have students point out the differences. (The cartoon reads "I do too!" whereas on the recording he says, "Me too!"; the cartoon reads "Neither am I!" whereas on the recording he says, "Me neither!") Explain that the form on the recording is considered more informal English. Point out that the form in the cartoon is standard English and students should use this form when writing and speaking, although they may hear native speakers using the informal form.

Beyond the Sentence: Combining Ideas (p. 255)

This section is intended to give students practice with the meaning and use of grammar as it functions naturally in paragraphs and conversations.

- Put students in pairs to read the explanation and the two sample paragraphs for the main idea. Have them compare the two paragraphs and decide which one is better.

- Bring the class back together and talk about which paragraph is better and why. (The second paragraph is better because it avoids repeating the same information. Instead, it uses additions.)

ADDITIONAL ACTIVITIES

The purpose of these activities is to provide freer practice opportunities for students to use additions and rejoinders.

Speaking: Find Someone Who . . .

- Ask each student to list five pieces of personal information. Tell them to write negative as well as affirmative sentences (e.g., *I was born in January. I don't like sports. I have five brothers and sisters. My father is a sales rep. I never eat meat.*).

- Circulate to help with grammar and vocabulary as students write their statements.

- Then tell students to circulate and share their information with classmates. Their objective is to find someone like themselves. Encourage them to speak with several different students, and tell them to take notes because they will report their findings to the class.

- Before they begin, model the exercise with volunteers.

  Instructor: I read a lot.
  Student 1: So do I.
  Student 2: I do too.

  Instructor: I don't like spinach.
  Student 1: Neither do I.
  Student 2: I don't either.

- Bring the class together and have students report what they have in common with their classmates (e.g., *I read a lot and Fumiko does too. I don't have any brothers, and neither does Hanna.*).

Writing: Describing Similar People

- Have students think of two people they know who are alike in many ways, for example, their sister or brother and themselves, or two friends, or two roommates. Describe their similarities. They can begin their paragraphs like this:

  My sister and I are very much alike. She has brown hair, and so do I. She is tall, and so am I. She likes to work out at least three times a week, and I do, too. . . .

- Circulate, helping as necessary with vocabulary and grammar.

- Ask a few volunteers to read their paragraphs to the class.

Returning to Grammar in Discourse

The purpose of this activity is to check students' understanding of key meanings and uses of the target structures in the chapter by having them return to the letter at the beginning of the chapter and apply what they have learned.

- Write the following extracts from the letter on the board (or type them up and photocopy them before class). Have students work in pairs to find them in the letter. Make sure they read the complete sentences that these extracts come from.

  1. *Humans shouldn't live in fear of their lives, and animals shouldn't, either.*
  2. *I'm upset, and I'm sure others are too.*
  3. *People also say that humans can appreciate beauty, but animals can't.*
  4. *I don't agree, and neither do many scientists.*

- Now write the following items on the board:
  a. *combines similar information*
  b. *combines contrasting information*

- Have students think about the meaning and use of the combined sentences in each extract and match each one to the letter of the item above that best describes it. (1. a; 2. a; 3. b; 4. a)

- Bring the class together. Call on pairs to give their answers, and have them offer explanations. If students still have problems, revisit the Meaning and Use Notes.

14 Nouns and Quantity Expressions

Overview

Count nouns have both singular and plural forms. They may be preceded by a number, *a/an*, *the*, or no article (e.g., *one egg, an egg, the egg, eggs*). They can also be preceded by general quantity expressions such as *several*, *many*, *a few,* and *few* in affirmative sentences and *many* in negative statements and questions (e.g., *I have a few friends. I don't have many friends. Do you have many friends?*). Noncount nouns cannot be counted and do not have plural forms. *The* or no article (Ø) can come before noncount nouns, as well as general quantity expressions (e.g., *a great deal*, *much* in negative sentences and questions), *a little* and *little,* and specific quantity expressions (e.g., *a cup of sugar*).

Form: Countability as a concept does not exist in all languages; for example, there is no count/noncount distinction in Chinese. Moreover, languages that do distinguish may consider some nouns count that are noncount in English or vice versa. Students may add *-s* to a noncount noun (e.g., **I cut my hairs.*) or they may use *much* in affirmative statements (e.g., **I like much salt on my food.*).

A GRAMMAR IN DISCOURSE

Mood Foods

A1: Before You Read

- Ask *What are some of your favorite foods?* List them on the board. Be sure there are count and noncount nouns. (You may have to add some of your favorite foods to accomplish this.) Keep this list on the board for later reference.

- Ask students if they think certain foods affect how they feel. Have them talk about their ideas and share personal experiences.

A2: Read

- Make sure that students understand that the chart should be read row by row, from left to right. Read the first row aloud as an example.

- Have students read the magazine article individually. Meanwhile, draw the following chart on the board:

IF YOU . . .	EAT OR DRINK . . .	
1. have to study later,	a. an egg.	(1. d)
2. feel nervous,	b. ginkgo biloba.	(2. c)
3. need energy quickly,	c. a cup of mint tea.	(3. a)
4. need to improve your memory,	d. tomato juice with cayenne pepper.	(4. b)

- Put students in pairs to match the items in each column. Have two sets of pairs switch papers and check each other's work. Then have them swap back.

- Call on students to read the answers in complete sentences (e.g., *If you feel nervous, drink a cup of mint tea.*). Discuss any disagreements or problematic items.

A3: After You Read

- Ask students to do this exercise individually and note the places in the article where they found their answers.

- Put students in pairs to compare their answers.

- Circulate, note any problematic items, and go over them with the whole class.

- Review the answers with the class. If there are any disagreements, ask students to find and read the portion of the article that contains the answer.

- For a follow-up activity, ask students if they know of any other foods that may help change someone's mood. Have them share their knowledge with the class.

Nouns and Quantity Expressions

EXAMINING FORM

Method 1

(For students not familiar with the structure)

- **Questions 1–3:** Write these nouns on the board: *information, books, water, student, chalk, sports.* Ask students to tell you which of these nouns can have a number in front of them. *(books, student, sports)*

- Call on students to give each of these nouns a number. *(two books, one student, four sports)* Ask students what these nouns are called. (count nouns)

- Ask students what nouns such as *water, chalk,* and *information* are called. (noncount nouns)

- Put students in groups to answer the questions. Have students refer to the charts to check their answers and familiarize themselves with the new structures. (1. count nouns: *calorie, calories;* noncount noun: *milk;* 2. *little energy, a lot of energy, a few prunes, a great deal of protein, some people*)

- Review the answers and discuss any difficult or problematic items.

Method 2

(For students familiar with the structure)

- Have students do the exercise in pairs.

- Give students a few minutes to refer to the charts to check their answers and review the structures.

- Call on students to go over the exercise. Discuss any disagreements and have students make any necessary corrections.

FORM CHARTS

- Refer students to the list of their favorite foods that you wrote on the board at the beginning of the lesson.

- Call on students to tell you if the foods are count or noncount nouns. Underline the count nouns and circle the noncount nouns.

- Have students work in small groups to select three count nouns from the list and write three sentences using an article (*a, an,* or *the*), a

number, a general quantity expression, or a specific quantity expression. Tell them to include one question using *how many.*

- Ask students to select three noncount nouns from the list and write three sentences using *the,* no article, a general quantity expression, or a specific quantity expression. Tell them to include one question using *how much.* Refer students to the charts to check their sentences.

- Bring the class together. Call on different groups to read their sentences. Correct form where necessary. When helpful, write problematic sentences on the board and elicit corrections. Answer any questions.

Informally Speaking: Reducing *Of* in Informal Speech (p. 269)

- Choose two students to read the text in the speech bubbles. Then tell the class you will play the recording and that they should listen to how the underlined form in the cartoon is different from what they hear. If needed, play the recording more than once.

- Have students point out the differences. (The first bubble reads "a lot of" and "plenty of," whereas on the recording these are pronounced "alotta" and "plennya"; the second bubble reads "a lot of," whereas on the recording this is pronounced "alotta.") Explain that the form on the recording is considered more informal English. Point out that the form in the cartoon is standard English and students should use this form when writing and speaking, although they may hear native speakers using the informal form.

C) MEANING AND USE 1

General Quantity Expressions

EXAMINING MEANING AND USE

- The difference in meaning between *few/little* and *a few/a little* can be confusing for many students. Therefore, it's a good idea to do this activity as a class.

- Call on individual students to read the sentences aloud. Then read the questions and call on students to answer. (1. quantity expressions: *many, few, lots of, a lot of*; Ben, Josh, and Tony have a large number of friends; Eva has a small number of friends; 2. quantity expressions: *little, a little*; 2a)

- Call on students to answer the following questions:

  Which expression means that there is not enough of something? (few/little)

  Which expression means that there is enough of something? (a few/a little)

- Put students in pairs to list the general quantity expressions. Have them refer to the Notes if they need help. Call on them to read their lists and write the expressions on the board.

- Ask students to write what they have in their refrigerator, using quantity expressions. Give them some examples: *I have a few eggs. I don't have much milk.*

- Call on students to write their sentences on the board. Discuss any disagreements and have students make any necessary corrections.

MEANING AND USE NOTES

- Write these count nouns on the board: *friends, illnesses, bad grades, good grades, nice clothes.* Call on students to make statements using general quantity expressions such as *few, a few, many, a lot of* and one of the count nouns.

- Write these noncount nouns on the board: *money, leisure time, intelligence, fear.* Call on different students to make statements with general quantity expressions such as *little, a little, not much, some, lots of,* and one of the noncount nouns. Refer them to the Notes if they need help.

D) MEANING AND USE 2

Specific Quantity Expressions

EXAMINING MEANING AND USE

- Put the students into pairs to read the recipe and answer the questions. (1. No. There are no specific quantities. You need to know exactly how much of each ingredient to use. 2. *a cup of, a half teaspoon of, a tablespoon*)

- Have students rewrite the recipe using specific quantity expressions. Tell them to use their imagination if they do not know how to make pancakes. Also tell them that they can add extra ingredients (e.g., *one banana, a cup of berries*).

- Give students a few minutes to refer to the Notes to check their work.

- Call on students to read their pancake recipes aloud. Discuss any disagreements and have students make any necessary corrections.

- For an optional activity, have students take notes while they listen to each other's recipes and decide which recipe is the best or most unusual.

MEANING AND USE NOTES

- Put students into groups. Write these nouns on the board and assign one noun to each group. Tell them to list as many specific quantity expressions as they can think of for their noun. Model an example: *coffee—a cup of, two pounds of, a pot of.*

  grapes (a bunch of, a bowl of, a pound of, two bags of)

  sugar (a cup of, two teaspoons of, one container of, two boxes of)

  paper (a sheet of, ten pieces of, a box of, a pile of, a pad of)

  bread (a loaf of, a slice of, a piece of, a basket of)

  mustard (a teaspoon of, a tablespoon of, a cup of, a jar of)

- Ask a member of each group to come to the board and list their noun and its specific quantity expressions.

- Review each list. Ask the other groups if they can think of any other expressions that are not on the list. Elicit them and add them to the list.

ADDITIONAL ACTIVITIES

The purpose of these activities is to provide opportunities for freer practice using count and noncount nouns with general and specific quantity expressions.

Speaking: Planning a Meal

- Bring in supermarket ads from various local supermarkets. Divide the class into groups and give each group an ad. Have each group plan an imaginary luncheon, dinner, or class party. Tell them to figure out which foods they will need to buy, which general or specific quantities of each food they will need, and how much the event will cost.

- Circulate, helping with vocabulary, pronunciation, and quantity expressions.

- Have each group report to the class what they will need and how much it will cost.

Writing: Favorite Dish

- Ask students to work individually to write a recipe for their favorite dish. Have them list the ingredients and the quantities (to the best of their knowledge).

- Circulate, helping them with vocabulary as necessary.

- Call on students to read their recipe to the class without telling the class what it is. Have the class guess the name of the dish.

Returning to Grammar in Discourse

The purpose of this activity is to check students' understanding of key meanings and uses of the target structures in the chapter by having them return to the magazine article at the beginning of the chapter and apply what they have learned.

- Write the following extracts from the magazine article on the board (or type them up and photocopy them before class). Have students work in pairs to find them in the article. Make sure they read the complete sentences that these extracts come from.

    1. *You have little energy in the morning.*
    2. *Have some cheese . . .*
    3. *Don't have a cup of coffee.*
    4. *. . . have a few pieces of mint candy.*
    5. *Eggs and cheese have a great deal of protein . . .*

- Now write the following items on the board:

    a. *a large quantity/amount*
    b. *a small quantity/amount*
    c. *a specific quantity/amount*

- Have students think about the meaning of the quantity expression in each extract and match each one to the letter of the item above that best describes it. (1. b; 2. b; 3. c; 4. b; 5. a)

- Bring the class together. Call on pairs to give their answers, and have them offer explanations. If students still have problems, revisit the Meaning and Use Notes.

15 Indefinite and Definite Articles

Overview

The indefinite article *(a/an)* is used before a singular count noun when it is mentioned for the first time and does not represent a specific person or thing (e.g., *They bought a new house.*). The definite article *(the)* is used in several different ways. For example, it is used before a singular or plural noun that has already been mentioned (e.g., *They bought a new house. The house is very large.*). It is also used when other information identifies the noun (e.g., *Please give me the book on the table.*).

Form: Some languages use the definite article where it is omitted in English. You may hear students say **The women should not work outside the home. *The nature is beautiful.*

A GRAMMAR IN DISCOURSE

Meat-Eating Plants

A1: Before You Read

- Ask the class if they know about any unusual plants. Ask *What makes these plants unusual?* Have students talk about what they know.

- Tell them to scan the article to find the name of the plant and what the plant eats. (Venus Flytrap, insects)

A2: Read

- This article may be challenging for some students. Ask them to read the article carefully and underline vocabulary or expressions that they do not know. Refer students to the glossary. Write any other words or phrases they still do not know on the board, and review their meanings with the class.

- Write these sentences on the board:

  Carnivorous plants attract _____.

When an insect lands on a Venus Flytrap,

_____.

- Put students in pairs. Tell them to find the answers in the article and complete the sentences.

- Call on students to read their sentences aloud. Complete the sentences on the board as students read their answers. Discuss any disagreements.

A3: After You Read

- Have students work in pairs to complete the task. Remind them to note the places in the article where they found their answers.

- Ask two sets of pairs to get together and compare answers. If there are any disagreements, ask students to read the part of the article that contains the answer.

- Go over any difficult items with the class and have students make necessary corrections.

- For a follow-up activity, ask *Would you like to have one of these plants in your home? Why or why not?*

B FORM

Indefinite and Definite Articles

EXAMINING FORM

Method 1
(For students not familiar with the structure)

- **Questions 1 and 2:** Put students into pairs and have them complete the tasks.

- Have two sets of pairs compare and discuss their answers. (1. a: A, the, a; b: a; c: the; 2. count nouns: *fly, plant, leaf, parts;* noncount noun: *air;* In these examples, *a* is used with singular count nouns, *the* is used with a plural count noun, and *the* is used with a noncount noun.)

- Call on students to read the answers. Discuss any problematic items.

Method 2
(For students familiar with the structure)

- Put students into pairs and have them complete the tasks.

- Give them a few minutes to refer to the charts to check their answers and review the structures.

- Call on students to read their answers aloud. Discuss any problematic items.

FORM CHARTS

- Have students work in groups. Tell them to reread the bulleted notes labeled "Indefinite Article" and "Definite Article."

- While students are working, write these sentences on the board:

  I am looking for _____ taxi. _____ taxi on the corner is free.

  I love _____ flowers. I have _____ rose bush in my garden.

  Judy needs _____ information on exotic plants. _____ information in this book will be helpful to her.

  There is _____ pink rose and _____ red rose in the vase. I prefer _____ pink rose.

- Have the groups work together to complete these sentences. Refer them to the charts if they need help.

- Call on students to read the sentences aloud. Discuss any disagreements and have students make any necessary corrections.

C MEANING AND USE 1

Indefinite and Definite Articles

EXAMINING MEANING AND USE

- Have students work in pairs to answer the questions. (specific: 1b and 2b; general: 1a and 2a)

- Give students a few minutes to refer to the Notes to check their answers.

- Call on students to read the questions and answers aloud. Discuss any disagreements

and have students make any necessary corrections.

- Write these sentences on the board:
  1. *Let's go down to the basement. I'm looking for a lamp.*
  2. *Let's go down to the basement. I'm looking for the green lamp.*

- Ask students to compare the sentences and explain how they are different. (Sentence 1 refers to any lamp. Sentence 2 refers to a specific lamp—the green one.)

MEANING AND USE NOTES

- Divide the class into groups. Assign each group a Note about indefinite articles (1A–1C). Ask them to write a mini-conversation that illustrates the Note that they were given. Then call on different groups to read their mini-conversations.

- Keep students in the same groups, or divide the groups into pairs if you have a smaller class. Assign each group or pair a Note about definite articles (2A–2F). Ask them to write a mini-conversation that illustrates the point that they were given. Call on students to read their mini-conversations.

Vocabulary Notes: Phrases such as *In School* and *In the School* (p. 292)

- Have students close their books. Write these sentences on the board: *He is in class now. He is in the class.*

- Ask students to explain the difference in meaning. (Adding *the* describes the physical place where a person is.)

- Tell students to open their books and read all six sentences. Discuss the differences in meaning.

D MEANING AND USE 2

Nouns in General Statements

EXAMINING MEANING AND USE

- Have students work in pairs to answer the questions. (1. 1a and 2a; 2. 1b and 2b)

- Give students a few minutes to refer to the

Notes to check their answers and review the uses of articles with nouns in general statements.

- Call on students to read the questions and answers aloud. Discuss any disagreements and have students make any necessary corrections.

MEANING AND USE NOTES

- Write the following sentences on the board. Have students work with their partner to match each sentence with one meaning in the Notes.

  1. *Lions have very sharp teeth.* (1A)
  2. *I love flowers.* (1E)
  3. *Male lions hunt for food.* (1B)
  4. *The buffalo used to be extinct.* (1C)
  5. *A cat is a solitary animal.* (1D)

- Keep students in pairs. Write these nouns on the board: *music, book, elephant,* and *rose.* Ask students to write three sentences. Tell them that each sentence must illustrate a different point in the Notes.

  Examples:

  Unfortunately, music is not important in our public schools.

  Books are an important part of our lives.

  The elephant has a long memory.

  A rose is a symbol of beauty.

- Have students write their sentences on the board and explain which point the sentence represents. Discuss and make any necessary corrections.

⬤ ADDITIONAL ACTIVITIES

The purpose of these activities is to have students practice using indefinite and definite articles in a less-structured setting.

Speaking: How's Your Memory?

- Without letting students watch you, assemble several different items (about 25) on a table or desk. Some possibilities include a cup, a pen, a piece of paper, a key, a box of paper clips, an orange, a coin, a feather, a ring, an apple, and a needle. They should all be objects that students can name.

- Give students 30 seconds to study the items and the arrangement, and then cover the items with a piece of cloth or paper.

- Give students one minute to make a list of everything that they remember.

- Have the class stand up and call on students one by one to name an item. Make sure they use the correct article (e.g., *a key, an orange*).

- Any student who cannot remember an item or does not use the correct article has to sit down. When no one can remember any more items, call on students to tell you the arrangement of the items and record them on the board (e.g., *The orange was next to the pen. The paper was inside the book.*).

- Remove the cover. Have students compare the notes on the board to the arrangement of the items. Who has the best memory?

Speaking: Listen and Draw

Model this activity by drawing your own picture and asking students to draw it as you describe it: *I drew an apple and a pear. The apple is in the center of the paper and the pear is above the apple.*

- Ask students to draw on a piece of paper a picture of at least three objects or shapes. The drawing can be abstract or realistic. However, if it is abstract, it must have easily describable forms (circles, diamonds, and so on).

- Put students in pairs. Tell them not to show their pictures to their partner.

- Have one student from each pair describe his or her picture while the partner draws it. Then have them compare the two pictures.

- When they are finished, have them switch roles.

Writing: Health Matters

Tell students to imagine they write a column called "Health Nut" for a local newspaper. They have just received the letter below. Write the letter on the board. Have students write a reply to the letter (in 1 or 2 paragraphs). First, tell them to think about foods that this person eats, and ask students why they are good or bad. Then have them think about foods they think are healthful. Finally, have students give this person advice on what she should and should not eat and why.

Dear Health Nut,

I am a teenager. My favorite foods are pizza and hamburgers. I also like to eat potato chips, candy, and soda. My parents say that these foods are not good for me, but I feel fine. What do you think? Are these foods good or bad? What should I eat?

Thanks,

Junk Food Jan

Returning to Grammar in Discourse

The purpose of this activity is to check students' understanding of key meanings and uses of the target structures in the chapter by having them return to the magazine article at the beginning of the chapter and apply what they have learned.

- Write the following extracts from the magazine article on the board (or type them up and photocopy them before class). Have students work in pairs to find them in the article. Make sure they read the complete sentences that these extracts come from.

1. *<u>A black fly</u> hovers in the air over a strange-looking plant.*
2. *. . . <u>the fly</u> lands on one of the plant's flat, red leaves.*
3. *Suddenly, <u>the leaf</u> moves!*
4. *<u>The plant</u> that ate this fly is called . . .*
5. *<u>A plant</u> that is carnivorous actually eats meat.*
6. *It traps and eats <u>insects</u>, and . . .*

- Now write the following items on the board:
  a. *a general class of a noun*
  b. *noun mentioned for the first time*
  c. *noun mentioned again*

- Have students think about the use of the underlined noun in each extract and match each one to the letter of the item above that best describes it. (1. b; 2. c; 3. c; 4. c; 5. a; 6. a)

- Bring the class together. Call on pairs to give their answers, and have them offer explanations. If students still have problems, revisit the Meaning and Use Notes.

16 Adjectives

Overview

This chapter introduces the placement and order of adjectives (e.g., *the big book, The book is big. The big, green leather book is on the desk.*). Students will also learn about the difference between adjectives that end in *-ing* and *-ed*. Adjectives ending in *-ing* express a certain emotional effect that something has on someone (e.g., *The play is boring.*). Adjectives ending in *-ed* show that someone is affected emotionally in this way (e.g., *The audience was bored.*).

Form: Students may find the placement of adjectives challenging. Some adjectives can only follow stative verbs (e.g., *he is afraid*, not **the afraid man*). Other adjectives can come only before a noun (e.g., *her future husband*, not **her husband future*). If there is more than one adjective in a sentence, students may order the adjectives incorrectly (e.g., *the round, yellow sun*, not ** the yellow, round sun*).

A GRAMMAR IN DISCOURSE

Unusual Gifts for Unusual People

A1: Before You Read

- Ask for a show of hands for this question: *How many of you have ever bought anything from a catalog?* Also ask if they ever purchased anything on-line (on the Internet).

- Ask students to describe their experiences. (What did they buy? Were they happy with their purchases? Why or why not? Was it easy to return them? What are the advantages and disadvantages of shopping from a catalog or on-line versus going into a store?)

A2: Read

- Review the words in the Glossary. Then have students read the catalog descriptions. Tell

them to remember as much as they can about each item. Once they have finished reading, have them close their books.

- On a piece of paper, write a list of adjectives from the catalog descriptions. Do not put them in the order in which they appear. Make copies of the list for each student.

long-lasting	(potholders)
challenging	(crossword puzzle)
special	(thermometer)
unusual	(thermometer)
fascinating	(crossword puzzle)
strong	(crossword puzzle)
leather	(potholders)
washable	(potholders)

- Divide students into groups. Give each group member a copy of the list of adjectives. Tell them to identify the item in the catalog that each adjective describes.

- Model the exercise. Write *long-lasting* on the board and ask *Which item does* long-lasting *describe?* (potholders)

- Have students review the catalog to check their answers.

Cultural Notes

Americans love to shop. However, they also love convenience, so many people shop by catalog. Thousands of different companies have no physical stores at all. They simply send out catalogs and wait for customers to call in or fax their orders. Shopping on the Internet (shopping on-line) has become very popular in recent years. You can purchase almost anything on-line, even a car.

A3: After You Read

- Have students do this exercise individually and then compare their answers with a partner. Remind them to note the places in the catalog descriptions where they found their answers.

- Go over any difficult or problematic items with the whole class.

B) FORM

Adjectives

EXAMINING FORM

Method 1
(For students not familiar with the structure)

- **Questions 1–3:** Put students in pairs to complete the tasks.
- Review the answers with the class.
  (1. adjectives: *fascinating, strong, gold*; nouns: *clues, paper, tag*; The adjective comes before the noun. 2. Possible answers are *challenging crossword puzzle*; *additional help*; *light, compact guitar*; *wooden body*. 3. *washable*; It follows a stative verb. It describes *potholders*.)
- Then ask *Can adjectives come before a noun?* (Yes) *Can adjectives come after a noun?* (Yes)

Method 2
(For students familiar with the structure)

- Have students do the exercise in pairs.
- Give students a few minutes to refer to the charts to check their answers and review the structures.
- Call on students to go over the exercise. Discuss any disagreements, and have students make any necessary corrections.

FORM CHARTS

- Put students into groups. Write the sentences below on the board. Ask them to look at the bulleted notes after the charts and answer these questions for each sentence: *Is the adjective before or after the noun? Which bulleted note does each underlined phrase illustrate?*

  You <u>seem fine</u>. (after, bullets 5 and 6)

  Let's eat <u>somewhere inexpensive</u>. (after, bullet 4)

  I need <u>four tall men</u>. (before, bullet 2)

  Did you ever eat <u>grilled fish</u>? (before, bullet 2 under "Formation")

  The window is <u>36 inches wide</u>. (before and after, bullet 3)

- Call on students to read a sentence and answer the questions. Discuss any disagreements or problematic items. Have students refer to the charts to check their answers and familiarize themselves with the new structures.
- Have each group write one sentence for each point in the bulleted notes.
- Bring the class together. Call on students to write their sentences on the board. There should be at least ten sentences on the board, one for each point.
- Go over each sentence with the class. Ask students to identify and correct any errors. You may have to help them if an error is difficult to correct. Answer any questions.

C) MEANING AND USE

Describing with Adjectives

EXAMINING MEANING AND USE

- Have students work in pairs to answer the questions. (quality/opinion: *expensive, favorite*; size: *large*; color: *blue*; origin: *Italian, European*; material: *leather, cotton*; kind/purpose: *riding, racing*)
- Give students a few minutes to refer to the Notes to check their answers.
- Put two sets of pairs together and have them compare their answers. Review the answers with the class and discuss any problematic or difficult items.

MEANING AND USE NOTES

- Put students in pairs. Write the phrases below on the board. Have students decide if the phrases are correct or incorrect. Refer students to the Notes to check their answers.

  the blue round ball (incorrect—the round blue ball)

  an expensive new car (correct)

  the big brown bear (correct)

  beautiful blond hair (correct)

  Indian, spicy food (incorrect—spicy Indian food)

- Call on students to tell you if the phrases are correct or incorrect. If a phrase is incorrect, have the student come to the board and correct it.
- Ask students to read the Notes about *-ing* and *-ed* adjectives.
- Demonstrate the meaning of *-ed/-ing* adjectives in the following ways:

  1. Give confusing directions (e.g., *Go to the corner. Drive two blocks; then take a right, a left, and another left, until you see two traffic lights. Turn right twice and then left at the second light*). Write *confused/confusing* on the board. Have students write two sentences using these adjectives. (*The directions are confusing. I am very confused.*) Call on students to read their sentences aloud.

  2. Shout at the class in a very loud voice with a very angry look on your face. Repeat the activity, using *frightened/frightening*.

  3. Tell students to listen carefully and then begin to read in a very monotonous tone. Repeat the activity, using *bored/boring*.

ADDITIONAL ACTIVITIES

The purpose of these activities is to provide practice using adjectives in the correct position and in the correct order.

Speaking: Giving Your Opinion

- Write these nouns and adjectives on the board:

  Nouns
  bears
  horror movies
  history
  television
  sports
  cities

  Adjectives
  interesting/interested
  exciting/excited
  frightening/frightened
  confusing/confused
  boring/bored
  fascinating/fascinated
  amazing/amazed

- Put students in pairs and have them take turns asking questions to find out their partner's opinion. Tell them to use the nouns and adjectives on the board.
- Model the activity. Ask *Do you think history is interesting?* Give examples of some possible answers: *No, I don't. I think it's boring.* OR *Yes, I think it's very interesting.*
- Ask students to report their partners' opinions to the class (e.g., *Ana thinks history is very interesting.*).

Writing: Putting Adjectives Together

- Write at least 20 adjectives on the board. They should cover many different descriptive categories. For example:

tall	*cheap*	*plastic*	*Swedish*
elegant	*hanging*	*black*	*intelligent*
cotton	*little*	*complicated*	*romantic*
fascinating	*large*	*square*	*classical*
handsome	*living*	*noisy*	*wooden*

- Put students in groups. Tell them that they are going to have a contest.
- Ask them to think of nouns that can be described by putting together at least two of the adjectives listed on the board. Give them an example: *a cheap, plastic belt*.
- Explain the rules: They have five minutes to write as many adjective-noun combinations as they can. They must use at least two adjectives in each combination. They cannot use any adjective more than once. They get one point for each correct combination. The group that scores the most points wins.
- Select a student to record the scores on the board. Call on each group to read their adjective-noun combinations, and have the class decide if each one is correct or incorrect.

Returning to Grammar in Discourse

The purpose of this activity is to check students' understanding of key meanings and uses of the target structures in the chapter by having them return to the catalog entries at the beginning of the chapter and apply what they have learned.

- Write the following extracts from the catalog entries on the board (or type them up and photocopy them before class). Have students work in pairs to find them in the entries. Make sure they read the complete sentences that these extracts come from.

  1. *This challenging crossword puzzle can take months to finish.*
  2. *The puzzle is printed on strong paper . . .*
  3. *Galileo was the first to make this unusual . . . thermometer.*
  4. *It has a wooden body and neck, . . .*
  5. *. . . each ball has a gold tag . . .*
  6. *. . . with large numbers.*

- Now write the following items on the board:
  a. *quality*
  b. *opinion*
  c. *size*
  d. *color*
  e. *material*

- Have students identify the adjective in each extract, think about its meaning, and match each one to the letter of the item above that best describes it. (1. b; 2. a; 3. b; 4. e; 5. d; 6. c)

- Bring the class together. Call on pairs to give their answers, and have them offer explanations. If students still have problems, revisit the Meaning and Use Notes.

17 Adverbs

Overview

Adverbs take many different forms and are used in various ways. Among their many meanings and uses, they can express how or in what manner (e.g., *She left suddenly.*); possibility (e.g., *Perhaps I'll go to Seattle.*); time (e.g., *I'll go next week.*); opinion (e.g., *Surprisingly, I got there in time.*); degree (e.g., *He talks so fast.*); excessive degree (e.g., *I usually cook steaks too long.*); and sufficient or insufficient degree (e.g., *My husband doesn't cook steaks enough.*). The adverb *too* is often confused with *very.* It is important that students understand that *too* has a negative meaning. *Too* is used when the degree of the adjective is undesirable (e.g., *The TV is too loud.*).

Form: Teachers, as well as students, may not always be able to identify an adverb. Adverbs can modify a verb, an adjective, or another adverb.

A) GRAMMAR IN DISCOURSE

The Personality Compass

A1: Before You Read

- Elicit from students some adjectives that describe their personality (e.g., *friendly, shy, honest, talkative*). List them on the board.

- Put students into pairs. Ask them to talk about their personalities using words like those on the board. Circulate, helping as necessary with vocabulary.

- Bring the class together and call on students to describe their partner's personality.

A2: Read

- Tell students to read the article and underline any of the traits that they think apply to them.

- Put students in groups. Have them identify the category they belong to (Norths, Souths, Easts, or Wests) and explain why they belong to it.

- Call on students to share their personality analysis with the class.

Cultural Notes

Americans are very fond of self-help books. These books are often written by psychologists, doctors, or other professionals who give practical advice on how individuals can solve their problems and live a happier life. This article is a summary of a self-help book that deals with personality analyses.

A3: After You Read

- Tell students to look at the list of jobs. Make sure that they know what each job is.

- Put them in pairs to discuss the answers. When they are finished, call on different pairs to report their answers. If students disagree, ask them to explain their decisions.

- For a follow-up activity, list other jobs on the board (e.g., *teacher, computer programmer, brain surgeon, graphic artist, store clerk*). Lead a class discussion about the personality type of each job.

B) FORM 1

Adverbs of Manner, Possibility, Time, and Opinion

EXAMINING FORM

Method 1
(For students not familiar with the structure)

- **Question 1:** Divide students into groups and have them complete the first task. Call on students to read the answers aloud. Write the seven *-ly* adverbs on the board: *fortunately, quickly, carefully, extremely, enthusiastically, especially, usually.*

- **Questions 2 and 3:** Have students complete the second and third tasks. Review the answers with the class. (2. *quickly, carefully, enthusiastically;* 3. They come after the main verb.)

- Ask the groups to select four *-ly* adverbs listed on the board and write a sentence for each. Call on students to write the sentences on the board and go over them with the class. Discuss any disagreements and make corrections as necessary.

- Have students refer to the charts to check their answers and familiarize themselves with the new structures.

Method 2
(For students familiar with the structure)

- Have students do the exercise in pairs. Give students a few minutes to refer to the charts to check their answers and review the structures.

- Call on students to go over the exercise. Discuss any disagreements and have students make any necessary corrections.

- Ask students for additional *-ly* adverbs of manner and list them on the board. Ask pairs to select four adverbs from the list on the board and write a sentence for each.

- Put two sets of pairs together and have them review the sentences they wrote. If students disagree on the correctness of a sentence, ask them to write it on the board and review it with the class.

FORM CHARTS

- Have students read the charts individually. Meanwhile, write the word *Adverbs* on the board. Under it draw four columns and label them *Manner, Possibility, Time,* and *Opinion.*

- Divide the class into four groups and assign one type of adverb to each group. Tell them to write two sentences using two different adverbs of their assigned type. Remind them to review the bulleted notes. Circulate to help with grammar and vocabulary.

- Bring the class together. Call on a member from each group to write their sentences in the

appropriate column on the board. Have students read their sentences aloud. If there are any errors, ask the class to correct them. Call on students from different groups to reread the sentence, placing the adverb in a different correct location (if it is possible). Discuss any disagreements.

C MEANING AND USE 1

Adverbs of Manner, Possibility, Time, and Opinion

EXAMINING MEANING AND USE

- Ask students to work individually to answer the questions. (1. *hard, unfortunately; Hard* describes how the action happened; *Unfortunately* gives an opinion. 2. *definitely, maybe;* 2a.)

- Give students a few minutes to refer to the Notes to check their answers.

- Have them exchange answers with a partner and check each other's work. Tell them to discuss any disagreements.

- Call on students to read the answers aloud. Review any problematic items and have students make any necessary corrections.

MEANING AND USE NOTES

- Write these sentences on the board:

  He plays the piano well because he practices daily.

  Have you seen him lately?

  Alberto carelessly left his wallet in the taxi, but fortunately, another passenger found it and returned it to him.

  I'll probably go to the movies with you, but I'm definitely not joining you for dinner.

- Have students work with a partner to underline the adverb(s) in the sentences and identify them as adverbs of manner, possibility, time, or opinion.

- Tell them to read the Notes to check their answers.

- Go over any problematic items with the class.

D) FORM 2

Adverbs of Degree

EXAMINING FORM

- Have students do the exercise in pairs.
- Give students a few minutes to refer to the charts to check their answers and review the structures. (1. 1a: adverb modified by *pretty*; 1b: adjective modified by *very*; 2. *So* is followed by an adjective; *such* is followed by an article + adjective + noun.)
- Ask pairs to compare their answers with another pair. Call on students to go over the exercise. Discuss any disagreements and have students make any necessary corrections.

FORM CHARTS

- Ask students for additional adverbs of degree and list them on the board (e.g., *really, extremely, very, somewhat*).
- Ask pairs to select three adverbs listed on the board and write a sentence for each.
- Put two sets of pairs together and have them go over their sentences.
- If students disagree on the correctness of a sentence, ask them to write it on the board and review it with the class.

E) MEANING AND USE 2

Adverbs of Degree

EXAMINING MEANING AND USE

- Have students work individually to answer the questions. (1. Sara; 2. *that the river froze; that I couldn't start my car*)
- Give students a few minutes to refer to the Notes to check their answers. Then have them compare answers with a partner.
- Call on students to read the questions and answers aloud. Discuss any disagreements and make any necessary corrections.

MEANING AND USE NOTES

- Write these sentences on the board:

  I have a terrible headache because the music is _____ loud.

  The soup is _____ that I can't eat it.

  The ice cream is _____ that my teeth hurt.

  It was _____ a cold day that I stayed inside my house.

  She is _____ tired because she didn't sleep at all last night.

  He ate _____ that he had a stomachache.

  They had _____ on their first date that they met the next day.

- Have students work in pairs to complete the sentences. Remind them to review the Notes to check their answers.
- Bring the class together and call on students to read their sentences aloud. Discuss any problem areas and have students make necessary corrections.

F) FORM 3

Too and *Enough*

EXAMINING FORM

- Have students complete the tasks individually.
- Call on students to read their answers aloud. (1. a and d = adverbs; b and c = adjectives; The adverbs modify verbs; The adjectives come after the verb *be*; 2. *Too* comes before the adjective or adverb; *Enough* comes after the adjective or adverb.)

FORM CHARTS

- Put students in pairs to write two sentences using *too* and *enough*.
- Ask students to write their sentences on the board. Review each sentence and have the class decide if the sentence is correct. If not, call on students to correct the errors.
- Write these sentences on the board:

  I'm too happy to see you. (incorrect)

  He is not enough fast to play tennis. (incorrect)

She is old enough to drive. (correct)

The soup is too hot to eat. (correct)

- Ask students to look at the charts to decide which are incorrect. Have them rewrite the incorrect sentences on the board. Discuss any disagreements and make any necessary corrections.

G MEANING AND USE 3

Contrasting *Too* and *Enough*

EXAMINING MEANING AND USE

- Put students in pairs to complete the tasks. (a: positive; b: negative)

- Have two sets of pairs compare answers. Refer them to the Notes to check their answers.

- Write these sentences on the board:

  I ate too much chocolate cake. (negative)

  I slept enough. (positive)

  I bought too many new clothes. (negative)

  I have enough clothes. (positive)

- Ask the pairs to underline the adverb in each sentence and decide which sentences are positive and which are negative. Then have two sets of pairs compare their answers. Discuss any disagreements or problematic items.

MEANING AND USE NOTES

- Write these sentences on the board. Have students complete them individually.

  It was _____ hot to run outside. (too)

  It wasn't cool _____ to run outside. (enough)

  These shoes don't fit. They are _____ big. (too)

  This shirt doesn't fit. It's not big _____. (enough)

- Call on several students to write their completed sentences on the board. Discuss any disagreements and make any necessary corrections.

ADDITIONAL ACTIVITIES

The purpose of these activities is to provide opportunities for students to practice using adjectives and adverbs correctly.

Speaking: A Guessing Game

- Divide the class into teams. Tell each team to think of three famous people.

- Ask them to write four clues for each famous person. Tell them to use adjectives and adverbs in the clues.

- Have two teams play together. The challenging team gives one clue at a time. The other team scores four points for guessing correctly after the first clue, but only one point for guessing after the fourth clue.

- Model the activity with the class. Give them these clues:

  1. *This person was very smart.*

  2. *He spoke German and English extremely well.*

  3. *He is so famous that everyone knows his face.*

  4. *His ideas are so complicated that many people cannot understand them.*

  Q: Is it Albert Einstein?

  A: Yes, it is. (score: 1 point)

- Have teams take turns giving clues and guessing.

Writing: A Biography of a Famous Person

- The first part of this activity is best done as homework. Have students research and prepare a list of important events in the life of a famous person from their country. Ask them to bring their lists to class.

- Look over their lists, correct them as necessary, and offer suggestions for improvement.

- Then, using this list of events, have students write a short essay in class highlighting the important events of their famous person's life. Remind them to pay close attention to adverbs and the order of events as they write. Circulate, helping as necessary with vocabulary and grammar.

- Ask a few volunteers to read their essays to the class.

Returning to Grammar in Discourse

The purpose of this activity is to check students' understanding of key meanings and uses of the target structures in the chapter by having them return to the magazine article at the beginning of the chapter and apply what they have learned.

- Write the following extracts from the magazine article on the board (or type them up and photocopy them before class). Have students work in pairs to find them in the article. Make sure they read the complete sentences that these extracts come from.

    1. *They are so confident and independent that . . .*

    2. *. . . they can make decisions quickly.*

    3. *Their motto is "Get the job done fast."*

    4. *Wests are . . . very creative.*

    5. *. . . one type is usually stronger than the others.*

    6. *Their motto is "Don't be afraid to try something new today."*

    7. *Fortunately, there is a test that helps these companies do this.*

- Now write the following items on the board:

    a. *manner*

    b. *possibility*

    c. *time*

    d. *degree*

    e. *opinion*

- Have students identify the adverb in each extract, think about its meaning, and match each one to the letter of the item above that best describes it. (1. d; 2. a; 3. a; 4. d; 5. b; 6. c; 7. e)

- Bring the class together. Call on pairs to give their answers, and have them offer explanations. If students still have problems, revisit the Meaning and Use Notes.

18 Comparatives

Overview

There are many different ways to express differences or similarities between two people, objects, ideas, places, or actions. Differences between two items can be expressed by using comparative forms of adjectives, adverbs, and nouns (e.g., *old–older*, *carefully–more carefully*, and *more/fewer people*). Similarities are expressed by using an adjective or adverb with *as . . . as* (e.g., *as old as, as carefully as*) or by using a noun with *as much/many . . . as* (e.g., *as much money as, as many people as*).

Form: The form of comparatives can present several problems for students. Key challenges include

- using the correct function word. *(He speaks better than Josh.)*

- using the correct comparative form. *(She is younger than I am.* Not **She is more young than I am.* Not **These shoes are gooder than those.)*

- using only one comparative form. (Not **He goes more faster than we do.)*

See Appendix 11 for a list of adjectives that take *more* or *-er*. See also Appendix 12 for a list of irregular adjectives.

A GRAMMAR IN DISCOURSE

Early to Rise Makes Teens . . . Less Attentive?

A1: Before You Read

- Read the proverb to the students. Ask them to guess the meaning of these words: *rise, wealthy,* and *wise.*

- Ask *Do you agree with this proverb? Why or why not?* Call on several students to share their

opinions with the class. Be sure to select students with opposing opinions.

- Ask if they have a similar proverb in their native country or a proverb that may have the opposite meaning. Write them on the board. You may wish to include the proverb "The early bird catches the worm."

- Put students in small groups to discuss their proverbs and ideas for a few minutes. Have a representative from each group summarize the opinions of their group.

A2: Read

- Have students read the article individually.

- Put students into groups. Tell them to underline all the reasons why sleeping later is a good idea. *(Students are more awake in class. The students participate more enthusiastically, and classes seem to go more smoothly. Counselors say that students seem happier and that they are nicer to one another. There is a better climate throughout the school building.)*

- Call on students to read the sentences aloud.

A3: After You Read

- Ask students to do this exercise individually and to note the places in the article where they found their answers. Then have students compare their answers with a partner's. Go over any difficult items with the whole class and have students make necessary corrections.

- For a follow-up activity, copy this outline on the board, allowing space for students to fill it in:

    I. Problem

    II. A way to solve the problem

    III. Positive results of solving the problem

- Call on students to write the answers in the outline on the board. Have them read their answers aloud.

B FORM 1

Comparatives

EXAMINING FORM

Method 1

(For students not familiar with the structure)

• Write the column heads *Adjectives* and *Adverbs* on the board. Put *older* and *more alert* under *Adjectives*, and *later* and *more smoothly* under *Adverbs*. Tell students that these are examples of comparative forms of adjectives and adverbs. Call on students to read the charts aloud.

• **Question 1:** Have students find the four underlined examples of comparative adjectives and adverbs. Ask individuals to come to the board and add them to the chart. (*Closer* and *more awake* are adjectives; *longer* and *more easily* are adverbs.)

• Ask *What ending is added to some adjectives or adverbs to form the comparative? (-er)* Then ask *What word is used with other adjectives or adverbs to form the comparative? (more)*

• **Question 2:** Put students in pairs and tell them to look back at the newspaper article and underline more adjectives and adverbs that have the comparative form. Ask students to come to the board to write the comparative forms in the correct columns. Go over the answers and discuss any difficult or problematic items.

Method 2

(For students familiar with the structure)

• Have students do the exercise in pairs.

• Give them a few minutes to refer to the charts to check their answers and review the structures.

• Call on students to go over the exercise. Discuss any disagreements and have students make any necessary corrections.

• Ask students to write other examples of these forms, and have them read them aloud.

FORM CHARTS

• Copy these charts on the board:

ADJECTIVES	
warm	
pretty	
handsome	
expensive	
good	
bad	

ADVERBS	
late	
early	
quickly	
badly	
well	
far	

NOUNS	
cats	
rain	

• Have students work in pairs to write the comparative form of these words. Refer students to Appendix 12 if necessary.

• Call on students to write the comparative forms on the board.

• Put students into groups. Ask them to look at the list of words on the board and try to write the rules about the formation of the comparative form. If they need help, ask them to think about the number of syllables and final sounds.

• Bring the class together and call on students to read their rules. Write their rules on the board.

• Ask students to compare their rules with the rules in the chart and make any corrections or additions that are necessary. Discuss any disagreements and make corrections as necessary.

Making Comparisons

EXAMINING MEANING AND USE

- Have students work in pairs to answer the questions. (a = larger amount; b = smaller amount)

- Give students a few minutes to refer to the Notes to check their answers and review the uses of comparatives. Then have two pairs compare their answers.

- Call on students to read the questions and answers aloud. Discuss any disagreements and have students make any necessary corrections.

MEANING AND USE NOTES

- Write these sentences and cues on the board.

  1. *My watch is $200. His is $85.*

     a. *(more)* My watch is more expensive than his.

     b. *(less)* His watch is less expensive than my watch (OR than mine).

  2. *Amy got an A in history. Gina got a C.*

     a. *(smart)* Amy is smarter than Gina.

     b. *(good/student)* Amy is a better student than Gina.

  3. *He has two bottles of milk in his refrigerator. She has one.*

     a. *(more)* He has more bottles of milk. OR He has more milk.

     b. *(less)* She has fewer bottles of milk. OR She has less milk.

  4. *Jenny is 22 years old. I am 26.*

     a. *(young—formal)* Jenny is younger than I.

     b. *(young—neutral)* Jenny is younger than I am.

     c. *(young—informal)* Jenny is younger than me.

- Have students work in pairs to write sentences using the comparative form.

- Have them exchange papers with another pair and check their answers. Then have them swap back.

- Call on students to write their sentences on the board. Discuss any disagreements and have students refer to the Notes to check their answers and make any necessary corrections.

As . . . As with Adjectives, Adverbs, and Nouns

EXAMINING FORM

Method 1

(For students not familiar with the structure)

- **Question 1:** Have students underline the adjectives and circle the adverbs. Write the headings *Adjectives* and *Adverbs* on the board. Then call on individuals to read the sentences aloud and say which adjectives or adverbs it has. Write them on the board in the correct column. (adjectives: *new, young*; adverbs: *fast, loudly*)

- **Question 2:** Have students find the sentences that end in an auxiliary or a verb. (b and d) Call on individuals to read the sentences aloud and identify the auxiliary or verb. Call on a student to read the sentence that ends with a noun (a) and the one that ends with an object pronoun (c).

- Have students refer to the charts to check their answers and study the new structures.

Method 2

(For students familiar with the structure)

- Have students work in pairs to answer the questions.

- Give students a few minutes to refer to the charts to check their answers and review the structures.

- Call on students to go over the exercise. Discuss any disagreements and have students make any necessary corrections.

FORM CHARTS

- Put students in pairs. Have them take turns reading the charts aloud.

- Ask them to write two sentences of each type below, similar to the examples in the charts:

  As . . . as *using adjectives*

  As . . . as *using adverbs*

  As . . . as *using noncount nouns*

  As . . . as *using count nouns*

- Bring the class together. Call on students to write their sentences on the board.

- Go over each sentence. Ask the class to identify and correct any errors.

E) MEANING AND USE 2

As . . . As with Adjectives, Adverbs, and Nouns

EXAMINING MEANING AND USE

- Have students work in pairs to answer the questions. (1. a; 2. b)

- Give students a few minutes to refer to the Notes to check their answers.

- Call on students to read the questions and answers aloud. Discuss any disagreements and have students make any necessary corrections.

MEANING AND USE NOTES

- Have students work in pairs to write sentences using the *as . . . as* comparative form. Use the cues below:

  1. *My watch is $200. His is $200.*

     (expensive) My watch is as expensive as his (watch).

  2. *Amy got an A in history. Gina got an A.*

     (smart) Gina is as smart as Amy.

  3. *He has two bottles of milk in his refrigerator. She has one.*

     a. She doesn't have as many bottles as he (does). He has more bottles of milk.

     b. She doesn't have as many bottles of milk as he (has).

  4. *Jenny is 22 years old. I am 22.*

     a. *(old—formal)* Jenny is as old as I.

     b. *(old—neutral)* Jenny is as old as I am.

     c. *(old—informal)* Jenny is as old as me.

- Bring the class together and call on different pairs to share their sentences. Discuss any problem areas and have students make necessary corrections.

Vocabulary Notes: Using Descriptive Phrases with *As . . . As* (p. 361)

- Write these sentences on the board: *My father knows everything. He's as wise as an owl.* Elicit the meaning from the class.

- Explain that there are several of these comparisons in English and that they make oral descriptions more interesting. They are considered to be clichés, however, and should not be used in formal writing.

- Ask students if they have similar expressions in their languages. Elicit a few examples.

- Put students into small groups and have them create sentences using the various comparisons. Circulate, helping as necessary with vocabulary.

- Call on students from each group to read one of their sentences aloud. Discuss and make corrections as necessary.

- As an optional activity, add a few more expressions. Write them on the board and elicit or explain their meaning: *as pale as a ghost, as red as a beet, as bald as an eagle, as cool as a cucumber.*

ADDITIONAL ACTIVITIES

The purpose of these activities is to give students less structured practice in expressing similarities and differences between two people or things in a freer context.

Speaking: Comparing Apples and Oranges

- Write the names of common items on index cards (about ten items, two items per card). For example: *horse, elephant, apple, orange, winter,* and *summer.*

- Divide the class into two teams and give each team five cards. Ask each team to stand against the wall on opposite sides of the room.

- Call on a student to select one of their cards and give a comparison of the two items written on the card. If the first student is successful, ask the next student on the team to give you another comparison with a different adjective. Continue until a student makes a mistake or they have run out of items. For example:

    Student 1: *A horse is bigger than a chair.*

    Student 2: *A chair isn't as expensive as a horse.*

    Student 3: *A chair is more useful than a horse.*

- Give the team one point for each sentence that is grammatical and logical. Keep track of their score on the board.

- Repeat the activity with the other team. The team with the most points wins.

Speaking: Which Is Better?

- Decide on a topic that students can argue about without anyone getting insulted. For example, seasons of the year, sports or sports teams, pets, or famous people. Do not choose topics such as countries, regions, or professions.

- Tell students to choose their favorite item or person related to the topic that you specify.

- Have them circulate and find someone who disagrees with their choice of favorite. They should then try to persuade the other person to agree with them, using comparisons.

- Model the activity with a student:

    A: I think summer is better than winter.

    B: I don't. Summer is a lot hotter than winter, and winter sports are more exciting than summer sports.

    A: I don't agree. Winter is more boring because you have to stay in the house. Summer is more beautiful because everything is green.

Writing: Comparisons

Have students write a paragraph comparing one of the topics below or a topic of their own choice, which you approve. Circulate, helping as necessary with vocabulary and grammar. Then ask a few students to read their paragraphs to the class. Topics to compare include:

1. Your home town with the town where you are living now or the town where you would like to live.

2. The climate of your home town with the climate of the town where you are living now.

3. The alphabet/pronunciation/grammar of English with that of your native language.

4. Two famous people from the present or the past.

5. Two sports.

Returning to Grammar in Discourse

The purpose of this activity is to check students' understanding of key meanings and uses of the target structures in the chapter by having them return to the newspaper article at the beginning of the chapter and apply what they have learned.

- Write the following extracts from the newspaper article on the board (or type them up and photocopy them before class). Have students work in pairs to find them in the article. Make sure they read the complete sentences that these extracts come from.

    1. *. . . many high school students get less sleep than younger students.*

    2. *The students participate more enthusiastically, and . . .*

    3. *Counselors say that students seem happier and that they are nicer to one another.*

    4. *. . . late risers weren't as hardworking or successful as early risers.*

- Now write the following items on the board:

    a. *larger amount, degree, or size*

    b. *smaller amount, degree, or size*

- Have students think about the meaning of the comparison in each extract and match each one to the letter of the item above that best describes it. (1. b; 2. a; 3. a; 4. b)

- Bring the class together. Call on pairs to give their answers, and have them offer explanations. If students still have problems, revisit the Meaning and Use Notes.

19 Superlatives

Overview

There are many ways to express differences among three or more people, objects, ideas, places, or actions. The superlative form of adjectives, adverbs, and nouns is used to express differences among three or more items (e.g., *the oldest, the most carefully,* and *the most/the fewest people*).

Form: The form of superlatives can present several problems for students. Key challenges include

- using the correct superlative form (e.g., *the most expensive,* not **the expensivest*).
- remembering to use the article *the* (e.g., *Lake Superior is the largest lake in the United States.*).
- using irregular forms (e.g., *This is the worst grade I've ever received.*).

See Appendix 11 for a list of adjectives that take both forms of the superlative. See also Appendix 12 for a list of irregular adjectives and adverbs.

A GRAMMAR IN DISCOURSE

Strange but True

A1: Before You Read

- In addition to *Guinness World Records,* other places where one might find this type of information include encyclopedias, almanacs, and the Internet.
- Write this question on the board: *What is the highest mountain in the world?* Elicit the answer. (Mt. Everest, 29,028 feet, on the border between Tibet and Nepal)
- Put students into pairs and have them discuss the questions.

- Bring the class together and have each pair tell their guesses. Write their guesses on the board and discuss the answers.

A2: Read

- Ask students to read the article individually and underline the world records.
- Have students tell you the world records without looking back at the article.
- Write the following questions on the board. Put students in pairs and have them answer the questions:

  Who wrote the first Guinness World Records?

  Why is the book named Guinness?

  How many have been sold so far?

  What is the only other book that has sold more copies than Guinness World Records?

- Call on students to answer the questions aloud. Discuss any disagreements.

A3: After You Read

- Make a game of this exercise by telling students to do it as fast as they can.
- Have them work in pairs. Tell them to come to the board and write their names when they think that they have answered all the questions correctly.
- When most pairs have finished, call on the pair that finished first to start giving the answers. If a wrong answer is given, go to the next pair. Continue until a pair has given the last correct answer.
- For a follow-up activity, ask students to use the superlative form to describe something about their country, city, or town (e.g., the biggest rain forest, the best food, the fastest train).

B FORM

Superlatives

EXAMINING FORM

Method 1

(For students not familiar with the structure)

- **Questions 1–3:** Tell students to work in pairs to complete the tasks. When most pairs have finished, tell them to read the charts to check their answers and review the structures.

- Call on students to write their answers on the board. (1. the biggest, the strongest, the most valuable, the most expensive; 2. Add *the . . . -est,* or add *the most.* 3. Possible answers include *the driest, the fastest, the ugliest, the worst, the tallest,* and *the most dangerous.*)

- Have each pair list an adjective, an adverb, and a noun on a piece of paper. Circulate to provide assistance if needed. Tell students to exchange papers with another pair and ask them to write the superlative form of the words that the other pair has selected.

- Call on students to write the superlative forms on the board. Review the forms with the entire class and discuss any problematic items.

Method 2

(For students familiar with the structure)

- Have students work in pairs to answer the questions.

- Give students a few minutes to refer to the charts to check their answers and review the structures.

- Call on students to go over the exercise. Discuss any disagreements and have students make any necessary corrections.

- Tell each pair to list an adjective, an adverb, and a noun on a piece of paper. Have the pairs exchange papers, and ask them to write the superlative form of the words that the other pair has selected.

- Call on students to write the superlative forms on the board. Review the forms with the entire class and discuss any problematic or difficult items.

FORM CHARTS

- Write these sentences on the board. Ask students to rewrite the sentences using the superlative form:

  He speaks better than I do. (He speaks the best.)

  I work more carefully than the others. (I work the most carefully.)

  We had better luck than you did. (We had the best luck.)

- Refer students to the charts to check their answers. Then have them write their superlative sentences on the board. Review any difficult or problematic items and make corrections as necessary.

C MEANING AND USE

Superlatives

EXAMINING MEANING AND USE

- Call on a student to read the questions aloud. Select another student to give you the answers. (Sentence b compares three or more things in a group. Sentence a compares only two things.)

- Put students in pairs to write two sentences: one that compares only two items and one that compares three or more items.

- Have them read the sentences aloud. If you hear an error, write the sentence on the board and elicit the correct form.

MEANING AND USE NOTES

- Write the following sentences on the board. Some of the sentences have errors. Have students identify and correct the sentences containing errors. Tell them to refer to the Notes as they complete this exercise.

  He is the best cook. (correct)

  New York is the more exciting city I have ever visited. (the most exciting city)

  What building is the most tall in the world? (the tallest)

  All the students in the class study hard, but Thomas studies the hardest of all. (correct)

Rembrandt is one of the greatest artists. (correct)

Michelangelo is one of the more greatest artists that has every lived. (one of the greatest)

I'm the least tall in my family. (I'm the shortest in my family.)

- Call on students to read the sentences and say if they are correct or incorrect. If incorrect, have them read the correct form. Discuss any disagreements.

ADDITIONAL ACTIVITIES

The purpose of these activities is to provide practice using superlative forms in a freer context.

Speaking: The Best of the Century

- List the following topics on the board. Do not list the hints in parentheses.

  helpful medical discovery (antibiotics, vaccines, genetics, blood plasma)

  influential person (Winston Churchill, Eleanor Roosevelt, JFK, Nelson Mandela)

  infamous person (Stalin, Hitler, Pol Pot, Jeffrey Dahmer)

  great natural disaster (hurricane Andrew, Northridge earthquake, Mount Pinatubo eruption)

  important invention (the automobile assembly line, broadcasting, airplanes, computers, nuclear bombs)

  momentous turning point (end of apartheid, Japanese bombing of Pearl Harbor, end of World War II, fall of the Berlin wall)

  famous sports hero (Joe DiMaggio, Pelé Muhammad Ali, Serena Williams, Michael Jordan, Sammy Sosa)

  famous entertainer (Charlie Chaplin, Edith Piaf, Frank Sinatra, Elvis Presley, The Beatles)

- Divide the class into groups of three or four. Tell them it is their turn to be historians. Ask them to use superlative adjectives to rank people and events of the twentieth century according to the list of topics above. Use the hints in parentheses only if necessary.

- Call on the groups to compare and discuss their answers.

Writing Commercials

- Tell students to think of a product that they would like to advertise on TV. Then have them form pairs or small groups depending on how many people they need in their commercial.

- Ask them to write a one-minute television commercial about their product using comparative and superlative forms. Circulate, helping as necessary.

- Call on the groups to perform their commercials for the class.

20 Gerunds

Overview

A gerund is a verb form ending in *-ing* that functions as a noun. Like a noun, a gerund is a name of a thing, in this case, an activity. A gerund can be used as a subject of a sentence (e.g., *Skiing is fun.*), as a direct object (e.g., *I enjoy skiing.*), or as an object of a preposition (e.g., *We talked about skiing all night long.*). When gerunds are modified by adjectives or adverbs or are followed by objects, the entire group of words is called a gerund phrase. Gerund phrases can also be used as a subject of a sentence (e.g., *Drinking more than one cup of coffee a day can be bad for your health.*) or as an object of a sentence (e.g., *He is good at driving race cars.*).

Form: After certain verbs, either a gerund or an infinitive can be used as an object (e.g., *She loves to swim. She loves swimming.*). See Appendix 15 for a list of such verbs. You may hear students use both the gerund and the infinitive as the object of the sentence (*e.g., *I like to running.*).

A GRAMMAR IN DISCOURSE

10 Easy Ways to Start Saving Money

A1: Before You Read

- Ask for a show of hands for these questions: *How many people own one or more credit cards? How many wish they didn't have any credit cards?*

- Discuss the questions with the class. Ask students if they know of ways to save money more easily. List their ideas on the board.

A2: Read

- Tell students to read the article individually and underline three of the best ideas for saving money. Call on students to read aloud what they have underlined.

- Put students in groups and have them compare the money-saving ideas in the article with their ideas listed on the board. Ask each group to select the best idea and be prepared to explain their reason for making their selection.

- Call on students to share their group's decision and explain their reasoning.

A3: After You Read

- Ask students to do this exercise individually and to note the places in the article that provided the answers. Call on them to read a statement and say whether it is true or false. Then have them read the statement that gave them the answer. Discuss any disagreements and have students make any necessary corrections.

- For a follow-up activity, ask the class *Do you know what is the average amount of credit card debt that each American owes?* ($9,000) *Do you agree with the "Buy now, pay later" philosophy?*

B FORM 1

Gerunds as Subjects and Objects

EXAMINING FORM

Method 1
(For students not familiar with the structure)

- **Questions 1–3:** Put students in pairs to complete the tasks.

- Call on students to answer each question. (1. 1b is present continuous because it has a form of the verb *be (is)* with it; 1a is a gerund because it does not have a form of the verb *be* with it. 2. 2b has a gerund as subject, and the main verb is singular; 2a has a gerund as object of the verb. 3. Gerunds are singular because when they are subjects the verbs that follow them are singular.)

- Ask the class what sentences 1a and 1b tell them about gerunds. (A gerund looks like a present continuous verb. Both end in -*ing*, but the gerund does not have a form of the verb *be* with it.) Ask what sentences 2a and 2b tell them about gerunds. (A gerund can be used as a subject or an object of a sentence.) Ask what sentences 1a and 2b tell them about gerund subjects. Are they singular or plural? (They are singular because the verb is singular.) When you hear the correct answers, write them on the board.

Method 2
(For students familiar with the structure)

- Have students work in pairs to answer the questions.
- Give students a few minutes to refer to the charts to check their answers and review the structures.
- Call on students to go over the exercise. Discuss any disagreements and have students make any necessary corrections.

FORM CHARTS

- Have students work in pairs. Ask them to write four sentences: one that uses an affirmative gerund as a subject, one that uses a negative gerund as a subject, one that uses a gerund as an object, and one that uses a gerund phrase. Refer them to the charts if they need help.
- Call on students to write their sentences on the board. Go over each sentence with the class. Have them tell you if the sentence is correct or incorrect. If there is an error, ask another student to correct it.

C) FORM 2

Gerunds After Prepositions

EXAMINING FORM

- Before starting this activity, review prepositions. So far, students have learned prepositions of place, direction, and time. Ask them to name as many prepositions as they can and write them on the board. Elicit a sample sentence for each preposition that you write on the board.

- Tell students to underline the gerunds and circle the word that comes before each gerund.
- Call on students to tell you the gerund in each sentence (*swimming, getting, lying, making*) and what kind of word comes before each gerund (a preposition).
- Write this sentence on the board. Ask students to complete it with the word *before* or *after*. (after)

  Gerunds can come _____ prepositions.

FORM CHARTS

- Put students in pairs to read the charts. Meanwhile, write these questions on the board:

  What do you believe in?
  What don't you believe?
  What are you tired of?
  What are you afraid of?
  What are you interested in?

- Have students ask their partners these questions. Ask them to take notes so they can remember their partner's answers. Tell them that the answers must have a gerund after the preposition.
- Call on students to report their partner's answers to the class (e.g., *Stefan is tired of waiting in line in stores.*).

D) MEANING AND USE

Gerunds

EXAMINING MEANING AND USE

- Have students work in pairs to answer the questions. (1. a; 2. b; 3. c) Give students a few minutes to look at the Notes to check their answers and review the meanings and uses.
- Combine two pairs into groups. Have each pair discuss their answers with the other pair. Discuss any disagreements or problematic items.

- Ask each group to write an explanation of each Note in their own words. Tell them not to look at their books.
- Have each group write their explanations on the board. Review them, and for each meaning and use, have the class decide which is the easiest to understand and the most accurate.

MEANING AND USE NOTES

- Read the situations below to students. Tell them to make up mini-conversations using a gerund and one of these words or phrases: *would you mind, enjoy, like*. After each situation, call on students to read their conversations.

  1. You're in line at the bank and you need a pen. What do you ask the customer standing in line next to you?
  2. You'd like to start a friendship with someone in your class and you want to get to know him or her. What might you ask this person?
  3. You're having a conversation with a friend about a vacation you've taken. You friend wants to know about it. What could you say?

- Model the activity with this situation: You're riding on a bus and it's very hot. The window near your seat is closed. What do you ask the passenger sitting next to you?

  A: *Would you mind opening the window?*
  B: *No, not at all.*

⬤ **ADDITIONAL ACTIVITIES**

The purpose of these activities is to provide extra practice in using gerunds in less-structured situations.

Speaking: Designing a Survey

- Divide the class into groups of three or four. Tell the groups to choose a topic that they would like to survey the class about. Some examples include: leisure time activities, health, work habits.

- Ask them to write ten survey questions on this topic using gerunds as subjects or objects. For example:

  A: *What do you enjoy doing in your spare time?*
  B: *Playing basketball with my friends.*
  A: *How much time do you spend surfing the Net?*
  B: *About ten hours a week.*

- Let each group ask at least ten people their survey questions.
- Have them compile the results and share them with the class.

Returning to Grammar in Discourse

The purpose of this activity is to check students' understanding of key meanings and uses of the target structures in the chapter by having them return to the magazine article at the beginning of the chapter and apply what they have learned.

- Write the following extracts from the magazine article on the board (or type them up and photocopy them before class). Have students work in pairs to find them in the article. Make sure they read the complete sentences that these extracts come from.

  1. *Many people love making budgets . . .*
  2. *. . . but hate staying within them.*
  3. *This will help you save by showing you where your money goes.*
  4. *If you are tired of not having money in the bank, try . . .*
  5. *How much do you save by not buying lunch?*

- Now write the following items on the board:

  a. *tells how*
  b. *tells about liking an activity*
  c. *tells about disliking an activity*

- Have students think about the use of the gerund in each extract and match each one to the letter of the item above that best describes it. (1. b; 2. c; 3. a; 4. c; 5. a)

- Bring the class together. Call on pairs to give their answers, and have them offer explanations. If students still have problems, revisit the Meaning and Use Notes.

21 Infinitives

Overview

Like gerunds, infinitives describe activities expressed by verbs. Certain verbs are typically followed by infinitives (e.g., *I want to go soon.*). Infinitives can also express purpose (e.g., *I hope to go home [in order] to visit my parents.*). Since an infinitive usually occurs near the end of a sentence, the pronoun *it* can replace an infinitive as subject of the sentence. It has the same meaning as the infinitive it replaces (e.g., *It was difficult to learn Japanese.*). Although there are semantic differences between forms such as *I like swimming* (in general) and *I like to swim* (more specific), these may be too sophisticated for students at this level.

Form: Some verbs take only infinitives (e.g., *I want to go soon.*); others take only gerunds (e.g., *I enjoy skiing.*); and others can take both with no obvious difference in meaning (e.g., *She loves swimming. She loves to swim.*). A few verbs (e.g., *stop, remember, forget*) can take either a gerund or an infinitive, but the meaning changes. See Appendixes 13–15 for lists of these verbs.

A GRAMMAR IN DISCOURSE

The *Twenty-One* Quiz Show Scandal

A1: Before You Read

- Write the phrase *quiz show* on the board. Elicit or explain the concept. Ask the class to name some quiz shows and write the names on the board. One example that is known around the world is *Wheel of Fortune*.

- Discuss the questions with the class. Ask *Do you ever watch quiz shows? Why or why not? Would you like to be on a quiz show?*

A2: Read

- Tell students to read the article individually. While they are reading, they should decide if the producer was right or wrong.

- Ask students if they agree with Enright. Be sure to select students with opposing opinions. Have them justify their opinions.

A3: After You Read

- Put students into small groups. Assign each group a question to answer. Circulate, helping as necessary.

- Call on students to give their answers aloud. They do not need to agree as long as they can explain the reasons for their answers.

B FORM

Infinitives

EXAMINING FORM

Method 1
(For students not familiar with the structure)

- **Question 1:** Call on two students to write sentences 1a and 1b on the board. Have them underline the verbs. *(speak, told, to speak)* Ask the class if the correct words have been underlined and make corrections as necessary. Then ask *Which sentence is in the simple present?* (1a) *Which sentence has an infinitive?* (1b)

- **Question 2:** Call on two different students to write sentences 2a and 2b on the board and have them underline the verbs. *(wanted, to be, wanted, to cheat)* Ask the class if the correct words have been underlined and make corrections as necessary. Then ask *In which sentence does the infinitive directly follow the verb?* (2a) *In which sentence does the infinitive follow the object of the verb?* (2b) Ask *What is the object? (him)*

- Put students in pairs to look at lines 31–40 of the magazine article. Have them circle at least one verb + infinitive (*started to get, agreed to lose, decided not to keep*) and one verb + object + infinitive (*convinced Van Doren to cheat, told Stempel to give*).
- Call on students to write them on the board. Discuss any disagreements and have students make any necessary corrections.

Method 2
(For students familiar with the structure)

- Have students do the exercise in pairs.
- Give them a few minutes to refer to the charts to check their answers and review the structures.
- Call on students to go over the exercise. Discuss any disagreements and have students make any necessary corrections.

FORM CHARTS

- Write this sentence on the board: *In order to get the job, he had to lie.* Ask students to come to the board and rewrite it two different ways. (He had to lie [in order] to get the job. OR To get the job, he had to lie.)
- Ask another student to come to the board and make the phrase *get the job* negative. (He had to lie in order not to get the job.)
- Refer students to the charts to check their answers.
- Write this sentence on the board: *It is easy to get rich.*
- Ask students what the subject of the sentence is. (*It*) Ask them what it replaces. (*to get rich*) Note their ideas on the board. Then tell them to look for the answer in the charts.

C MEANING AND USE 1

Infinitives

EXAMINING MEANING AND USE

- Make sure students understand the meaning of *purpose*. Explain that it is similar to *reason* and answers the question *Why?* (e.g., *Why did he go to the store? To buy milk and bread.*).

- Have students work in pairs to answer the questions. (1. *to arrive, to eat, to leave;* 2. Sentences b and c express a feeling about an activity; sentence a expresses a reason.)
- Give students a few minutes to refer to the Notes to check their answers and review the uses of infinitives.
- Call on students to read the questions and answers aloud. Discuss any disagreements and have students make any necessary corrections.

MEANING AND USE NOTES

- Select individual students each to read one Note (1, 2A, 2B, 3A, or 3B) aloud.
- Divide students into small groups and have each group write five sentences, one for each Note.
- Ask them to read their sentences to another group. Tell them to note if they disagree about the form or meaning and use.
- Call on the groups to read their sentences aloud. Write any problematic sentences on the board. Let the entire class decide on the correctness of these sentences. Guide them to the correct answer if necessary.

D MEANING AND USE 2

Contrasting Gerunds and Infinitives

EXAMINING MEANING AND USE

- Most classes should do this as a class activity.
- Ask a student to read sentence 1a. Then ask *What did the person use to do every day?* (eat ice cream) Ask *Does this person eat ice cream now?* (No)
- Ask another student to read sentence 1b. Ask *Does this person eat ice cream every day?* (Yes) Then ask *Does this person weigh more or less?* (more)
- Ask students if *stopped eating* and *stopped to eat* mean the same thing. (No)
- Check students' comprehension by writing these two sentences on the board:

    Lisa stopped smoking. Susan stopped to smoke.

- Ask *Who is going to live longer?* (Lisa, because she does not smoke anymore.)
- Ask a student to read sentences 2a and 2b. Write *started raining* and *started to rain* on the board. Ask the class if they mean the same thing. (Yes)

MEANING AND USE NOTES

- Put students in pairs to write new pairs of sentences with the verbs in Note 1 *(enjoy, finish)*. Then ask pairs to read their sentences aloud.
- Have the pairs do the same for Notes 2 and 3.
- Tell them to read Note 4B. Then have the same pairs write two sentences: one to tell you something that they forgot to do and another to tell about something that they will never forget doing. Ask several pairs to read their sentences aloud. Write any problematic sentences on the board. Let the entire class decide on the correctness of these sentences. Guide them to the correct answer if necessary.

ADDITIONAL ACTIVITIES

The purpose of these activities is to provide practice in using gerunds and infinitives in less structured situations.

Writing and Speaking: Taking a Stand

- Ask students to think of a topic that they feel strongly about. If you want to avoid political controversy, you can suggest innocuous school-based topics (e.g., Doing homework is a waste of time. Students should be allowed to smoke in classrooms.).
- Tell students to look at Appendixes 13–15 for the lists of verbs and phrases that take infinitives and those that take gerunds. Have them find at least five of each type that they think they could use in a speech about their topic.
- Have them write the speech. As they are working, circulate to help them with vocabulary and grammar.

- Put students in pairs to practice presenting their speeches to each other.
- Call on several students to give their speeches.
- Depending on the level of your class, you may wish to videotape students as they give their speeches, but be sure to let them know in advance.

Returning to Grammar in Discourse

The purpose of this activity is to check students' understanding of key meanings and uses of the target structures in the chapter by having them return to the magazine article at the beginning of the chapter and apply what they have learned.

- Write the following extracts from the magazine article on the board (or type them up and photocopy them before class). Have students work in pairs to find them in the article. Make sure they read the complete sentences that these extracts come from.

    1. *Each week families turned on their TVs to watch their favorite quiz shows.*
    2. *Soon, however, people started to get tired of Stempel.*
    3. *. . . and would keep watching in order to see him.*
    4. *. . . two contestants tried to answer questions for points.*
    5. *To find out more about the scandal, as well as Stempel and Enright, watch . . .*

- Now write the following items on the board:

    a. *expresses a purpose*
    b. *can be replaced by a gerund*

- Have students think about the use of the infinitive in each extract and match each one to the letter of the item above that best describes it. (1. a; 2. b; 3. a; 4. b; 5. a)
- Bring the class together. Call on pairs to give their answers, and have them offer explanations. If students still have problems, revisit the Meaning and Use Notes.

22 Phrasal Verbs

Overview

Phrasal verbs are common in English and other Germanic languages but exist in few others, which makes them difficult for students. They consist of two or three words (e.g., *He lived up to his name.*). The meaning of a phrasal verb is idiomatic because its meaning is different from the individual meanings of the words that make up the phrasal verb. If the meaning can be understood from the common meanings of the two words, it is a verb + preposition combination (e.g., *He lived up the road.*) and not a phrasal verb. It is important that students understand the concept and categories of phrasal verbs because they are so common in the spoken language. Once students understand the categories of phrasal verbs, they can think of them as vocabulary.

Form: Phrasal verbs are either transitive (taking a direct object) or intransitive (not taking a direct object), and they are separable (the direct object can come between the verb and the particle) or inseparable (the direct object comes after the particle). Students can use the dictionary to find the meaning of a phrasal verb and whether it is separable. Encourage students to memorize the list of inseparable verbs in Appendix 17.

A) GRAMMAR IN DISCOURSE

"Eggstraordinary" Breakfasts Are Easy!

A1: Before You Read

- Find out what students eat for breakfast. If many students do not eat eggs for breakfast, ask them when they eat eggs, what kind of eggs they eat, and how they cook them. Elicit ideas from several students.

- Ask students if they have cooked eggs before and if they have had any problems cooking them.

A2: Read

- Write *eggstraordinary* on the board. Elicit or explain that it looks like the word *extraordinary*. Explain that it is not a real word, but a play on words.

- Before students start reading, ask them to scan the article quickly to find the basic steps to cooking eggs. (*Start out with fresh eggs. Heat up the pan. Cook the eggs. Take the eggs out and season them.*)

Cultural Notes

Eggs are one of the most common breakfast foods in the United States. Americans eat them fried, scrambled, poached, or boiled.

A3: After You Read

- Have students do this exercise individually and then compare their answers with a partner's. Remind them to note the places in the article where they found their answers.

- When most students have finished, ask students to read the steps beginning with number 1. If someone makes a mistake, call on another student.

- Go over any difficult or problematic items with the whole class.

B) FORM

Phrasal Verbs

EXAMINING FORM

Method 1
(For students not familiar with the structure)

- **Question 1:** Write the word *Verbs* on the board. Under it write the words *transitive* and *intransitive* side by side. If these terms are new to your students, make sure that they understand that both one-word and phrasal verbs can be transitive or intransitive.

- Tell students to answer question 1 individually. Then have them read their answers aloud. (1a has the object *stove.* 1b has no object; it is intransitive.) Write the verbs under the appropriate heading on the board.

- Explain that for any transitive verb, it can answer the question *What?* (e.g., What did you turn off? The stove.).

- **Question 2:** Ask students to write sentences 2a and 2b on the board. Tell them to circle the objects. *(the stove, the stove)*

- Ask students to tell you the difference between the objects in 2a and 2b. (In 2a, the object comes after the two-word verb. In 2b, it separates the two words.)

- Write the word *separable* on the board. Ask students what it means. (The two parts can be separated with a direct object.) Point out that many phrasal verbs are separable.

Method 2
(For students familiar with the structure)

- Have students do the exercise in pairs.

- Give students a few minutes to refer to the charts to check their answers and review the structures.

- Call on students to go over the exercise. Discuss any disagreements and have students make any necessary corrections.

FORM CHARTS

- Write these pairs of sentences on the board. Ask students to identify the ones with phrasal verbs. (1b and 2a)

    1a. The man turned off the road.

    1b. The man turned off the light.

    2a. He looked up the word.

    2b. He looked up at his mother.

- Ask students how they know which sentences have phrasal verbs. Discuss how you can tell a phrasal verb from a verb + preposition by

understanding their meaning. (For example, *off* in 1a is a preposition because it tells you where the man turned. It has a separate meaning from the verb *turned.* In 1b, however, *off* is a particle because it is part of the meaning of the two-word verb.)

- Write the sentences below on the board. Tell students that they all contain phrasal verbs. Ask them to use the information in the charts to find and underline the verb and decide if it is transitive or intransitive. If the verb is transitive, they should circle the object.

    I took care of the dog. (transitive)

    What went on last night? (intransitive)

    Please sit up straight. (intransitive)

    She put her jacket on. (transitive)

C MEANING AND USE

Phrasal Verbs

EXAMINING MEANING AND USE

- Tell students to look at the three sentences and find the common phrasal verb. *(pick up)* Write it on the board.

- Have students work in pairs to answer the questions. (1. c; 2. a; 3. b)

- Give students a few minutes to refer to the Notes to check their answers.

- Call on students to read the questions and answers aloud. Discuss any disagreements and have students make any necessary corrections.

MEANING AND USE NOTES

- Divide students into four groups and assign one Note (1A, 1B, 1C, or 2) to each group.

- Tell each group to read the Note and prepare to teach the information to the class. The groups should also write one new sentence for each phrasal verb in their assigned Note.

- Circulate as the groups work, pointing out any problems in their example sentences.

- Ask each group to present, and have the rest of the class check if the example sentences are correct. If not, work together to improve them.

- Discuss ways that students can guess the meaning from the context of the sentence, especially predictable meanings in Note 2. When guessing does not help, students will have to look up the word in an English-language dictionary.

ADDITIONAL ACTIVITIES

The purpose of these activities is to provide practice with using phrasal verbs in less-structured situations.

Writing: How Do You Use This?

- Have students bring in small kitchen or household appliances or gadgets that they use regularly, such as a toaster, an iron, or even a computer. If it is not possible to bring in the item, have them bring in a picture of one from a catalog or a magazine.

- Form small groups and give each group one of these gadgets. Let students choose a group based on an item they are familiar with.

- Tell the groups to pretend they are writing a manual about how to use this equipment. Have them write a short list of instructions. Circulate, helping the groups as necessary with vocabulary and grammar.

- Have groups present their demonstration on how to use their appliance or gadget.

Returning to Grammar in Discourse

The purpose of this activity is to check students' understanding of key meanings and uses of the target structures in the chapter by having them return to the website article at the beginning of the chapter and apply what they have learned.

- Write the following extracts from the website article on the board (or type them up and photocopy them before class). Have students work in pairs to find them in the article. Make sure they read the complete sentences that these extracts come from.

  1. *Do you try to get by without breakfast?*
  2. *Why put up with an ordinary breakfast . . .*
  3. *To cut down on fat, use less butter . . .*
  4. *Turn the heat down to low, so the eggs will cook slowly.*
  5. *. . . remember to start out with fresh eggs . . .*

- Now write the following items on the board:
  a. *reduce*
  b. *lower*
  c. *to manage*
  d. *begin*
  e. *tolerate*

- Have students think about the meaning of the phrasal verb in each extract and match each one to the letter of the items above that best describes it. (1. c; 2. e; 3. a; 4. b; 5. d)

- Bring the class together. Call on pairs to give their answers, and have them offer explanations. If students still have problems, revisit the Meaning and Use Notes.

Student Book Tapescript

CHAPTER 1

A2 (p. 4)

Please refer to the geography quiz in the Student Book.

B1: Listening for Form (p. 8)

Many people in Hawaii live in two different worlds—the world of traditional Hawaiian culture and the world of modern American culture. Keenan Kanaeholo is a typical Hawaiian. He lives on the island of Oahu. Like many Hawaiians, Keenan speaks two languages. At home he and his family don't speak English. They talk to each other in Hawaiian. Keenan works in a large hotel. At work he speaks English. Keenan's wife, Emeha, doesn't work in the hotel. She teaches at an elementary school. Both Keenan and Emeha like to dance. They go to discos on the weekends. Emeha also knows the hula, but Keenan doesn't.

B3: Pronouncing Verbs Ending in -s or -es (p. 9)

A. 1. lives
2. practices
3. works
4. closes
5. arranges
6. tells

C1: Listening for Meaning and Use (p. 12)

1. Professional ice-skaters, like myself, spend many hours practicing.
2. I usually get up at three o'clock in the morning so I can go to the ice rink and practice.
3. Most people are usually asleep at three in the morning!
4. After I practice ice-skating, I go to school.
5. I study until six every evening. Then I have dinner and go to bed.
6. Most teenagers visit with their friends after school. They generally have a lot of free time—that is, if they aren't professional ice-skaters!

 CHAPTER 2

A2 (p. 18)

Please refer to the leaflet in the Student Book.

B1: Listening for Form (p. 20)

1. Don't leave. It's early.
2. Turn right at the corner.
3. Don't study in the kitchen.
4. Come home before dinner.
5. Don't be angry with me, please.
6. Please turn off the light.

C1: Listening for Meaning and Use (p. 23)

1. A: Alex, please help me finish this report. I don't know what to write.
   B: I'm sorry, but I'm too busy today. Ask Mark. He's great at that kind of thing.
2. A: Don't forget your résumé.
   B: Oh! Please hand it to me. Thanks.

A: Sure. Call me after the interview, dear. And don't worry! I'm sure they'll hire you!
3. A: Excuse me, sir, can you please tell me where the nearest bank is?
   B: Uh, let's see . . . Turn right at the corner and then walk west for three blocks. Cross the street and you'll see it on your left.
   A: Thanks.
4. A: Do you need anything else, Ms. Fields?
   B: Yes, Jane, cancel my meeting with Mr. Gordon and please tell Bob I need to speak with him immediately.
5. A: Here, you hold my briefcase, and I'll get the car.
   B: Oh, wait! Get my bag, Eric. It's on the table.
   A: All right. Now hurry up. We're already late!
6. A: Come on! We're late!
   B: I'm coming. Wait for me in the car.
   A: Okay, but don't be long. The movie starts in 15 minutes.

 CHAPTER 3

A2 (p. 30)

Please refer to the magazine article in the Student Book.

B1: Listening for Form (p. 34)

1. We aren't living in Texas anymore.
2. I am trying to study for the test.
3. Steve and Julie are not meeting with the boss. I am.
4. Julie is sleeping upstairs.
5. He isn't working in California now.
6. I am not cooking dinner tonight!

C1: Listening for Meaning and Use (p. 38)

1. We are now climbing to 35,000 feet. We are traveling at a speed of about 600 miles per hour.
2. Ladies and gentlemen, we are currently serving food and beverages in the dining car at the back of the train.
3. Flight 220 to Pittsburgh is now boarding at Gate 17.
4. We are now closing. Please make your final selections and take your purchases to the counter.
5. Davis has the ball. He's moving down the field. Schmidt is chasing him. He's trying to get the ball away. Now Davis is shooting! Goal! England wins! The crowd is going crazy!
6. Ladies and gentlemen, we are now leaving the Port of New York. We hope you have a pleasant vacation with Sunshine Cruises.

 CHAPTER 4

A2 (p. 48)

Please refer to the book excerpt in the Student Book.

B1: Listening for Form (p. 52)

1. Dan invited us to the movies.
2. They didn't go to the hockey game.
3. She found 20 dollars on the street.
4. They didn't close the store at nine.
5. I went to work by car every day last week.
6. He played baseball for the New York Mets.

7. You got a haircut! It looks great!
8. We ate chocolate cake at the restaurant.

B3: Pronouncing Verbs Ending in -ed (p. 53)

1. waited
2. walked
3. rained
4. played
5. coughed
6. decided
7. jumped
8. answered

Informally Speaking (p. 56)

A: Didja forget my birthday? It was Saturday.
B: Oh, no! I'm really sorry!

B7: Understanding Informal Speech (p. 56)

1. A: Didja go to the party?
   B: Yes, I did.
   A: Didja have a good time?
   B: Yes, but today I'm very tired.
2. A: Didja eat lunch yet?
   B: Yes, I did.
   A: What didja have?
   B: A burger and fries.
3. A: Didja stay home last night?
   B: No, I went to a movie.
   A: Didja like it?
   A: No, it wasn't very good.
4. A: Why didja work so late?
   B: My boss needed help on a report.
   A: Didja finish it?
   B: Yes, it wasn't difficult.

C1: Listening for Meaning and Use (p. 58)

1. A: Why weren't you at work yesterday?
   B: My grandmother died over the weekend.
   A: Oh, I'm sorry.
2. A: Mom, it's raining! Could you drive me to the university?
   B: No, I can't. Take an umbrella. When I was your age, I walked to school every day.
   A: But these days no one walks when the weather is bad!
3. A: Did you see Kedra when you were in Philadelphia last week?
   B: Yes, I did. In fact, we had dinner together every evening.
   A: So how is she doing?
4. A: Where did you get that great dress?
   B: Oh, it's old. I bought it years ago.
   A: Well, you look great!
5. A: Did your mother have an exciting time in college?
   B: Yes, she took part in protests during the late 1960s and early '70s.
6. A: Does your grandfather speak French?
   B: Yes, he studied French for several years in high school and college.

D1: Listening for Form (p. 63)

1. They used to live next door to me.
2. We didn't use to eat out so much.

3. Did you use to exercise every day?
4. People used to be a lot more patient.
5. Why did he use to go there?
6. Who used to be your doctor?
7. She didn't use to call us so often.
8. What building used to be here?

E1: Listening for Meaning and Use (p. 66)

1. I used to live alone.
2. Our house used to be smaller.
3. We used to be good friends.
4. My husband used to cook dinner every night.
5. My children never used to enjoy school.
6. My family didn't use to help around the house.
7. My son Paul used to be afraid of dogs.
8. My husband and I used to want a lot of children.

🎧 CHAPTER 5

A2 (p. 70)

Please refer to the history book excerpt in the Student Book.

B1: Listening for Form (p. 73)

1. We were living in Texas at the time.
2. It wasn't raining yesterday.
3. They were leaving the house.
4. The cars weren't going very fast.
5. Where were they going?
6. Why was he crying?

C1: Listening for Meaning and Use (p. 77)

1. I lived in Japan for the first 20 years of my life.
2. Last summer I was living at the beach and writing a book.
3. Last weekend my father and I were painting our house. My father got angry because I spilled a bucket of paint on the carpet. Then the dog stepped in it and made a mess!
4. My air conditioner was broken for a long time, but I fixed it last month.
5. I wrote a ten-page paper last night and gave it to my teacher this morning.
6. I was taking flying lessons with a friend on Saturday morning. I was having a great time, but he was really nervous.

D1: Listening for Form (p. 81)

1. Some people left town before the storm began.
2. The weather forecaster warned us about the storm before it hit.
3. After the people left, the tornado hit the house.
4. When the storm began, we went into the basement.
5. The river overflowed when it rained.
6. The sky was beautiful after the storm ended.

E1: Listening for Meaning and Use (p. 84)

1. A: I'm sorry, Professor, I didn't finish my essay.
   B: Hmm. Why not?
   A: While I was writing it, the lights went out.
   B: Do you really expect me to believe that?

2. A: Did you have a good time at Josh's party last night?
   B: No. I was helping him in the kitchen while all our friends were dancing!
   A: That's too bad!
3. A: Where were you yesterday afternoon?
   B: I had a lot to do. After I helped my brother fix his car, I went to the grocery store for my mother.
4. A: How did you hurt yourself?
   B: At football practice. I was running down the field when I fell and twisted my ankle.
   A: Try to be more careful next time!
5. A: Oh, no! I failed my chemistry test! I'm never going to finish my college science requirement.
   B: You just don't study enough. Last weekend you were watching television while all of us were studying.
   A: That's not true.
6. A: Why didn't you call me last night?
   B: I didn't feel well. After I got home, I had dinner and went straight to bed.

CHAPTER 6

A2 (p. 90)

Please refer to the magazine article in the Student Book.

B1: Listening for Form (p. 94)

1. I have worked here for three years.
2. We haven't seen Yuji since August.
3. I'm sorry. Mr. O'Neill has left for the day.
4. Our class hasn't taken the exam yet.
5. It has rained every day this week!
6. Don't leave yet. You haven't eaten your breakfast.

Informally Speaking (p. 95)

A: Wow . . . Mark's changed a lot!
B: He's gotten his hair cut. He looks great!

B3: Understanding Informal Speech (p. 95)

1. John's been here for a long time.
2. Kedra and Rick've seen the movie already.
3. Paul's bought a new racing bicycle.
4. The guests've gone home.
5. The police've arrested the thief.
6. Where's she been?
7. Fresno's grown bigger since the 1930s.
8. Why's it taken so long?

C1: Listening for Meaning and Use (p. 98)

1. Elena has been a teacher here for ten years. She's always taught science, and this year she's teaching Russian, too.
2. Bob was a repair man here for ten years. He knew how to fix everything in the building.
3. I've loved pizza since I was a child. It's still my favorite food.
4. I hated vegetables when I was a child. I never ate them. Now I love them.
5. Silvio worked in an office last year, but he didn't like his job. He left after only eight months.
6. Susan has worked for a television broadcasting company since March. She's learning all about news reporting.

7. I lived in Berlin for a year. I had a really great time there and met lots of interesting people.
8. I've lived in Paris for two years, and I'm still discovering new places.

D1: Listening for Meaning and Use (p. 101)

1. Ming-woo has been to my house many times.
2. Donna and her family have often invited me to dinner.
3. They built that hotel a hundred years ago.
4. I've seen that old movie several times.
5. We met ten years ago.
6. She's seen the film several times.
7. He started to drive in 1996.
8. He's won five gold medals.
9. He's changed a lot in the last few years.
10. They lost a lot of money in the stock market last year.

CHAPTER 7

A2 (p. 112)

Please refer to the newspaper article in the Student Book.

B1: Listening for Form (p. 116)

A. 1. She's going to start school next year.
2. We're not going home tonight. The airline canceled our flight.
3. Where is he going tonight?
4. Take your umbrella. It's going to rain.
5. Are you going to watch TV tonight?
6. They hate that hotel so they're not going to stay there again.
7. We're going on vacation tomorrow.
8. I'm not going to the office next week. I'm on vacation.
9. Study hard, or you're going to fail the test.
10. I'm really excited! I'm going on a business trip to Brazil next month.

Informally Speaking (p. 118)

A: Are you gonna see Mary tonight?
B: No, I'm gonna study. I have a lot of homework.

B5: Understanding Informal Speech (p. 118)

1. We're gonna make dinner soon.
2. I'm gonna go to the beach.
3. We're not gonna see him in Seattle.
4. Our class is gonna meet next Wednesday.
5. The store is gonna close in five minutes.
6. Mark's gonna study at Lincoln University.
7. The children aren't gonna be happy about this.
8. They're gonna take the test tomorrow.

C1: Listening for Meaning and Use (p. 120)

1. I think she's going to get an A on the math test.
2. We're going to the football game tomorrow.
3. She's having dinner with Rick tonight.
4. You're going to love this movie!
5. She's going to be angry when she sees you here.
6. They're taking the three o'clock train to Vancouver tomorrow.
7. I don't think she's going to turn in her paper on time.
8. I'm going to study for the exam after dinner tonight.

D1: Listening for Form (p. 126)

1. They're not going to finish on time.
2. We'll leave after the show.
3. I'm going to visit her tomorrow.
4. They're having a party this weekend.
5. Where are you going on your vacation?
6. Will you be home on Saturday?
7. I'll help you paint the house this weekend.
8. We aren't going to see them next week.

Informally Speaking (p. 129)

A: Who'll pick up the kids from school?
B: I will. My boss'll let me leave early.

D5: Understanding Informal Speech (p. 129)

1. What'll you say to him tonight?
2. When'll Tony be home?
3. The students'll need paper and pencils for the test.
4. Who'll help me carry these bags?
5. Amy'll help you with your homework.
6. After the test, the teacher'll grade our papers.
7. John'll get the job. He's so qualified.
8. The game'll be over at ten o'clock.

E1: Listening for Meaning and Use (p. 131)

1. In 20 years there won't be enough gasoline for all of the cars.
2. Don't get up. I'll close the window for you.
3. Don't worry. I'll call you as soon as I get home.
4. I'm bored. I think I'll go see a movie.
5. Don't go out without your coat! You'll get sick.
6. I'll lend you the money. I told you that yesterday.

CHAPTER 8

A2 (p. 138)

Please refer to the magazine article in the Student Book.

B1: Listening for Form (p. 142)

1. When I see Elena, I'll give her the message.
2. We'll need more time if the test is very difficult.
3. Marcus and Maria will go to Budapest after they visit Prague.
4. She'll call us when she gets here.
5. You'll meet him if you go to the party.
6. If Matt gets a loan from the bank, he'll buy a new car.

C1: Listening for Meaning and Use (p. 144)

1. I'll look for a job before I graduate.
2. Before he gets here, we'll make dinner.
3. We'll go to the park after we go to the museum.
4. I'll call you after they leave.
5. Before I clean the house, I'll go shopping.

D1: Listening for Meaning and Use (p. 147)

1. A: Are you going to see Amy tonight?
   B: I think so. We might go to a movie. If we do, I'll call you.
2. A: I'm going to the store later today. Do you want anything?
   B: When you go, could you buy some ice cream?
3. A: What are you going to do this weekend?

B: I'm not sure. If it snows, we'll go skiing.
4. A: Your trip to Mexico sounds like it will be great!
   B: Yes, but the airlines are on strike. If the strike continues, I won't be able to go.
5. A: Has Mark asked Celia to marry him yet?
   B: No, not yet. But when he asks her, she'll say yes.
6. A: Is Jake going to rent the apartment?
   B: Well, if he doesn't find a roommate, he won't.

CHAPTER 9

A2 (p. 156)

Please refer to the magazine article in the Student Book.

B1: Listening for Form (p. 160)

Michael is blind. He can't see. He can do amazing things, however. He lives in Chicago, and he can walk around the city alone. Of course, he can't read the street signs, so sometimes he asks for help. After he has been somewhere with a friend, he can go there again by himself. Michael is good at sports, too. He's the best player on his bowling team, even though he can't see the bowling pins.

C1: Listening for Meaning and Use (p. 164)

1. I can't go today, but I can go tomorrow.
2. The children can play outside.
3. We could see the mountains from our hotel room.
4. She can play tennis very well.
5. The weather was cold, so they couldn't swim.
6. After the accident, she couldn't walk.

D1: Listening for Form (p. 168)

1. A: What will you do when you finish college?
   B: I might look for a job, or I may go to graduate school instead.
2. A: The traffic is moving very slowly. We won't get to the theater on time.
   B: We might. We still have plenty of time.
3. A: When is the package arriving?
   B: It could be here tomorrow, or it might not arrive until the next day.
4. A: Will there be many people at the meeting?
   B: I don't know. There may be just a few of us.
5. A: What do you think? Is it going to snow tonight?
   B: Well, according to the weather report, there could be a lot of snow, but the storm might not hit us at all.

E1: Listening for Meaning and Use (p. 171)

A: Let's talk about our trip. We need to make some decisions about what we want to see.
B: I want to see everything.
A: I know, but we won't be able to see everything. That's impossible.
B: Well, we're going to visit Disney World, right?
A: Of course we are! While we're there, we could also spend a day at the Epcot Center. People say that it's interesting.
B: We could do that, but we might not want to spend the time. I really want to go to Cape Canaveral.
A: Is that the place where they launch rockets?
B: That's right.

A: We'll go there for sure.

B: OK, so we'll go to Disney World and to Cape Canaveral, and we might go to Epcot Center. Where else could we go?

A: Well, we could go to the beach. Florida is famous for its beaches.

B: How about Miami Beach? That's supposed to be really nice.

A: It's nice, but it's about four hours away.

B: That doesn't matter, because I really want to go to the Everglades. I've never seen an alligator. Aren't the Everglades near Miami?

A: Yes, they are. Okay. We'll go to Miami Beach and to the Everglades. Is there anything else you want to see?

B: I really want to go to Key West. I hear it's a beautiful island off the coast.

A: We might be able to go, but we might not have time. We'll see.

🎧 CHAPTER 10

A2 (p. 178)

Please refer to the book excerpt in the Student Book.

B1: Listening for Form (p. 183)

1. A: Kevin, will you start dinner? I'm going shopping.
   B: Hmm . . . could you get some chocolate ice cream?
   A: I'd rather not buy more ice cream. You know we're both on a diet.

2. A: May I speak with Mrs. Thompson, please?
   B: No, I'm sorry. She's in a meeting. Could you call back in an hour?

3. A: Would you like a cup of coffee?
   B: No, thanks. I'd prefer a cup of tea.

4. A: I'd like to go to the beach with my friends this weekend, but I don't have any money. Can I borrow $50?
   B: No, you can't. You already owe me $100!

C1: Listening for Meaning and Use (p. 187)

A. 1. A: Will you help me carry these groceries into the house?
   B: Sure. So, what's for dinner?

2. A: Would you please look at my report and tell me if I've used the correct information?
   B: Certainly. Just put it on my desk and I'll look at it after lunch.

3. A: Can you give me a ride to Jake's party?
   B: I'm sorry, but I can't. I've decided not to go to the party.

4. A: Will you walk the dog? I'm in the middle of cooking dinner, and I think he needs to go out now.
   B: Sure. No problem. I want to go for a run before dinner anyway.

5. A: I'm having trouble finding that book you assigned us. Could you please lend me a copy?
   B: I'm sorry, but I don't have an extra copy. Have you checked in the main library?

6. A: Excuse me, could you tell me the time, please?
   B: Of course. It's 9:25.

B. Same as A above.

D1: Listening for Meaning and Use (p. 191)

1. A: Can I borrow your geography book?
   B: No problem, but don't lose it!

2. A: Could I please have until Friday to finish my paper?
   B: No. I'm sorry, but it's due tomorrow, just like everyone else's.

3. A: May I park here for just a few minutes?
   B: I'm sorry, miss, but you can't. The sign says "No Parking."

4. A: Can I use the phone now?
   B: No way. This is important. I'll let you know when I'm off.

5. A: May I leave a few minutes early today, or do you need me to stay for the meeting?
   B: You don't need to stay for the meeting. You can go home early.

6. A: Can I go skiing with my friends this weekend?
   B: Absolutely not.

7. A: Could I please get in line in front of you? My train is about to leave.
   B: Certainly. Go right ahead.

8. A: Could I try these clothes on?
   B: Of course. The fitting room is over there.

E1: Listening for Meaning and Use (p. 194)

1. We'd like two tickets, please.
2. I'm not doing anything now. Would you like some help?
3. I'd rather leave the party early than stay until the end.
4. I have my car today. Would you like a ride home?
5. John and I would prefer to stay in the city rather than move to the country.
6. I've just made a pot of coffee. Would you like some?
7. I'd like some coffee and a piece of apple pie, please.
8. The twins would prefer to have a chocolate cake for their birthday.

🎧 CHAPTER 11

A2 (p. 200)

Please refer to the on-line book review in the Student Book.

B1: Listening for Form (p. 205)

1. You shouldn't leave until the rain stops.
2. He has to get to work early.
3. We'd better go to the library now.
4. You must not start the car with your foot on the gas.
5. They don't have to go if they don't want to.
6. She should call if she isn't coming.
7. You've got to get a new car, Dad!
8. What do we have to buy for the party?

Informally Speaking (p. 207)

A: I awda get back to the library.
B: Yeah, I hafta go to class, anyway.

B5: Understanding Informal Speech (p. 207)

Conversation 1: At Matt's house

A: It's 9:00. We awda leave now.
B: The wedding is at 10:00. We don't hafta leave until 9:30.
A: But we've godda be there before the guests arrive.

Conversation 2: Later, at the church

A: Where's Matt? He hasta come soon! We're getting married in 15 minutes!

B: Maybe I awda call him at home.

C: Don't worry. He'll be here. We hafta stay calm and wait.

C1: Listening for Meaning and Use (p. 210)

1. A: You could have a small wedding.
   B: You ought to have a small wedding.
2. A: You should go to Paris for your honeymoon.
   B: You have to go to Paris for your honeymoon!
3. A: You'd better clean your room before you go out.
   B: You should clean your room before you go out.
4. A: You ought to sign up for classes next week.
   B: You must sign up for classes next week.
5. A: You'd better let them know that you'll be late.
   B: You could let them know that you'll be late.
6. A: You shouldn't play your music this loud.
   B: You'd better not play your music this loud.
7. A: You've got to do some work this weekend.
   B: You ought to do some work this weekend.
8. A: You should try to call her.
   B: You might try to call her.

D1: Listening for Meaning and Use (p. 215)

1. A: I'm calling for information about getting a driver's license. Do I have to take an eye test?
   B: Yes, you must take an eye test in order to get your driver's license.
2. A: Do I have to take the test at the Department of Motor Vehicles?
   B: No, you don't have to take the test here. You can take the test at your eye doctor's.
3. A: I'm from Italy, and I have an Italian driver's license. Do I need a California license to drive in California?
   B: Not if you are just here on vacation. If you move here you should get a California license.
4. A: Can I pay with a credit card?
   B: No. You must pay in cash or with a check or money order.
5. A: I just got my learner's permit. I don't want to go to driving school because I have a car I can use. Is that OK?
   B: Yes, that's OK. You don't have to go to driving school.
6. A: Can I drive alone with a learner's permit? I don't have anyone to practice with.
   B: Sorry, there must be a licensed driver in the car with you at all times. You must not drive alone.

🎧 CHAPTER 12

A2 (p. 224)

Please refer to the magazine article in the Student Book.

B1: Listening for Form (p. 229)

1. A: You're surprised to see me, aren't you?
   B: Yes, I am. What are you doing here?
2. A: You didn't bring an umbrella, did you?
   B: No, I didn't. I didn't think it would rain.
3. A: My father doesn't need an operation, does he?
   B: Yes, I'm afraid that he does.

4. A: You can go to the movies tonight, can't you?
   B: I'm sorry, but I can't. I've got a lot of work to do.
5. A: There isn't any more ice cream, is there?
   B: No, there's not. Dad ate it all.
6. A: I'm not playing the music too loud, am I?
   B: No, you're not. I like it.

Informally Speaking (p. 230)

A: Not very good, is he?
B: No, he's absolutely awful.

B4: Understanding Informal Speech (p. 230)

1. Funny, aren't they?
2. Not happily married, is she?
3. Very expensive, isn't it?
4. Great athletes, aren't they?
5. Not warm enough, are you?
6. Beautiful, isn't it?

C1: Listening for Meaning and Use (pp. 232–233)

A.
1. We spent too much money, didn't we?
2. That's a very expensive restaurant, isn't it?
3. You didn't walk here, did you?
4. He has Ms. Walker for history, doesn't he?
5. You couldn't watch my children for an hour, could you?
6. You've never met the Smiths, have you?

B. Same as A above.

🎧 CHAPTER 13

A2 (p. 240)

Please refer to the letter to a newspaper editor in the Student Book.

B1: Listening for Form (p. 244)

1. Humans have rights, but animals don't.
2. Humans can communicate in writing, but animals can't.
3. Humans have families, and apes do too.
4. Some apes like to watch sunsets, but some don't.
5. Not all humans are kind, and some apes aren't either.
6. Humans can change their environment, and some animals can too.
7. Humans feel emotions, and some animals do too.
8. Humans can appreciate beauty, and some animals can too.
9. Steve doesn't know a lot about apes, and I don't either.
10. I think apes should have rights, but Nicole doesn't.

C1: Listening for Form (p. 248)

1. Los Angeles is a big city, and so is Chicago.
2. He didn't need a hotel room, and neither did I.
3. February doesn't have 31 days, and neither does April.
4. Teresa should go home, and so should you.
5. Carol can't ski, and neither can I.
6. They've left, and so has she.

D1: Listening for Meaning and Use (p. 251)

1. Horses sleep standing up, but cats don't.
2. Elephants live for a long time, and so do parrots.

3. Cows are plant-eaters, and giraffes are too.
4. Tigers don't live in groups, but gorillas do.
5. Monkeys have tails, but chimpanzees don't.
6. Turtles aren't warm-blooded, and snakes aren't either.

Informally Speaking (p. 252)

A: I want to try bungee jumping.
B: Me too!
A: I'm not sure about this!
B: Me neither!

D3: Understanding Informal Speech (p. 252)

1. A: I didn't like that movie.
   B: Me either.
2. A: We go to the beach every summer.
   B: Us too.
3. A: I don't want to move to the city.
   B: Me neither.
4. A: We're thinking about sending the kids to camp this summer.
   B: Us too.
5. A: My parents are coming to graduation. What about your parents?
   B: Them too.
6. A: I can walk on my hands.
   B: Me too.
7. A: I hear Mark got a raise. What about Gina?
   B: Her too.
8. A: I'm not a very good cook. What about you?
   B: Me neither.
9. A: I speak German.
   B: Her too.

CHAPTER 14

A2 (p. 262)

Please refer to the magazine article in the Student Book.

B1: Listening for Form (p. 267)

A. 1. There isn't much news at all.
2. The interviews are today.
3. I need a little information.
4. Three people called.
5. The children are noisy.
6. Milk is healthy.
7. Have a sandwich.
8. Coffee sometimes tastes weak.

B. *Conversation 1*
A: Do you have any news about those jobs you applied for?
B: Yes. I've had several interviews. I'm sure I'll get an offer, but I need some information about the companies before I decide.

Conversation 2
A: Were there many people in the park?
B: There were a lot of children! I forgot that summer vacation started last week.

Conversation 3
A: Would you like a glass of milk with your sandwich?
B: No, thanks. I'd rather have a cup of coffee.

Conversation 4
A: How much food should I buy?
B: There are a lot of people coming. You should buy lots of food.

Informally Speaking (p. 269)

A: Well, Liz, we have alotta gas and plennya time.
B: Good thing we also have alotta friends.

B4: Understanding Informal Speech (p. 269)

1. Lotsa people enjoy playing golf.
2. A fewa my friends are coming over tonight.
3. If you're going to Las Vegas, take plennya money.
4. This dishwasher uses a great deala hot water.
5. Are you hungry? There's alotta food left over from the party.
6. There are lotsa lakes in Minnesota.
7. He took alotta classes last year.
8. We won't be late. We have plennya time.

C1: Listening for Meaning and Use (p. 272)

1. I can't go. I have a lot of work to do.
2. We have little milk left. Can you stop at the store on your way home?
3. There are no cars in the parking lot.
4. I don't have much homework to do this weekend.
5. Don't worry. There's plenty of food for the party.
6. I've got a few books on photography. Would you like to borrow one?
7. There isn't any caffeine in this drink.
8. Our teacher gives too many tests. All I do is study!
9. I don't have much money. Did you bring your wallet?
10. Jenny has so many friends! She's really popular.

D1: Listening for Meaning and Use (p. 277)

1. For my favorite spaghetti sauce, I use a can of tomatoes.
2. I also need a pound of ground beef.
3. For seasoning, I add some salt.
4. I usually chop several onions to cook with the ground beef.
5. Then I add a little cream.
6. This makes the right amount of sauce for a box of spaghetti.
7. I boil a gallon of water and then put the spaghetti in.
8. When the spaghetti is done, I mix it with the sauce and serve it with some bread.

CHAPTER 15

A2 (p. 282)

Please refer to the book excerpt in the Student Book.

B1: Listening for Form (p. 285)

1. David wants to be a scientist.
2. Botany is the study of plants.
3. Many insects eat plants.
4. I can only stay for an hour.
5. Please put the books on the table.
6. Could you get me a fork, please?
7. Would you like an apple?
8. I gave the children some candy.

9. Can I borrow a pen, please?
10. There are flowers in every room.

C1: Listening for Meaning and Use (p. 289)

1. I bought a little present for you. Do you want to open it?
2. The children are playing in the park.
3. We want to buy a new car.
4. Did the teacher come today?
5. I'll be at the restaurant at seven.
6. I met a really nice man yesterday.
7. I'm going to the bank. I'll be back in an hour.
8. There's an interesting article in the newspaper. You should read it.
9. Do you know where the car keys are?
10. I have a meeting at 3:30.

D1: Listening for Meaning and Use (p. 294)

1. Teachers don't like grading tests.
2. The kids love dogs. We should get one.
3. A girl gave me the information.
4. The dolphin is a very intelligent animal.
5. A radio station shouldn't have too many advertisements.
6. The doctor moved to a new hospital with better facilities.

 CHAPTER 16

A2 (p. 302)

Please refer to the catalog entries in the Student Book.

B1: Listening for Form (p. 306)

Conversation 1
A: That movie was really entertaining!
B: Did we see the same movie? Sure, it had a lot of famous stars, but I thought it was boring. The man next to me was asleep during most of it.

Conversation 2
A: How was the amusement park?
B: Well, the kids seemed excited to be there, but I thought some of the rides were frightening.
A: How long did you stay?
B: We were there all day. When we left, the kids were fine, but the adults were tired and hungry.

C1: Listening for Meaning and Use (p. 310)

1. The movie was very exciting.
2. Don't take that history class. The teacher is really boring.
3. The frightening dog barked at us.
4. I was very tired after I finished teaching the class.
5. She looked surprised when she saw me at the door.
6. The class was very interested in the book.
7. It's an amazing film.
8. The climb up the mountain was exhausting.
9. The frightened child cried for help.
10. The book was very disappointing.

CHAPTER 17

A2 (p. 318)

Please refer to the magazine article in the Student Book.

B1: Listening for Form (p. 322)

1. I haven't seen Jim recently.
2. David always drives very carefully.
3. She did a careless job.
4. We have an unexpected visitor.
5. Anna read the article slowly.
6. When I talked to you this morning, you seemed angry about something.
7. We got to the theater late, but luckily there were still some tickets left.
8. I might not take my vacation this summer, but I'm certainly taking it before the end of the year.

C1: Listening for Meaning and Use (p. 326)

1. I saw her recently.
2. It hardly snowed last night.
3. He's been coming to our meetings a lot lately.
4. We're probably going to Mexico this summer.
5. I'm studying hard this year.
6. Some buses are arriving late.

D1: Listening for Form (p. 329)

1. She cooks so well that everyone wants to eat at her house.
2. He's very busy right now.
3. We're such good friends that I can tell her anything.
4. The kids were having such a good time that they didn't want to leave.
5. They were so tired that they fell asleep during the movie.
6. The test was so hard that I don't think anyone passed.
7. She spoke so softly that I couldn't hear her.
8. We arrived really early for the concert.

E 1: Listening for Meaning and Use (p. 332)

1. My neighbor plays his music so loudly that I can't sleep at night.
2. She's such a strong swimmer that she wins every race.
3. Wow! You got here quite fast.
4. She's doing pretty badly in my class.
5. The lines at the supermarket were so long.
6. Gina's somewhat young to wear makeup, isn't she?

F1: Listening for Form (p. 336)

1. You're too young to drive.
2. This cake is too sweet for me.
3. They don't work hard enough at school.
4. He drives too fast, and it makes me nervous.
5. Don't buy those sweaters. They're too expensive.
6. He's not tall enough to play basketball.

G1: Listening for Meaning and Use (p. 338)

1. He's too sloppy to help me cook for the party.
2. He didn't do well enough to pass the course.
3. She's well enough to leave the hospital.
4. She didn't stay out too late.

CHAPTER 18

A2 (p. 346)

Please refer to the newspaper article in the Student Book.

B1: Listening for Form (p. 350)

1. A: Should we take a bus to the theater?
   B: No, let's go by subway. The subway will get us there more quickly than the bus will.
2. A: Does Paula's husband still work?
   B: No, he's retired. He's older than she is.
3. A: How did you do on your test today?
   B: Not very well. Next time I'll study harder.
4. A: How's your new apartment?
   B: I like it. And it's more convenient than my old one.
5. A: I need someone careful for this job. Should I have Bill do it?
   B: Try Barbara first. Bill's a good worker, but she's more careful than he is.
6. A: Would you prefer to live in a small town or a big city?
   B: I'm not sure. Cities are exciting. But I think people in small towns are friendlier than people in cities.

C1: Listening for Meaning and Use (p. 354)

1. A: Dan is 15 and Mike is 13.
   B: Who is younger?
2. A: Ana's coat cost $40 and Rick's cost $49.
   B: Which coat was less expensive?
3. A: Our team scored three goals. Their team scored five goals.
   B: Which team played better?
4. A: Betty got a 60 on her test. Her classmates got 80s and 90s.
   B: Who did worse?
5. A: Maria lives five miles from town. Frank lives three miles from town.
   B: Who lives closer to town?
6. A: When I take the B4 bus, I usually can't find a seat. When I take the D2 bus, I can always find a seat.
   B: Which bus is less crowded?

D1: Listening for Form (p. 357)

1. A: Do you like going to a small college?
   B: My college isn't small. It's as big as your college.
2. A: Can I read that book after you're through reading it?
   B: Yes, but it's going to take me a while to finish it. I don't read as quickly as you do.
3. A: Don't tell me that you're tired already! We've just been hiking an hour.
   B: I'm not as young as you are.
4. A: How's your new car?
   B: Not great. It seems to have as many problems as my old car.
5. A: How is math this year?
   B: It's hard. The other kids already did this stuff. I can't work as fast as they can.

E1: Listening for Meaning and Use (p. 359)

1. A: The Atlanta Braves aren't as good as the New York Yankees.
   B: According to the speaker, which baseball team is better?

2. A: Russian isn't as difficult as Chinese.
   B: According to the speaker, which language is less difficult?
3. A: Carlene runs as fast as Janet.
   B: According to the speaker, who runs faster?
4. A: Techno computers aren't as expensive as Quantum computers.
   B: According to the speaker, which computers are more expensive?
5. A: Teenage girls have as many problems as teenage boys do.
   B: According to the speaker, who has more problems?
6. A: Teachers work as hard as nurses.
   B: According to the speaker, who works harder?
7. A: Paul's children don't watch as much television as Bob's children do.
   B: According to the speaker, whose children watch more television?
8. A: Rattlesnakes aren't as dangerous as king cobras.
   B: According to the speaker, which snakes are less dangerous?

 CHAPTER 19

A2 (p. 366)

Please refer to the magazine article in the Student Book.

B1: Listening for Form (p. 370)

1. Elephants are the largest mammals on land.
2. Dolphins seem to be the friendliest mammals in the sea.
3. Tigers hunt more silently than wolves.
4. Cheetahs are the worst climbers of all the big cats.
5. Zebras run faster than giraffes.
6. Chimpanzees are the most intelligent apes.

C1: Listening for Meaning and Use (p. 374)

Situation 1
A: You have three daughters. . . . Is Megan your oldest daughter?
B: Yes, she is. Caitlin's the youngest. And poor Alison is stuck in the middle.

Situation 2
A: Is there a restaurant nearby?
B: Well, Sun Palace is the nearest restaurant, but it's not so good. Isabelle's is farther, but it's better. Or you could try Seaview. It's the farthest of the three, but it's the best.

Situation 3
A: We need one more person for the basketball team. Who looked the best in the practice game?
B: I'm not sure. Pete made the most baskets. But Tom made more baskets than a lot of the boys, and on defense he played the best of all. I thought Ed would be good, but he made the fewest baskets.

 CHAPTER 20

A2 (p. 382)

Please refer to the magazine article in the Student Book.

B1: Listening for Form (p. 385)

1. Shopping is my favorite activity. I could do it all the time!
2. We started saving money a few years ago. We want to buy a house.
3. We don't see Dana much these days. She's working two jobs.
4. Dan likes eating in expensive restaurants. I don't know how he can afford it.
5. I avoid buying clothes that aren't on sale.
6. We'll be here all summer. We're not taking a vacation this year.
7. Not having my car is very inconvenient. I hope I get it back from the mechanic soon.
8. I'm spending more money these days. Everything seems to cost more.

C1: Listening for Form (p. 388)

1. Are you interested in going to a movie tonight?
2. You should drink tea instead of drinking coffee.
3. John is talking about quitting his job.
4. I'm looking forward to taking Mr. Johnson's class.
5. I'm tired of watching TV.

D1: Listening for Meaning and Use (p. 390)

1. I hate taking tests first thing in the morning.
2. You can probably find cheaper plane fares by looking on the Internet.
3. Would you mind holding the door for me?
4. You can pay for many of your expenses by getting a part-time job.
5. I don't mind living alone.
6. You can lose weight by eating less and exercising more.

🎧 CHAPTER 21

A2 (p. 396)

Please refer to the magazine article in the Student Book.

B1: Listening for Form (p. 400)

1. I want to go to the movies tonight.
2. You'll need scissors to open this envelope.
3. They want a new car, too, but they can't afford one.
4. Let's go to the mall today.
5. He promised not to come back until next week.
6. She has gone to France many times.
7. It can be difficult to say good-bye to good friends.
8. To be there by six, you should get up at four.

C1: Listening for Meaning and Use (p. 403)

1. They hate to go to the mall on the weekends.
2. We left home early in order to avoid the traffic.
3. He loves to hike in the mountains.
4. We went to the train station to say good-bye to them.
5. She doesn't like to drive on icy roads.

6. She really wants to go to Europe this summer.
7. He phoned her to see if she was all right.
8. He took a conversation course to improve his speaking skills.

D1: Listening for Meaning and Use (p. 406)

1. A: We stopped to talk.
   B: We stopped talking.
2. A: He likes to dance.
   B: He likes dancing.
3. A: I remembered to write down the number.
   B: I remembered writing down the number.
4. A: We hated to go to school.
   B: We hated going to school.
5. A: Did you forget to give him money?
   B: Did you forget giving him money?
6. A: They've started to take English classes.
   B: They've started taking English classes.

🎧 CHAPTER 22

A2 (p. 412)

Please refer to the website article in the Student Book.

B1: Listening for Form (p. 416)

1. Did you remember to take out the garbage?
2. He wants to be a doctor when he grows up.
3. My pen ran out of ink, so I had to borrow one from my friend.
4. I always look up words in the dictionary when I do my homework.
5. I give up. I can't do this math problem.
6. He made out a check for $20.
7. Please turn off that light.
8. He doesn't get along with his boss.

C1: Listening for Meaning and Use (p. 419)

1. Take off your coat and have a seat.
2. I'm going to take off early today.
3. School is going to let out at 3:00.
4. This skirt's too tight; I need to let it out.
5. I'm busy on Friday, so I have to turn down the invitation.
6. I can't hear a word you're saying; you'll have to turn down that radio.
7. I'm feeling much better since I started to work out.
8. Don't worry. Everything will work out fine.
9. Kristen will be happy if she and her best friend make up.
10. If you don't want to go to the meeting, just make up some excuse.
11. I hurt my back last week, and I can't pick up anything over five pounds.
12. Did you pick up any Japanese expressions when you were in Tokyo last year?

Student Book Answer Key

CHAPTER 1

A3: After You Read (p. 5)

2. T
3. F
4. F
5. F
6. T

Examining Form (p. 6)

1. The form in 1b has an *-s* added to the base form of the verb.
2. The negative verb form in 2b uses *doesn't* + base form of the verb. The others use *do* + the base form of the verb.

3. Affirmative Forms

line 1:	is	line 17:	buy	line 27:	carry
line 2:	's	line 19:	like	line 28:	heats
line 3:	contains	line 21:	are	line 29:	get
line 4:	has	line 22:	swim	line 29:	use
line 12:	is	line 23:	heats	line 31:	means
line 13:	is	line 25:	use	line 33:	is
line 16:	eat	line 26:	use		

Negative Forms
line 32: don't need
line 34: doesn't go (down)

4. Yes/No question: a
   Information question: b
   Differences: The *Yes/No* question starts with *do;* the information question starts with a *Wh-* word. The *Yes/No* question is in the third-person singular and uses *does* before the subject + base form of the verb; the information question is in the third-person plural and uses *do* before the subject + base form of the verb.
   Similarities: Both use *do/does* before the subject + base form of verb.

B1: Listening for Form (p. 8)

2. is
3. lives
4. speaks
5. don't speak
6. talk
7. works
8. speaks
9. doesn't work
10. works
11. like
12. go
13. knows
14. doesn't

B2: Working on Affirmative and Negative Statements (p. 8)

2. isn't
3. has
4. has
5. hide
6. is
7. doesn't have
8. doesn't need

9. eats
10. play
11. put
12. move
13. run
14. live
15. are

B3: Pronouncing Verbs Ending in *-s* or *-es* (p. 9)

A.

		/s/	/z/	/ɪz/
2.	practices			✓
3.	works	✓		
4.	closes			✓
5.	arranges			✓
6.	tells		✓	

B4: Forming *Yes/No* Questions (p. 10)

A. 2. Does your teacher speak your language?
3. Do you have a lot of homework?
4. Do you use a dictionary?
5. Do you speak English outside of class?
6. Does your school have computers?

B. Answers will vary.

B5: Changing Statements into Questions (p. 10)

A. 2. Who has a test today?
3. What does a power plant make?
4. Where is Niagara Falls?
5. Who drives Lee to school every day?
6. Who does Dan drive to school every day?
7. When is it hot in Chicago?
8. Where is the eucalyptus tree from?

B. 2. Does Kim have a test today?
3. Does a power plant make electricity?
4. Is Niagara Falls in North America?
5. Does Dan drive Lee to school every day?
6. Does Dan drive Lee to school every day?
7. Is it hot in Chicago in the summer?
8. Is the eucalyptus tree from Australia?

Examining Meaning and Use (p. 11)

1. c
2. a
3. b

C1: Listening for Meaning and Use (p. 12)

	PERSONAL ROUTINE	GENERAL TRUTH
2.	✓	
3.		✓
4.	✓	
5.	✓	
6.		✓

C2: Talking About Routines (p. 13)

A. Answers will vary.

B. Answers will vary.

C3: Asking for Definitions (p. 13)

A. 2. A: What does the word *glacier* mean?
B: The word *glacier* means "a large body of ice that moves slowly over land."

3. A: What does the word *greenhouse* mean?
B: The word *greenhouse* means "a glass building used for growing plants."

4. A: What does the word *climate* mean?
B: The word *climate* means "the typical weather conditions of a place."

5. A: What does the word *geyser* mean?
B: The word *geyser* means "a hot spring that shoots water into the air."

6. A: What does the word *volcano* mean?
B: The word *volcano* means "a mountain from which hot melted rock, gas, smoke, and ash can escape from a hole in its top."

B. Answers will vary.

C4: Expressing Factual Information (p. 14)

A. 2. weighs
3. carries
4. has
5. move
6. starts
7. push
8. jumps
9. jumps
10. stays
11. pushes
12. gets
13. is
14. goes

B. Answers will vary.

D1: Thinking About Meaning and Use (p. 15)

Topics to check are 4, 7, and 8.

D2: Editing (p. 15)

Which large American city ~~are~~ *is* on three islands? New York City! New York is on Manhattan Island, Long Island, and Staten Island. Most people ~~thinks~~ *think* of Manhattan when they think of New York City. This is because Manhattan ~~have~~ *has* the tall buildings that New York is famous for. Sometimes people travel from Staten Island to Manhattan by boat. However, most people in New York *do* not use boats to go from one part of the city to another. Large bridges ~~connects~~ *connect* the islands. Trains and cars also ~~uses~~ *use* long tunnels under the water to move between the islands. In fact, New Yorkers usually forget that they ~~lives~~ *live* on an island.

CHAPTER 2

A3: After You Read (p. 18)

2. F   3. T   4. T   5. T   6. F

Examining Form (p. 20)

1. Underline: bears, Do not climb, do not attack, Lie
Circle: Bears, bears
Sentences b and d do not seem to have a subject.

2. line 5: Talk   line 21: be quiet
line 5: sing   line 23: do not climb
line 5: clap   line 25: do not keep
line 9: Don't hike   line 26: Put them
line 11: stay inside line 26: hang them
line 12: close   line 29: Remove
line 14: don't get out line 32: Burn
line 15: stay calm   line 35: Remember
line 16: move backward line 36: Be safe
line 20: don't fight line 37: Don't be sorry
line 20: lie still

B1: Listening for Form (p. 20)

2. Turn
3. Don't study
4. Come
5. Don't be
6. turn

B2: Forming Sentences with Imperatives (p. 21)

2. Don't leave your notebook at home.
3. Be ready for the test tomorrow.
4. Try to answer all the questions.
5. Do not talk during the test.

B3: Working on Affirmative and Negative Imperatives (p. 21)

A. Ideally, students will check items 3, 4, and 6, but answers may vary. For example, some students may not feel it's bad advice to look up every new word or to write a translation of every new word.

B. Answers may vary. If students produce different answers, ask them to justify their ideas.
2. Write English definitions for new words.
3. Try to use new words in conversation.
4. Don't look up every new word you read.
6. Don't write a translation of every new word.

B4: Building Sentences (p. 21)

Imperative:
Don't listen to him!
Don't speak to him!
Don't speak Korean!
Don't chew gum!
Speak to him!
Speak Korean!
Chew gum!

Simple Present:
She goes late.
She goes to him.
She is late.
She is Korean.
They listen to him.
They speak to him.
They speak Korean.
They chew gum.

Examining Meaning and Use (p. 22)

1. d   2. c   3. a   4. b

C1: Listening for Meaning and Use (p. 23)

2. b
3. a
4. c
5. b
6. b

C2: Giving Warnings and Commands (p. 24)

2. Please put your seatbelt on.
3. Watch out for the ball!
4. Sit down and be quiet.
5. Don't step on the truck!
6. Stop! Police!

C3: Making Requests (p. 25)

Answers will vary. Some examples are:
2. Please be on time for the meeting.
3. Please open your suitcase.
4. Dance with me!
5. Please take out the garbage.
6. Buy me a large popcorn, please.

C4: Giving Advice (p. 25)

Answers will vary. Some examples are:
2. Call the doctor. Don't worry.
3. Stop at the next gas station. Don't drive fast.
4. Listen to relaxing music. Don't drink coffee after dinner.
5. Go out and meet people. Don't sit at home.
6. Take an aspirin. Don't listen to loud music.

C5: Giving Instructions (p. 25)

Answers will vary. Some examples are:
Walk the dog twice a day.
Don't leave the lights on, please.
Please take the mail out of the mailbox every day.
Please bring in the newspaper.
Remember to water the plants.
Pay the rent on the first of the month.
Don't forget to take out the trash every night.
Please check the voice mail for new messages.
Keep the windows closed at night.

C6: Understanding Uses of the Imperative (p. 26)

Answers will vary. Some examples are:
A. 2. Watch your step, sir.
3. Please don't worry about me.
4. Please sign the receipt, ma'am.
5. John, (you) wash the dishes. And Alex, (you) dust the furniture.
6. Watch out for the broken glass!
7. Have a sandwich, Josh.
8. Don't work so hard, Uncle Bob.
9. Wait for me in the lobby.
10. Watch out for that bus!

B. *You* might be used (with or without the names) in sentence 5 to make it clear that the speaker is talking to two different people, each of whom is assigned a different task. In the other situations, only one person is being addressed, so it is not needed.

D1: Thinking About Meaning and Use (p. 27)

2. appropriate
3. Look out! A car is coming!

4. Please sit down, Grandma.
5. Give me all your money!
6. Turn off the television, please.

D2: Editing (p. 27)

2. Don't be noisy!
3. Don't listen to her.
4. Megan, close the door, please.
5. correct
6. Don't leave now!

CHAPTER 3

A3: After You Read (p. 30)

2. T
3. F
4. T
5. F
6. F

Examining Form (p. 32)

1. Underline: is, is carrying. The first is simple present. The second is present continuous.
2. Two words are necessary to form the present continuous. The ending *-ing* is added to the base form of the verb
3. line 6: are . . . receiving
   line 8: is . . . moving
   line 13: are . . . giving
   line 18: is not carrying . . .
   line 19: is carrying
   line 25: is carrying

B1: Listening for Form (p. 34)

2. a
3. d
4. c
5. b
6. b

B2: Forming Statements and *Yes/No* Questions (p. 34)

A. 2. Hector's working in a factory.
3. Maria isn't working in a factory.
4. She's teaching Spanish.
5. Hector's studying English at night.
6. They aren't living in an apartment.
7. They're renting a small house.
8. Maria and Hector are learning about life in Canada.

B. Answers will vary slightly. Some examples are:
2. A: Is Hector working in an office?
   B: No, he isn't. He's working in a factory.
3. A: Is Maria working in a factory?
   B: No, she isn't. She's a teacher.
4. A: Is Maria teaching Spanish?
   B: Yes, she is.
5. A: Is Hector studying Spanish at night?
   B: No, he isn't. He's studying English.
6. A: Are they living in an apartment?
   B: No, they aren't. They are renting a small house.
7. A: Are they renting a large house?
   B: No, they aren't. They're renting a small house.

8. A: Are they learning about life in the United States?
   B: No, they aren't. They're learning about life in Canada.

B3: Writing Information Questions (p. 35)

2. Who is talking on the telephone?
3. What is Ben reading?
4. Where is Eric studying?
5. What are their children playing?
6. Why are the children yelling?
7. How is he feeling today?
8. What are they doing now?

Examining Meaning and Use (p. 36)

1. b
2. c
3. a

C1: Listening for Meaning and Use (p. 38)

2. on a train
3. in an airport
4. in a store
5. on television or the radio
6. on a ship

C2: Understanding Meaning and Use (p. 38)

2. T
3. F
4. T
5. T
6. F

C3: Describing Activities in Progress (p. 39)

Answers will vary. Some examples are:
In picture 1, a man and woman are waiting at the bus stop. In picture 2, they are entering the bus.
In picture 1, a man is waiting with his dog. In picture 2, the man is shouting at a thief.
In picture 1, a dog is standing still. In picture 2, it is running after the thief.
In picture 1, a woman is walking across the street. She is carrying a purse. In picture 2, she is shouting for help. She is not carrying a purse.
In picture 1, a police officer is helping a woman. He is putting her groceries in a bag. In picture 2, he is running after the thief.

C4: Using Adverbs and Time Expressions with the Present Continuous (p. 40)

Answers will vary. Some examples are:
2. My best friend is taking driving lessons these days.
3. Some of my friends are still living with their parents.
4. My English class is studying the present continuous right now.
5. My family is living in Boston nowadays
6. I am still working part-time in the evenings.
7. I am living in the dormitory this year.
8. My neighbor is still complaining about my music.

C5: Contrasting Routines with Activities in Progress (p. 41)

Answer will vary. Some answers are:
2. Celia teaches ballet. Now she's shopping for food.
3. Linda and Kedra wait on tables. Now they're going to the movies.

4. Greg teaches math. Now he's playing the violin.
5. David cooks in a restaurant. Now he's fishing.
6. Ed and Reiko work in a hospital. Now they're bowling.

C6: Distinguishing Between States and Actions (p. 42)

2. don't know
3. hurts OR is hurting
4. aches OR is aching
5. look
6. think
7. 'm having
8. 'm thinking

C7: Distinguishing Differences in Meaning (p. 42)

2. D
3. S
4. D
5. D
6. D

D1: Thinking About Meaning and Use (p. 43)

2. a	6. c
3. a	7. b
4. b	8. b
5. c	

D2: Editing (p. 44)

Dear Donna,

I love Sunrise Inn. It is ~~having~~ *has* a very restful atmosphere. Right now I ~~sit~~ *'m sitting* under a large tree in the garden. I ~~don't~~ *I'm not* worrying about anything. The sun ^*is* shining, a cool breeze ~~blows~~ *is blowing* and birds ^*are* singing. I ~~have~~ *'m having* a wonderful vacation!

What ~~do~~ *are* you ~~do~~ *doing* these days? Are you ~~work~~ *working* hard? Is Ted still ~~being~~ angry at you? Are you ~~have~~ *having* good weather?

Write and tell me your news.

Myles

CHAPTER 4

A3: After You Read (p. 48)

2. T
3. T
4. F
5. F
6. T

Examining Form (p. 50)

1. Underline: questioned, protested, believed
2. The simple past of regular verbs is formed by adding -d or -ed to the base form of the verb.
3. line 9: made
   line 11: led
   line 15: wrote
   line 20: went
   They are different in that they do not add -d or -ed to the base form of the verb.

B1: Listening for Form (p. 52)

2. didn't go
3. found
4. didn't close
5. went
6. played
7. got
8. ate

B2: Working on Regular Verb Forms (p. 52)

2. lived
3. protested
4. carried
5. believed
6. wanted
7. supported
8. listened

B3: Pronouncing Verbs Ending in *-ed* (p. 53)

		/t/	/d/	/ɪd/
2.	walked	✓		
3.	rained		✓	
4.	played		✓	
5.	coughed	✓		
6.	decided			✓
7.	jumped	✓		
8.	answered		✓	

B4: Working on Irregular Verb Forms (p. 54)

A.
2. lay
3. ran
4. rose
5. flew
6. fell
7. made
8. paid
9. gave
10. became

B. Answers will vary. Some examples include:

Yes/No Questions:
Did the first airplane flight take place on December 17, 1903?
Did Orville Wright stand up in the middle of the airplane?
Did Wilbur run alongside the airplane?
Did the plane rise smoothly in the air?
Did the plane fly for several hours?
Did the flight make history?
Did the public pay attention to the Wright brothers at first?
Did the Wright brothers became famous?

Wh- Questions:
When did the first airplane flight take place?
Who lay face down in the middle of the plane?
Who ran alongside the plane?
Where did the plane rise smoothly into the air?
How long did the plane fly?
When did the plane fall to the ground?
When did the Wright brothers become famous?

C. Answers will vary.

B5: Building *Yes/No* Questions in the Simple Past (p. 55)

Did it win?
Did it leave?
Did it start on time?
Did the children win?
Did the children leave?
Did the children start on time?
Did Maria win?
Did Maria leave?
Did Maria start on time?
Did the party start on time?
Was it first?
Was it fun?
Was Maria first?
Was Maria nervous?
Were you first?
Were you nervous?
Was the party fun?
Were the children first?
Were the children nervous?

B6: Working on *Yes/No* Questions and Short Answers in the Simple Past (p. 55)

A.
2. did
3. Was
4. was
5. didn't
6. did
7. were
8. didn't
9. Did
10. did
11. didn't
12. was

B7: Understanding Informal Speech (p. 56)

1. 2. Did you have
2. 1. Did you eat
   2. did you have
3. 1. Did you stay
   2. Did you like
4. 1. did you work
   2. Did you finish

Examining Meaning and Use (p. 57)

Sentence a talks about the present.
Sentences b and c talk about a situation that started and ended in the past.
Sentence c talks about a situation that happened a short time ago.
Sentence b talks about a situation that happened a long time ago.

C1: Listening for Meaning and Use (p. 58)

A.

		RECENT PAST	DISTANT PAST
2.	walked to school		✓
3.	saw Kedra	✓	
4.	bought the dress		✓
5.	took part in protests		✓
6.	lived in France		✓

B.

		HAPPENED ONCE	HAPPENED REPEATEDLY
2.	walked to school		✓
3.	saw Kedra		✓
4.	bought the dress	✓	
5.	took part in protests		✓
6.	lived in France		✓

C2: Making Excuses (p. 58)

A. 2. I'm sorry. I forgot the name of the restaurant.
3. I'm sorry. I had an important meeting at work.
4. I'm sorry. My car ran out of gas.
5. I'm sorry. My watch stopped.
6. I'm sorry. I had a terrible headache.

B. Answers will vary.

C3: Guessing What Happened (p. 59)

Answers will vary. Some examples are:
2. Maybe she didn't like the food.
3. Perhaps he won a lot of money.
4. Perhaps he had a car accident.
5. Maybe his son got excellent grades in school.
6. Perhaps he received bad news.

C4: Using Time Expressions with the Simple Past (p. 60)

Answers will vary. Some examples are:

A. 2. I washed the dishes yesterday.
3. I talked to a friend on the telephone last night.
4. I ate in a restaurant the day before yesterday.
5. I spoke English outside of class this morning.
6. I went to a movie last week.
7. I received an e-mail this morning.
8. I took a vacation a while ago.

B. Answers will vary.

C5: Using Time Expressions with Tense Changes (p. 61)

Answers will vary. Some examples are:
2. Now
3. This morning
4. Last night
5. these days
6. last week

Examining Form (p. 62)

1. a. He (didn't) use to visit his parents so often.
   b. (Did) she use to like the class?
   c. We used to swim every morning.
   d. Where (did) you use to live?
2. We use the form *used to* with affirmative statements. We use the form *use to* with negative statements and information questions with *did/didn't*. (We also use *used to* with *Wh-* question words in the subject position. See Form charts on page 63.)

D1: Listening for Form (p. 63)

	USED TO	DIDN'T USE TO	DID . . . USE TO
2.		✓	
3.			✓
4.	✓		
5.			✓
6.	✓		
7.		✓	
8.	✓		

D2: Rewriting Statements and Questions with *Used To* (p. 64)

2. Did you use to be in the army?
3. I didn't use to go to the movies very often.
4. He didn't use to be a good student.
5. Did your family use to rent a beach house every summer?
6. We used to visit our parents on weekends.

D3: Completing Conversations with *Used To* (p. 64)

Conversation 1
2. We used to have

Conversation 2
1. Did Satomi use to date
2. they used to be

Conversation 3
1. I didn't use to like
2. He didn't use to be

Examining Meaning and Use (p. 65)

1. 1a
2. 2a suggests that Mary's present situation is different from the past.
   2b does not suggest anything about Mary's present situation.

E1: Listening for Meaning and Use (p. 66)

2. a
3. a
4. b
5. b
6. a
7. b
8. a

E2: Comparing the Past and the Present (p. 66)

Answers will vary. Some examples are:
2. Women didn't use to work outside the home. Nowadays many women have jobs.

3. In the past most people didn't use to go to college. Now many people do.
4. Many years ago supermarkets didn't use to stay open late. Now some are open 24 hours a day.
5. People didn't use to move away from their families. These days people live far away.
6. In the past most people used to get married very young. Nowadays many people get married in their thirties.

E3: Remembering Your Past (p. 66)

Answers will vary.

F1: Thinking About Meaning and Use (p. 67)

2. a
3. b
4. b
5. a
6. a

F2: Editing (p. 67)

2. We didn't ~~needed~~ _need_ any help.

3. Ana ~~taked~~ _took_ the cake to Miguel.

4. Where did they ~~went~~ _go_?

5. correct

6. Who ~~give~~ _gave_ you a present?

7. When did ~~left he~~ _he leave_?

8. correct

9. The test ~~were~~ _was_ on Saturday.

10. What ~~did~~ happened here?

CHAPTER 5

A3: After You Read (p. 71)

1. A hurricane hit the city of Galveston, Texas.
2. Galveston is on an island near the Texas coast.
3. Most people went to friends' and relatives' houses away from the water.
4. The house collapsed because a huge wave hit it.
5. They built a seawall.

Examining Form (p. 72)

1. line 8:   were living
   line 13: was moving
   line 16: was getting
   line 16: were getting
   line 21: was getting
   line 23: was going on
   line 24: was making
   line 26: were drifting
   line 27: were flying
2. Two words are necessary to form the past continuous. The two forms of *be* that are used are *was* and *were*. The ending *-ing* is added to the base form of the verb.

B1: Listening for Form (p. 73)

2. a   3. a   4. c   5. b   6. a

B2: Forming Statements with *Yes/No* Questions in the Past Continuous (p. 74)

A. Answers will vary. Some examples are:
2. Alex was listening to the music.
3. Myles and Reiko were talking in the kitchen
4. Kevin was opening the refrigerator.
5. Kalin and Kim were looking at a photo album.
6. Nicole and her dog, Sparks, were playing on the rug.

B. Answers will vary.

B3: Forming Information Questions in the Past Continuous (p. 75)

2. How was your grandfather feeling last night?
3. Who was leading the meeting this morning?
4. What was Mr. Gonzalez teaching last semester?
5. Where were you living five years ago?
6. Why were Dan and Ben fighting on Saturday?

B4: Asking and Answering Information Questions in the Past Continuous (p. 75)

Answers will vary.

B5: Building Past Continuous and Simple Past Sentences (p. 75)

Past Continuous
Carlos was sleeping.
Carlos was studying.
You weren't sleeping.
You weren't studying.
Ana and Rose weren't sleeping.

Simple Past
Carlos was early.
Carlos didn't call.
You had a cold.
You didn't call.
You weren't early.
Ana and Rose had a cold.
Ana and Rose didn't call.
Ana and Rose weren't early.

Examining Meaning and Use (p. 76)

1. b
2. a

C1: Listening for Meaning and Use (p. 77)

		ONGOING	COMPLETED
2.	write a book	✓	
3.	paint the house	✓	
4.	fix the air conditioner		✓
5.	write a paper		✓
6.	take flying lessons	✓	

C2: Describing Activities in Progress at the Same Time (p. 77)

Answers will vary.

C3: Describing Past Situations (p. 78)

Conversation 1
2. owned

Conversation 2
1. Did
2. know
3. arrived
4. was taking
5. weren't

Conversation 3
2. wasn't paying
3. was thinking

Conversation 4
1. saw
2. was
3. doing
4. was looking

C4: Introducing Background Information with the Past Continuous (p. 79)

A. Answers will vary. Some examples are:
2. They were standing in line. The line was moving slowly.
3. They were hurrying down the hall. They were telling jokes and laughing.
4. He was yelling at me. Everyone in the office was listening.
5. Some students were sitting at the tables. Others were standing in line and waiting for their food.
6. The wind was blowing hard. People were hurrying home.

B. Answers will vary.

Examining Form (p. 80)

1. Underline: was; didn't worry, got; ended, was
Sentences b and c have two verbs.
2. Circle: when he got the news; After the storm ended

D1: Listening for Form (p. 81)

2. before it hit
3. After the people left
4. When the storm began
5. when it rained
6. after the storm ended

D2: Forming Sentences with Past Time Clauses (p. 81)

2. a   3. e   4. b   5. c   6. d

D3: Practicing Punctuation with Past Time Clauses (p. 82)

A terrible storm hit last night <u>while my friend was staying at my house</u>. All the lights went out <u>when lightning struck the house</u>. <u>While I was looking for matches,</u> I tripped over a rug. I heard a knock on the door. I went to the door and answered it. A strange man was standing outside. He was wearing a hood. The wind was blowing the trees back and forth <u>while the storm was raging</u>. <u>When I saw the stranger,</u> I became nervous. Then, <u>when he began to speak,</u> I recognized his voice. It was my friend's father.

D4: Changing the Position of Past Time Clauses (p. 82)

2. Reiko got a cramp in her leg while she was swimming.
3. My sister ate pizza for breakfast when she woke up this morning.
4. While I was driving to work, it started to rain.
5. After she finished high school, Eva became a ballet dancer. OR After Eva finished high school, she became a ballet dancer.

Examining Meaning and Use (p. 83)

1. c
2. a
3. b

E1: Listening for Meaning and Use (p. 84)

	SIMULTANEOUS	INTERRUPTED	IN SEQUENCE
2.	✓		
3.			✓
4.		✓	
5.	✓		
6.			✓

E2: Understanding Time Clauses (p. 84)

Answers may vary slightly. Some examples include:
2. A: *While* is used for simultaneous activity. You can't drive away while you're looking for your car keys.
   B: It should be, "When/After Ben found his car keys, he drove away."
3. A: It isn't very dark when the sun comes up.
   B: It should be, "Before the sun came up, it was very dark."
4. A: You normally dance *after* the band starts to play.
   B: It should be, "Everyone danced when/after the band started to play."
5. A: People fill the pool with water *before* they swim.
   B: It should be, "Before we went swimming, they filled the pool with water."

E3: Writing About Events in Sequence (p. 85)

Answers will vary. Some examples are:
1. they wanted to buy it right away.
   they loved it.
2. she spent two hours getting ready.
   she saw several of her friends.
   she went to a friend's house.
3. he left, he bought a camera.
   he got there, he took a tour of the city.
   he got back, he showed his photos to his friends.

E4: Expressing Simultaneous, Interrupted, and Sequential Events (p. 85)

Answers will vary. Some examples are:
2. I spilled my soda on the floor.
3. I was taking a shower.
4. the phone rang.
5. she began to study harder
6. we ordered pizza and played cards until 3:00 A.M.

F1: Thinking About Meaning and Use (p. 86)

2. a. No
   b. It's not clear.
3. a. It's not clear.
   b. It's not clear.
4. a. It's not clear.
   b. It's not clear.
5. a. It's not clear.
   b. It's not clear.
6. a. No
   b. It's not clear.
7. a. No
   b. It's not clear.
8. a. No
   b. Yes
9. a. No
   b. No
10. a. No
    b. Yes

F2: Editing (p. 87)

2. I'm so sorry about your mug. I ~~was dropping~~ *dropped* it.
3. They ~~were owning~~ *owned* a house before they had children.
4. It *was* ^snowing when we went to school.
5. correct
6. After he ~~was throwing~~ *threw* the ball, it hit the window.
7. What did he say to you while you ~~watched~~ *were watching* the movie?
8. Where were you going when I ~~was seeing~~ *saw* you yesterday?
9. She was reading ~~after~~ *before* she fell asleep.
10. correct

CHAPTER 6

A3: After You Read (p. 91)

A. The following should be circled: Bouvet Island, Clipperton, the Paracel Islands.

B. 2. c
   3. a
   4. b
   5. d

Examining Form (p. 92)

1. 1b and 2a are in the simple past.
   1a and 2b are in the present perfect.
   Two words are necessary to form the present perfect.
2. Underline: crossed (1a); flown (2b).
   The form *crossed* resembles the simple past. The form *flown* is irregular.
3. In affirmative statements:
   line 2: has visited
   line 3: has been
   line 5: has crossed
   line 12: have traveled
   line 13: has cost
   line 14: has spent
   line 15: has . . . taken
   line 18: has continued
   line 24: have been
   line 34: has said
   line 37: 's been
   line 41: you've seen
   line 42: you've seen

   In negative statements:
   line 18: No, he hasn't.
   line 19: hasn't visited
   line 32: has never . . . stated

   In *Yes/No* questions:
   line 17: Has . . . stopped

   In information questions:
   line 36: has . . . visited

B1: Listening for Form (p. 94)

2. haven't seen
3. has left
4. hasn't taken
5. has rained
6. haven't eaten

B2: Working on Irregular Past Verb Forms (p. 94)

	BASE FORM	SIMPLE PAST	PAST PARTICIPLE
2.	get	got	gotten
3.	take	took	taken
4.	buy	bought	bought
5.	leave	left	left
6.	cost	cost	cost
7.	show	showed	shown/showed
8.	be	was/were	been
9.	go	went	gone
10.	eat	ate	eaten
11.	make	made	made
12.	do	did	done
13.	see	saw	seen
14.	think	thought	thought
15.	grow	grew	grown
16.	spend	spent	spent

B3: Understanding Informal Speech (p. 95)

2. have seen
3. has bought
4. have gone
5. have arrested
6. has . . . been
7. has grown
8. has . . . taken

B4: Completing Conversations with the Present Perfect (p. 96)

Conversation 1
3. Have
4. been

5. haven't
6. 've
7. been

Conversation 2
1. haven't seen
2. 's been
3. has
4. been
5. have been
6. has gotten
7. have had

B5: Building Sentences (p. 96)

A. Present perfect:
She has been to a restaurant.
She has been a good friend.
She has waited for a long time.
She has learned English.
They have been to a restaurant.
They have waited for a long time.
They have learned English.

Simple past:
She waited for a long time.
She learned English.
She went for a long time.
She went to a restaurant.
They learned English.
They waited for a long time.
They learned English.
They went for a long time.
They went to a restaurant.

B. Present perfect:
She hasn't been to a restaurant.
She hasn't been a good friend.
She hasn't waited for a long time.
She hasn't learned English.
They haven't been to a restaurant.
They haven't waited for a long time.
They haven't learned English.

Simple past:
She didn't wait for a long time.
She didn't learn English.
She didn't go for a long time.
She didn't go to a restaurant.
They didn't learn English.
They didn't wait for a long time.
They didn't learn English.
They didn't go for a long time.
They didn't go to a restaurant.

Examining Meaning and Use (p. 97)

1. 1b and 2b began and ended in the past. 1a and 2a began in the past and have continued up to the present.
2. 1b and 2b are in the simple present. 1a and 2a are in the present perfect.

C1: Listening for Meaning and Use (p. 98)

	PAST SITUATION THAT CONTINUES TO THE PRESENT	SITUATION THAT BEGAN AND ENDED IN PAST
2.		✓
3.	✓	
4.		✓
5.		✓
6.	✓	
7.		✓
8.	✓	

C2: Using *For* and *Since* (p. 98)

A. 2. since
3. for
4. since
5. for
6. since
7. for
8. for
9. since
10. for

B. 2. Betty has worked at Happy Systems for ten years.
3. Paul has studied French for two semesters.
4. I have been married to Kalin since last August.
5. Liz and Sara have known Celia for many years.

C3: Talking About How Long (p. 99)

A. A: How long has he been married?
B: He's been married since 1992/for . . . years.
A: How long has he had a business?
B: He's had a business since 1995/for . . . years.
A: How long has he known his best friend?
B: He's known his best friend since 2000/for . . . years.
A: How long has he lived in the U.S.?
B: He's lived in the U.S. since 1990/for . . . years.
A: How long has he owned a house?
B: He's owned a house since 1998/for . . . years.

B. Answers will vary.

Examining Meaning and Use (p. 100)

1. 1b and 2b; simple past
2. 1a and 2a; present perfect

D1: Listening for Meaning and Use (p. 101)

	DEFINITE TIME IN THE PAST	INDEFINITE TIME IN THE PAST
2.		✓
3.	✓	
4.		✓
5.	✓	
6.		✓
7.	✓	
8.		✓
9.		✓
10.	✓	

D2: Contrasting Definite and Indefinite Past Time (p. 102)

A. Answers will vary. Some examples are:
2. had dinner with some students from Kenya.
3. he wore a tuxedo to school.
4. moved to the United States so I could have a better life.
5. he gave us an hour to take a test with two hundred questions.

B. Answers will vary. Some examples include:
2. He has had a lot of jobs.
3. She has been in a lot of shows.
4. I have done a lot of chores today.
5. They have lived in many places.

D3: Asking Questions About Indefinite Past Time (p. 103)

Answers will vary. Some examples are:
2. How many times has your car broken down?
   Have you ever been in an accident with your car?
3. Have you had previous experience with young babies?
   Have you ever taken a course in first aid?
4. Have you ever shared an apartment before?
   Has anyone ever complained about your music?
5. Have you made any new friends?
   Have you found a new job?

D4: Describing Progress (p. 103)

Answers will vary. Some examples are:
He's disconnected the telephone.
He hasn't packed all his clothes.
He hasn't thrown away the trash.
He hasn't contacted the post office.
He's called his mother and given her his new address.
He hasn't cleaned the oven.
He hasn't left the key with the superintendent.

D5: Using Adverbs with the Present Perfect (p. 104)

A. *Conversation 1*
2. No, I still haven't asked her.

Conversation 2
1. Have you ever played golf?
2. No, I've never played golf.

Conversation 3
1. Has she bought the tickets yet?
2. No. She's already made the reservations, but she hasn't bought the tickets yet. OR No. She's made the reservations already, but she hasn't bought the tickets yet.

Conversation 4
1. Have you raised any money yet?
2. Yes. We've raised $2,000 so far. We still haven't finished.

Conversation 5
1. Has Rick left yet?
2. Yes, he's already left. OR Yes, he's left already.

Conversation 6
1. Have you made any friends at school yet?
2. No, I've been too busy so far. OR No. So far, I've been too busy.

E1: Thinking About Meaning and Use (p. 106)

2. a
3. b
4. a
5. a
6. a
7. b
8. a

E2: Editing (p. 107)

Rita and Bob ~~have been~~ [are] the most-traveled people I know. They ~~went~~ [have gone] almost everywhere. Rita ~~has been~~ [is] a photographer, and Bob ~~has been~~ [is] a travel writer, so they often travel for work. They [have] been to many countries, such as Nepal and India. They have also ~~travel~~ [traveled] to Turkey, Greece, and Bulgaria. They have[n't] [seen] ~~see~~ some places yet, though. For example, they still haven't visited New Zealand. This year they've ~~been already~~ [already been] away from home a total of three months, and it ~~has been~~ [is] only June. In January Rita ~~has gone~~ [went] to Kenya while Bob ~~has toured~~ [toured] Indonesia. Then they both ~~have~~ traveled to Argentina and Norway. Right now they're at home. They ~~were~~ [have been] here for two weeks already. Two weeks at home is like a vacation for Rita and Bob.

CHAPTER 7

A3: After You Read (p. 113)

WHICH CANDIDATE . . .	MONROE	OVERMEYER	KELLY
1. isn't going to raise taxes?	✓		
2. is a woman?	✓		
3. runs a large company?		✓	
4. promises to bring jobs to the state?		✓	
5. is a mayor?			✓
6. wants to raise taxes?			✓

Examining Form (p. 114)

1. line 25: Overmeyer is going to win
   line 38: he is going to help
   line 56: I'm going to sit down
2. The form *are going to* is used with *we*
   The form *is going to* is used with *he*
   The form *am going to* is used with *I*
3. line 1: I'm voting for

B1: Listening for Form (p. 116)

2. We're not going
3. is he going

4. It's going to rain
5. Are you going to watch TV
6. they aren't going to stay
7. We're going
8. I'm not going
9. you're going to fail
10. I'm going

B2: Working on *Be Going To* (p. 116)
2. are going to take
3. is not going to apply
4. is going to be
5. is not going to be
6. is going to stay
7. is going to live
8. are going to enjoy

B3: Building Present Continuous Statements (p. 117)
I am going to Europe next summer.
I am going to Europe tomorrow.
I am going to Europe tonight.
I'm giving a test tomorrow.
I'm giving a test tonight.
I'm taking a test tomorrow.
I'm taking a test tonight.
I am going to a restaurant tomorrow.
I am going to a restaurant tonight.
My friends are taking a test tomorrow.
My friends are taking a test tonight.
My friends are going to Europe next summer.
My friends are going to Europe tomorrow.
My friends are going to Europe tonight.
My friends are going to a restaurant tomorrow.
My friends are going to a restaurant tonight.
Our teacher is giving a test tomorrow.
Our teacher is giving a test tonight.
Our teacher is going to Europe next summer.
Our teacher is going to Europe tomorrow.
Our teacher is going to Europe tonight.
Our teacher is going to a restaurant tonight.
Our teacher is going to a restaurant tomorrow.

B4: Forming Questions with *Be Going To* (p. 117)
2. Are they going to call tomorrow?
3. Are you going to graduate this semester?
4. Are you going to move to Canada?
5. Where is he going to study tonight?
6. When are they going to call?
7. When are you going to graduate?
8. Where are you going to move?

B5: Understanding Informal Speech (p. 118)
2. am going to go
3. are not going to see
4. is going to meet
5. is going to close
6. is going to study
7. are not going to be
8. are going to take

Examining Meaning and Use (p. 119)
1. a, c
2. b

C1: Listening for Meaning and Use (p. 120)

	INTENTION / PLAN	PREDICTION
2.	✓	
3.	✓	
4.		✓
5.		✓
6.	✓	
7.		✓
8.	✓	

C2: Making Predictions with *Be Going To* (p. 121)
Answers will vary. Some answers are:
2. I think he's going to ask her to marry him.
   I think she's going to say yes.
3. I think he's going to write a letter.
   I think he's going to do his homework.
4. I think they're going to play basketball.
   I think she's going to win.
5. I think the hair stylist is going to give her a new style.
   I think she's going to look great with short hair.
6. I think she's not going to catch the ball.
   I think her team is going to lose the game.

C3: Using Future Time Expressions (p. 122)
Answers will vary. Some examples are:
2. A: When is your best friend going to visit you?
   B: He's going to visit me during Spring Break
3. A: When are you going to finish your homework?
   B: In a half hour.
4. A: When are your friends having a party?
   B: They're having a party next weekend.
5. A: When are you checking your e-mail?
   B: In a few minutes.
6. A: When is your history teacher giving a test?
   B: He's giving a test the week after next.
7. A: When is your family going to take a vacation?
   B: Next summer.
8. A: When are you going to clean your apartment?
   B: I'm going to clean my apartment this weekend.

C4: Talking About Intentions and Plans (p. 123)
A. Answers will vary. Some examples:
2. I'm going to the movies the day after tomorrow.
3. I'm going to go to Vancouver next spring.
4. I'm going to go home in six months to see my parents.
5. I'm studying Italian next year.
6. I'm leaving in an hour.

B. Answers will vary.

C5: Thinking About Intentions and Plans (p. 123)
A. Students should check items 3, 4, 7, 8, 9, 10, and 12.

B. Answers will vary.

C6: Planning a Meeting (p. 124)
A. Answers will vary.

B. Answers will vary.

Examining Form (p. 125)

1. a. (I)'ll <u>decide</u> in a few weeks.
   b. (He) will probably <u>raise</u> taxes.
   c. (They) will <u>vote</u> for him.
   d. Will (Overmeyer) <u>keep</u> his promises?
2. No.
3. *Will* goes before the subject in a question.

D1: Listening for Form (p. 126)

	BE GOING TO	PRESENT CONTINUOUS	WILL
2.			✓
3.	✓		
4.		✓	
5.		✓	
6.			✓
7.			✓
8.	✓		

D2: Completing Conversations with *Will* (p. 127)

Conversation 1
2. we will

Conversation 2
1. Will we be
2. we'll be

Conversation 3
1. you'll be
2. I won't

Conversation 4
1. I'll do
2. you won't

Conversation 5
1. I'll never learn
2. I'll show

Conversation 6
1. you'll find
2. It will be
3. I'll try

D3: Asking *Yes/No* Questions with *Will* (p. 128)

A. 2. Will we have a final exam?
   3. Will we get grades for class participation?
   4. Will we use a textbook?
   5. Will we have a lot of tests?
   6. Will we use the language lab?

B. Answers will vary.

C. Answers will vary.

D4: Building Sentences (p. 128)

What will you talk about after class today?
What will your boss talk about at the meeting?
What will be ready?
When will dinner be ready?
When will you be ready?
When will you be at the meeting?
When will you graduate from college?
When will your boss be ready?

When will your boss graduate from college?
Where will you be after class today?
Where will you go after class today?
Where will your boss be after class today?
Where will your boss go after class today?
Who will you talk about after class today?
Who will you talk about at the meeting?
Who will your boss talk about after class today?
Who will your boss talk about at the meeting?
Who will be at the meeting?
Who will be ready?
Who will graduate from college?

D5: Understanding Informal Speech (p. 129)

2. When will
3. students will
4. Who will
5. Amy will
6. teacher will
7. John will
8. game will

Examining Meaning and Use (p. 130)

1. c   2. a   3. b

E1: Listening for Meaning and Use (p. 131)

	PROMISE	PREDICTION	QUICK DECISION
2.			✓
3.	✓		
4.			✓
5.		✓	
6.	✓		

E2: Contrasting *Be Going To* and *Will* (p. 132)

Conversation 1
2. I'm going to visit

Conversation 2
1. Maria is going to have

Conversation 3
1. I'll answer

Conversation 4
1. Will you marry
2. I will

E3: Making Quick Decisions (p. 132)

Answers will vary. Some examples are:

Conversation 2
B: I'll open the door for you.

Conversation 3
B: I'll lend you some money.

Conversation 4
B: I'll help you clean it.

Conversation 5
B: Don't worry. I'll lend you my notes.

E4: Making Promises (p. 133)

Answers will vary. Some examples are:
2. I'll never forget to lock the house again.

3. I'm sorry. I promise I won't forget my homework again.
   I promise.
4. Don't worry. I promise you it won't hurt.
5. I'll pay the whole bill next month.

E5: Making Predictions (p. 133)

Answers will vary. Some examples are:
2. Space travel is going to be very common. People will
   live on Mars and go to the moon for vacation.
3. People will live in peace. Governments will not go to
   war.
4. Cars will use solar energy. Planes will fly to Europe in
   three hours.
5. Education will become very expensive. Computers are
   going to replace teachers.
6. There's going to be another international economic
   crisis. Poverty will increase around the world.

F1: Thinking About Meaning and Use (p. 134)

2. b
3. b
4. a
5. b
6. b
7. b
8. a

F2: Editing (p. 135)

2. What ~~she is~~ *is she* going to study?

3. correct

4. Betty ~~studying~~ *is going to study* with some famous chefs next year.

5. Someday maybe Betty ~~is being~~ *will be/is going to be* a famous chef, too.

6. correct

7. After these classes she certainly ~~wills~~ *will* know all about

   restaurant management.

8. Maybe in a few years Betty ~~owns~~ *will own* a restaurant.

9. What kind of food ₍*will*₎ her restaurant ~~will~~ serve?

10. I predict it ~~is serving~~ *will serve* Chinese.

CHAPTER 8

A3: After You Read (p. 139)

Students should check items 4 and 6.

Examining Form (p. 140)

1. a. I'll see him (before I leave.)
   b. (When they graduate,) they're going
      to look for work.
   c. We're going to have dessert
      (after we finish dinner.)
2. First word of each dependent clause:
   before; When; after
   The simple present is used.
3. *If*
4. Future Time Clauses
   line 20: When the weather is cold, . . .
   line 22: . . . when the weather is hot.

If Clauses
If the robots find water, . . .
If a room is empty, . . .

B1: Listening for Form (p. 142)

2. 'll need, is
3. will go, visit
4. 'll call, gets
5. 'll meet, go
6. gets, 'll buy

B2: Building Sentences (p. 142)

Future forms in main clauses may vary.
After Megan finishes class, she'll have lunch
(OR she's going to have lunch).
After Megan finishes class, she'll call you
(OR she's going to call you).
Before she leaves the house, she'll have lunch
(OR she's going to have lunch).
Before she leaves the house, she'll call you
(OR she's going to call you).
If we win the prize, we'll get a lot of money.
If you study hard, you'll pass the test
(OR you're going to pass the test).
When we get to the movies, we'll save
you a seat.

B3: Working on Future Time Clauses and *If* Clauses (p. 143)

A. 2. After she graduates,
   3. , we'll look for a house.
   4. They'll visit the Eiffel Tower

B. 2. I'll call
   3. , I'll go to work.
   4. If you don't study,

B4: Completing Sentences with Future Time Clauses and *If* (p. 143)

2. leaves
3. I'll decorate (OR I'm going to decorate)
4. go
5. will get (OR is going to get)
6. goes
7. comes
8. won't be (OR aren't going to be)
9. ask
10. won't be
11. is
12. 'll call

Examining Meaning and Use (p. 144)

Underline: we get the results; the teacher will review the
homework; he comes home from the hospital
The words *when, before,* and *after* tell the order of the
events. (When a time clause begins with *when* or *after*, the
event in the time clause happens first. When a time clause
begins with *before*, the event in the time clause happens
second.)

C1: Listening for Meaning and Use (p. 144)

2. 2, 1
3. 2, 1
4. 2, 1
5. 2, 1

C2: Talking About Two Future Events (p. 145)

A. 2. I'll take the next level
3. When the semester is over
4. when I save enough money
5. When I move to the U.S.
6. after I take the final exam

B. Answers will vary.

C3: Describing Future Events in Sequence (p. 145)

Answers will vary.

Examining Meaning and Use (p. 146)

1. *If* clauses (underlined): If you take some aspirin; if you help me with my homework
   Main clauses (circled): you'll feel better; I'll take you out to dinner.
   The *if* clauses describe a possible situation in each sentence.
   The main clause describes a possible result.
2. 1a gives advice.
   1b makes a promise.
3. 2b

D1: Listening for Meaning and Use (p. 147)

	POSSIBLE	CERTAIN
1.	✓	
2.		✓
3.	✓	
4.	✓	
5.		✓
6.	✓	

D2: Giving Warnings (p. 148)

Answers will vary. Some examples are:
2. if you touch the stove
3. You'll be living in the dark
4. you'll catch a cold
5. You'll be hungry all day
6. You'll be tired
7. if you come to work late
8. If you run down the stairs

D3: Giving Advice (p. 148)

Answers will vary. Some examples are:
1. If you take the bus, you'll save ten minutes.
2. If you get good grades, you'll get into a good university.
   If you take part in student organizations, you'll improve your chances.
3. If you're polite to her, she'll respect you more.
   If you talk to her, maybe you'll solve some of your problems.
4. If you find a roommate, you won't have any problems.
   If you get a part-time job, you'll be able to pay the rent.

D4: Making Promises (p. 149)

Answers will vary. Some examples are:
2. A: If you lend me the car, I'll mow the lawn.
   B: If you finish your homework, you can borrow the car.
3. A: If you don't give me a ticket, I'll never speed again.
   B: If you speed, you'll have an accident.

4. A: If you give me another chance, I'll never be late again.
   B: If you're late again, you won't have a job.

D5: Making Predictions (p. 149)

Answers will vary. Some examples are:
If the man falls on the telephone cord, the woman may fall off the ladder.
If the woman falls off the ladder, she'll drop the dishes.
If she drops the dishes, there will be glass all over the floor.
If the dishes break, the child will cut his feet.
If the child reaches the counter, the fish will fall on the floor.
If the fish falls on the floor, the cat will eat it.
If the cat eats the fish, the family will go to a restaurant for dinner.

E1: Thinking About Meaning and Use (p. 150)

2. a
3. a
4. b
5. b
6. a
7. b
8. a
9. a
10. a

E2: Editing (p. 151)

2. If I ~~won't~~ *don't* feel better soon, I'll go to the doctor.

3. correct

4. I'm going to check the prices on-line before I'~~m going~~ ~~to~~ buy a camera.

5. correct

6. He's going to drive to Dallas if the weather ~~will improve~~ *improves.*

7. When I'~~ll~~ get my paycheck, I'll pay my bills.

8. They'll cancel the picnic if it ~~will~~ rain*s* tomorrow.

9. When the phone ~~is going to ring~~ *rings* I'll answer it.

10. correct

CHAPTER 9

A3: After You Read (p. 157)

2. T   3. T   4. F   5. F   6. T

Examining Form (p. 158)

1. The base form of the verb follows *can* and *could*.
2. line 3: can't do
   line 9: could not defeat
   line 14: couldn't jump
   line 19: cannot write
   The unusual feature of *cannot* is that we write it as one word.
   The contracted forms of *can* and *could* are *can't* and *couldn't.*

B1: Listening for Form (p. 160)

2. can
3. can
4. can't
5. can
6. can't

B2: Building Sentences with *Can* and *Can't* (p. 161)

People can bark.
People can swim.
People can't bark.
Fish can swim.
Fish can't climb trees.
Fish can't bark.
Dogs can bark.
Dogs can swim.
Dogs can't climb trees.

B3: Forming Statements and Questions with *Can* and *Could* (p. 161)

2. We could take them to the airport.
   Could we take them to the airport?
3. His parents can speak several languages.
   Can his parents speak several languages?
4. Your sister can speak Mandarin.
   Can your sister speak Mandarin?
5. She can help us with this problem.
   Can she help us with this problem?

B4: Completing Conversations with *Be Able To* (p. 161)

1. 3. I wasn't
   4. was able to do
2. 1. wasn't able to come
   2. 'll be able to help
3. 1. was
   2. able to practice
   3. was able to play
4. 1. Will
   2. be able to call
   3. 'll be able to see

Examining Meaning and Use (p. 162)

1. a
2. c
3. b

C1: Listening for Meaning and Use (p. 164)

2. a
3. a
4. b
5. a
6. a

C2: Talking About Future Abilities (p. 164)

Answers will vary.

C3: Distinguishing Between *Can* and *Be Able To* (p. 164)

2. Paul can drive us to school tomorrow morning.
3. *No change is possible.*
4. *No change is possible.*
5. The doctor can see you at three o'clock this afternoon.
6. *No change is possible.*

C4: Talking About Past Abilities (p. 165)

A. Answers will vary.

B. Answers will vary.

C5: Comparing Long Periods of Time and Single Events (p. 165)

A. 2. *No change is possible.*
   3. Before he hurt his knee, he could run five miles a day.
   4. Even as a young child, she could swim well.
   5. We couldn't get to the concert on time last night.
   6. Could you see the fireworks from your window the other night?
   7. Matt couldn't find his keys this morning.
   8. *No change is possible.*

B. Sentences 2 and 8 cannot be rewritten with *could* because they are affirmative sentences that describe a single event.

C6: Talking About Skills (p. 166)

A. Answers will vary. Some examples are:
   2. Can you/Do you know how to change a tire?
   3. Can you/Do you know how to use a computer?
   4. Can you/Do you know how to sew on a button?
   5. Can you/Do you know how to play the guitar (or another instrument)?
   6. Can you/Do you know how to play baseball?
   7. Can you/Do you know how to speak French?
   8. Can you/Do you know how to drive a motorcycle?

B. Answers will vary.

Examining Form (p. 167)

1. Sentences a and c contain modals.
   Underline: *might, may*
   Sentence c contains a verb in the simple present.
2. a. He might not walk again.
   b. He doesn't have the strength of one hundred men.
   c. Researchers may not find a cure.

   Negative statements with modals use the modal + *not* + base form of verb.

   Negative statements in the simple present use *do/does* + *not* + base form of verb.

D1: Listening for Form (p. 168)

1. 2. may
2. 1. might
3. 1. could
   2. might not
4. 1. may
5. 1. could
   2. might not

D2: Forming Affirmative and Negative Statements (p. 169)

A. 2. You could win the game next Saturday.
   3. Bob and Carol might get married next year.
   4. It could rain tomorrow.
   5. Sara will cook dinner tonight.
   6. We may go to the beach on Sunday.
   7. Yuji will come at six o'clock.
   8. Kim and Josh might have a party.
   9. Lynn could graduate next semester.
   10. Victor may stay home next weekend.

B. 2. *Cannot be made negative.*
3. Bob and Carol might not get married next year.
4. *Cannot be made negative.*
5. Sara won't cook dinner tonight.
6. We may not go to the beach on Sunday.
7. Yuji won't come at six o'clock.
8. Kim and Josh might not have a party.
9. *Cannot be made negative.*
10. Victor may not stay home next weekend.

Sentences 2, 4, and 9 can't be made negative because *could not* is not used to show future possibility.

Examining Meaning and Use (p. 170)

Sentence b is the most certain.
Sentences a, c, d, and e are less certain.

E1: Listening for Meaning and Use (p. 171)

2. ?
3. ✓
4. ✓
5. ✓
6. ?

E2: Using Modals for Future Possibility (p. 172)

2. Will
3. might
4. might not
5. might
6. Maybe
7. may be
8. 'll

E3: Contrasting *May Be* and *Maybe* (p. 172)

2. The weather may be better on the weekend.
3. We may be able to get tickets to the baseball game.
4. Maybe this will be an exciting game.
5. They may not be home this evening.
6. Maybe the final exam won't be very difficult.
7. Maybe he will be stuck in traffic.
8. They may be able to help us clean the attic.

E4: Expressing Future Possibility (p. 173)

A. Answers will vary. Some examples are:

Conversation 2
1. may be able to get a part-time job and save some money.

Conversation 3
1. It could snow tonight.

Conversation 4
1. could have steak
2. could have pasta

Conversation 5
1. Maybe I'll go to the Bahamas. OR I may go to the Bahamas.

B. Answers will vary.

F1: Thinking About Meaning and Use (p. 174)

2. b
3. a
4. a
5. b
6. a
7. b
8. a

F2: Editing (p. 175)

. . . The beach isn't far from his house. Josh can ~~to~~ walk there. He is a great swimmer. He could swim when he was three years old! My roommate Nicole doesn't know how to swim, so I will probably teach her this weekend. Nicole will be able to swim by the end of the summer if she practices every day. Maybe ~~May be~~ we'll go sailing, too. Last Saturday Josh and I were ~~was~~ able to go sailing because the weather was great. We could see dolphins near the boat. They were beautiful. Unfortunately, we couldn't touch them. If we're lucky, we will be able to ~~can~~ see some dolphins at the beach this weekend.

CHAPTER 10

A3: After You Read (p. 179)

Students should check items 3, 5, and 6.

Examining Form (p. 180)

1. line 11: Can <u>we</u> talk another time?
line 17: Would <u>you</u> consider giving me a raise?
line 21: Could <u>we</u> discuss a raise sooner?
line 23: Can <u>you</u> please ask Kristen to come into my office when you leave?
Subjects: (see underlined words above)
The base form of the verb follows the subject in each question.

2. line 13: I would rather talk to you now, if possible.
line 19: I would like to wait until your review.
Would rather is followed by the base form of the verb.
Would like is followed by an infinitive.

B1: Listening for Form (p. 183)

1. 2. could
3. 'd rather not
2. 1. May
2. Could
3. 1. Would
2. like
3. 'd prefer
4. 1. 'd like
2. Can
3. can't

B2: Building Questions with Modals (p. 183)

Can you give me a ride?
Could I come with you?
Could you give me a ride?
Would you give me a ride?
Would you prefer some coffee?
Would you prefer to leave now?
Would you like to leave now?
Would you like some coffee?
Would you rather eat later?

B3: Completing Conversations (p. 184)

1. 2. Where can I leave
2. 1. May I help

2. I'd like to get
3. 1. Can I park
   2. Visitors can't park
4. 1. Will you answer
   2. I can't
5. 1. Would you like to go
   2. I'd rather stay
6. 1. Would you like to order
   2. Would you prefer

B4: Working on Negative Sentences (p. 185)

2. We'd prefer not to exercise in the morning.
3. I don't want to call you later.
4. They'd rather not live in the suburbs.
5. He'd prefer not to buy a new computer.
6. He doesn't want to finish his work now.

B5: Writing Short Conversations (p. 185)

B's answers will vary. Some examples are:
2. A: Who would you prefer to meet, a famous athlete or a famous writer?
   B: I'd prefer to meet a famous athlete.
3. A: Where would you like to eat dinner tonight, at home or in a restaurant?
   B: I'd like to eat in a restaurant.
4. A: What would you rather do tonight, watch TV or go out?
   B: I'd rather go out.
5. A: How would you rather travel, by car or by plane?
   B: I'd rather travel by car.
6. A: What would you like to buy, a laptop computer or a digital camera?
   B: I'd like to buy a digital camera.
7. A: What would you rather eat, cookies or cake?
   B: I'd rather eat cookies.
8. A: Where would you prefer to live, in a big city or in a small town?
   B: I'd prefer to live in a small town.

Examining Meaning and Use (p. 186)

Sentence b is the most polite. Sentence a is the least polite.

C1: Listening for Meaning and Use (p. 187)

A.

	INFORMAL	FORMAL
2.		✓
3.	✓	
4.	✓	
5.		✓
6.		✓

B. 2. f 3. d 4. a 5. e 6. c

C2: Using the Telephone (p. 188)

A. 2. b 3. b 4. a 5. a 6. a

B. Answers will vary.

C3: Making Formal and Informal Requests (p. 189)

A. Answers will vary.

B. Answers will vary.

C4: Agreeing to and Refusing Requests (p. 189)

Answers will vary. Some examples are:
2. A: Can you help me move this weekend?
   B: Sure, no problem.
3. A: Will you lend me $50 until next week?
   B: Sorry, I need to pay my rent this week.
4. A: Could you give me a larger room please?
   B: I'm sorry. We have no empty rooms.
5. A: I was sick yesterday. Would you lend me your notes?
   B: Sure, but I'll need them back tomorrow morning.
6. A: Could you repair the car by the end of the week?
   B: I'm sorry, we're really busy right now, but I could have it ready for you on Monday.

Examining Meaning and Use (p. 190)

1. 1a asks for permission. 1b asks about ability.
2. 2b is more formal.

D1: Listening for Meaning and Use (p. 191)

2. h   4. g   6. c   8. f
3. e   5. a   7. b

D2: Asking For Permission (p. 192)

2. May I pet your dog?
3. Can I use my laptop now?
4. Can I have this piece of cake?
5. Could I hold the baby, please?
6. Could I join you at this table?

D3: Asking For and Giving or Refusing Permission

Answers will vary. Some examples are:
2. A: May I see this apartment again in the daytime?
   B: Certainly.
3. A: Could I please borrow your car this afternoon?
   B: I'm sorry. I need it.
4. A: Could I have some of this pizza?
   B: Sure. Go right ahead.
5. A: Could I pay by check?
   B: I'm sorry. Only cash or credit cards are accepted.

Examining Meaning and Use (p. 193)

1. 1b sounds more polite.
2. 2b is an offer. 2a asks about likes or dislikes.

E1: Listening for Meaning and Use (p. 194)

	REQUEST	OFFER	PREFERENCE
2.		✓	
3.			✓
4.		✓	
5.			✓
6.		✓	
7.	✓		
8.			✓

E2: Making Offers and Stating Preferences (p. 195)

Answers will vary. Some examples are:
2. A: Would you prefer unleaded or super plus?
   B: Unleaded, please.
3. A: Would you like to dance?
   B: No, thanks. I'd rather not.

4. A: Would you prefer cake or pie?
   B: I'd prefer the cake, please.
5. A: Would you rather buy the white gloves or the black gloves?
   B: I'd rather buy the black ones.
6. A: Would you like some pizza?
   B: No, thanks. I'd rather not eat right now.

E3: Asking About and Stating Preferences (p. 196)

Answers will vary. Some examples are:
2. A: Would you rather have chicken or fish tonight?
   B: I'd prefer fish. We had chicken last night.
3. A: Would you prefer to stay late or come in early tomorrow?
   B: I'd prefer to stay late, if that's OK.
4. A: Would you rather fly to Rome or go by train?
   B: I'd prefer to go by train.
5. A: Would you prefer to do the dishes or vacuum?
   B: I'd rather do the dishes.

E4: Discussing Preferences (p. 196)

Answers will vary.

F1: Thinking about Meaning and Use (p. 197)

2. a
3. b
4. a
5. a
6. b

F2: Editing (p. 198)

2. You ~~could~~ *can* not borrow my van next week.

3. correct

4. You ~~mayn't~~ *may not* leave until the exam is over.

5. Where *would* ∧ you prefer to go this weekend?

6. I'd rather not ~~to~~ go now.

7. She'd like ∧*to* learn to drive.

8. correct

CHAPTER 11

A3: After You Read (p. 200)

2. F
3. T
4. T
5. F

Examining Form (p. 202)

1. line 4: must play
   The base form of the verb follows *must*.
2. line 11: should stop
   The base form of the verb follows *should*.
3. line 15: have to follow
   line 21: ought to know
   line 18: had better buy
   The base form of the verb follows each of these phrasal modals.

4. line 6: must not call
   line 15: should not follow
   line 19: don't have to play
   The negative of *have to* is formed by adding *do/does* + *not* before *have to* + main verb. The negative forms of *should* and *must* are formed by adding *not* between the modal and the base form of the main verb.

B1: Listening for Form (p. 205)

2. a
3. a
4. b
5. b
6. a
7. a
8. b

B2: Working on Questions (p. 205)

A. 2. Do we have to eat at twelve?
3. Should they bring a gift?
4. Does she have to go to class today?
5. Do you have to get a new passport?
6. Should he see a doctor?

B. 2. What does he have to write?
3. How long do you have to stay in the hospital?
4. When should we go to the gym?
5. Where do they have to take this form?
6. When should you talk to the professor?

B3: Writing Contracted Forms (p. 206)

2. No contraction is possible.
3. No contraction is possible.
4. He's got to study more.
5. You shouldn't wear jeans to work.
6. No contraction is possible.
7. You'd better not argue with him.
8. You've got to take a trip to the Caribbean!
9. He shouldn't waste any more time.
10. No contraction is possible.

B4: Writing Negative Statements (p. 206)

2. Jake doesn't have to do his homework now.
3. Visitors must not park here.
4. You'd better not tell your roommate the news.
5. Employees don't have to attend the sales meeting.
6. They shouldn't buy their son a car this year.
7. You must not get on that train.
8. You shouldn't ask for a raise.
9. He'd better not wait until tomorrow.
10. You don't have to be home early.

B5: Understanding Informal Speech (p. 207)

Conversation 1
2. have to
3. 've got to

Conversation 2
1. has to
2. ought to
3. have to

Examining Meaning and Use (p. 208)

1. a and e
2. d
3. b
4. c

C1: Listening for Meaning and Use (p. 210)

	SPEAKER A	SPEAKER B
2.		✓
3.	✓	
4.		✓
5.	✓	
6.		✓
7.	✓	
8.	✓	

C2: Making Suggestions (p. 211)

Answers will vary. Some examples are:
2. You could put an ad in the newspaper.
   You might go into stores to see if they need help.
3. We could take her to a movie.
   We might take her out to her favorite restaurant.
4. You could invite some friends over.
   You might join some clubs and try to meet people.

C3: Giving Your Opinion (p. 211)

A. B's answers will vary. Some examples are:
2. A: Should women with small children work?
   B: No, they shouldn't. I think they ought to stay home until the children go to school.
3. A: Should men do housework?
   B: Yes, I think they should do housework. They ought to share the work with their wives.
4. A: Should women invite men to go out?
   B: No, I think women shouldn't ask men out.
5. A: Should a married woman keep her family name or take her husband's last name?
   B: I think she should take her husband's last name, but maybe she should keep her family name for work.

B. Answers will vary.

C4: Giving Advice (p. 212)

A. Answers will vary. Some examples are:
2. Maybe you should call the doctor.
   You ought to stay home.
3. Perhaps you ought to get a tutor.
   You should study more.
4. Perhaps you should move.
   Maybe one of you could get a weekend job.

B. 2. You must go to the doctor tomorrow.
   You've got to stay home tomorrow.
3. You must get a tutor.
   You've got to study more.
4. You've got to move.
   You have to find a cheaper apartment.

C. Answers will vary.

C5: Giving Warnings (p. 213)

Answers will vary. Some examples are:
2. They had better not go fishing there.
3. He had better walk more slowly.
4. They had better know how to use their parachutes.
5. He had better take his umbrella.
6. She had better not tease the cat.

Examining Meaning and Use (p. 214)

1. 1a, 2a
2. 1b, 2b

D1: Listening for Meaning and Use (p. 215)

		NECESSARY	NOT NECESSARY	NOT ALLOWED
2.	Take the eye test at the Department of Motor Vehicles		✓	
3.	need a California license to drive in California		✓	
4.	pay with a credit card			✓
5.	go to driving school		✓	
6.	drive alone when you have a learner's permit			✓

D2: Explaining Signs (p. 216)

A. Answers will vary. Some examples are:
2. must not
3. don't have to
4. don't have to
5. must not
6. must
7. must not
8. must, don't have to

B. Answers will vary. Some examples are:
1. an apartment swimming pool
2. a restaurant or a supermarket
3. a museum
4. a doctor's office or a hair salon
5. a movie theater or an office building
6. a bank or a military base
7. the neighborhood around a hospital
8. a restaurant

D3: Writing about Rules and Laws (p. 217)

A. 2. You must wear a seatbelt.
3. You must not run.
4. You must not use cell phones here.
5. You must stop.
6. You must not swim here.

B. Answers will vary.

D4: Stating Necessity, Lack of Necessity, and Prohibition (p. 217)

Answers will vary. Some examples are:
2. We must bring our books to class.

3. We have to do our homework every night.
4. We don't have to look up every new word in a dictionary.
5. We must not cheat on tests.

E1: Thinking About Meaning and Use (p. 218)

2. a
3. b
4. a
5. b
6. a
7. b
8. a

E2: Editing (p. 219)

There are many wedding traditions in the United States. One of them is that the bride ought ^to^ wear "something old, something new, something borrowed, something blue, and a sixpence in her shoe." The old, new, borrowed, and blue parts are easy enough. However, a sixpence is an old English coin. It is impossible to find these days, so most people feel that the bride doesn't ~~has~~ ^have^ to use a sixpence—any coin will do. Another tradition is that the groom must not ~~to~~ see the bride before the wedding. People think that it is bad luck. In addition, many people think that first-time brides ought ^to^ wear white and second-time brides ~~could~~ ^should^ not. However, second and third marriages are so common these days that many brides feel they ~~must not~~ ^don't have to^ follow this rule. One final tradition is that when people get married, ~~they've~~ ^they have^ to save a piece of their wedding cake for good luck.

CHAPTER 12

A3: After You Read (p. 225)

2. T
3. F
4. F
5. T

Examining Form (p. 226)

1. line 21:   are you?
   line 35:   aren't you?
   line 40:   did you?
2. A negative tag question follows an affirmative statement. An affirmative tag question follows a negative statement.

B1: Listening for Form (p. 229)

2. a
3. a
4. b
5. b
6. a

B2: Working on Tag Questions (p. 229)

2. could you
3. did he
4. didn't I
5. am I
6. didn't she

B3: Using Tag Questions (p. 229)

A. 2. aren't you?
   3. don't you?
   4. haven't you?
   5. don't you?
   6. do you?

B. 2. Yes, I am. OR No, I'm not.
   3. Yes, I do. OR No, I don't.
   4. Yes, I have. OR No, I haven't.
   5. Yes, I do. OR No, I don't.
   6. Yes, I do. OR No, I don't.

B4: Understanding Informal Speech (p. 230)

2. a
3. b
4. b
5. a
6. a

Examining Meaning and Use (p. 231)

1. 1b shows that the speaker has a previous idea about the time of dinner. 1a shows that the speaker has no previous idea about the time of dinner.
2. The speaker is making a request in 2b. The speaker is expecting agreement in 2a.

C1: Listening for Meaning and Use (p. 232)

A. 2. That's a very expensive restaurant, isn't it?

   3. You didn't walk here, did you?

   4. He has Ms. Walker for history, doesn't he?

   5. You couldn't watch my children for an hour, could you?

   6. You've never met the Smiths, have you?

B.

	CERTAIN	UNCERTAIN
2.	✓	
3.		✓
4.		✓
5.		✓
6.	✓	

C2: Practicing the Intonation of Tag Questions (p. 233)

2. He's coming back, isn't he?

3. Oh, no! It's going to be really expensive, isn't it?

4. It's going to rain, isn't it?

5. You're welcome. You eat meat, don't you?

6. You didn't agree, did you?

C3: Expressing Doubt (p. 234)

2. A: Africa isn't the largest continent, is it?
   B: No, it's not. Asia is the largest continent.
3. A: Saturn isn't the farthest planet from the sun, is it?
   B: No, it isn't. Pluto is the farthest planet from the sun.
4. A: Toronto isn't the capital of Canada, is it?
   B: No, it isn't. Ottawa is the capital of Canada.
5. A: There aren't 31 days in November, are there?
   B: No, there aren't. There are 30.
6. A: They use pesos in Japan, don't they?
   B: No, they don't. They use yen.
7. A: Albert Einstein invented the telegraph, didn't he?
   B: No, he didn't. Samuel Morse invented the telegraph.
8. A: A yard is equal to 24 inches, isn't it?
   B: No, it isn't. It's equal to 36 inches.

C4: Making Polite Requests (p. 234)

2. You couldn't give me a ride to the clinic, could you?
3. You couldn't take care of my son after school today, could you?
4. You couldn't help me tonight with my paper for English class, could you?
5. You couldn't feed my cat next week, could you?
6. You couldn't lend me your car for the weekend, could you?

C5: Using and Answering Tag Questions (p. 235)

A. Answers will vary. Some examples are:
2. A: You live on Oak Street, don't you?
   B: Actually, I live on Maple Street.
3. A: You're from France, aren't you?
   B: No, I'm from Switzerland.
4. A: You've studied English for a long time, haven't you?
   B: That's right.
5. A: You speak German, don't you?
   B: That's right. And I also speak Italian.
6. A: You work, don't you?
   B: That's right, but only part time.
7. A: You like classical music, don't you?
   B: Not really. I prefer rock and roll.
8. A: You have a brother, don't you?
   B: No, I don't. Actually, I'm an only child.
9. A: You play tennis, don't you?
   B: That's right, and I love it.
10. A: You like to swim, don't you?
    B: Not really.

B. Answers will vary.

C6: Beginning Conversations (p. 236)

A. Answers will vary. Some examples are:
2. It's a beautiful day, isn't it?
3. The cashier is very slow, isn't he?
4. The band is great, isn't it?
5. The food isn't very good, is it?
6. There are a lot of people here, aren't there?

B. Answers will vary.

D1: Thinking about Meaning and Use (p. 237)

2. a   5. a
3. b   6. a
4. b

D2: Editing (p. 238)

2. I shouldn't tell the teacher, ~~could~~ *should* I?
3. There are many French speakers in Canada, aren't ~~they~~ *there*?
4. I'm not going to see you again, ~~are~~ *am* I?
5. correct
6. Frank didn't get married, did ~~Frank~~ *he*?
7. Barbara isn't traveling alone, ~~will~~ *is* she?
8. Your sneakers don't fit, ~~don't~~ *do* they?

CHAPTER 13

A3: After You Read (p. 241)

Students should check 3, 4, and 6.

Examining Form (p. 242)

1. Sentence b is a combination of two affirmative sentences. The words *and* and *too* connect the clauses.
2. Sentence c is a combination of two negative sentences. The words *and* and *either* connect the clauses.
3. Sentences a and d combine an affirmative and a negative sentence. The word *but* connects the two clauses in both sentences.
4. Circle: *and . . . too; and . . . either;* and *but. And . . . too* connects two affirmative clauses; *and . . . either* connects two negative clauses, and *but* connects an affirmative and a negative clause.

B1: Listening for Form (p. 244)

	AND . . . TOO	AND . . . EITHER	BUT
2.			✓
3.	✓		
4.			✓
5.		✓	
6.	✓		
7.	✓		
8.	✓		
9.		✓	
10.			✓

B2: Understanding Additions (p. 244)

2. I am hungry.
3. He doesn't watch a lot of television.
4. The teachers needed to leave early.
5. Their telephone wasn't working.
6. They couldn't speak French.
7. Holly doesn't enjoy jazz.
8. She liked the concert.
9. My uncle hasn't visited Iowa.
10. Josh isn't going to work this summer.

B3: Working on Form (p. 245)

2. do
3. doesn't

4. is
5. couldn't
6. was
7. haven't
8. wasn't
9. did
10. won't
11. shouldn't
12. hasn't

B4: Combining Sentences (p. 246)

2. I don't like getting up early, and Jane doesn't either.
3. Dan has a car, and Rita does too.
4. She was feeling sick, but he wasn't.
5. I didn't play sports in high school, and Carlos didn't either.
6. He's going to the conference, but she isn't.
7. Ana doesn't eat meat, and I don't either.
8. Soo-jin has studied chemistry, and Won-joon has too.

B5: Completing Sentences (p. 246)

Answers will vary. Some examples are:
2. a jacket / he is too
3. meat / she doesn't either
4. living in Mexico / you weren't
5. relax / he is too
6. finished my paper / she hasn't either

Examining Form (p. 247)

1. Underline: apes; apes
   Circle: are; are
   In 1a (with *and so*), the verb comes before the subject.
   In 1b (with *and . . . too*), the subject comes before the verb.
2. Underline: apes; apes
   Circle: are; are
   In 2a (with *and neither),* the verb comes before the subject. In 2a (with *and . . . either*), the subject comes before the verb.
3. *And so* connects two affirmative sentences. *And neither* connects two negative sentences.

C1: Listening for Form (p. 248)

2. and neither did I
3. and neither does April
4. and so should you
5. and neither can I
6. and so has she

C2: Combining Sentences (p. 249)

2. Science isn't an easy subject for me, and neither is math.
3. Children will enjoy that movie, and so will adults.
4. My sisters don't live at home anymore, and neither does my brother.
5. The stores here close early, and so do the restaurants.
6. We didn't know the answer, and neither did the teacher.

C3: Completing Sentences (p. 249)

A. Answers will vary. Some examples are:
2. and so is pizza
3. and so do animals
4. and neither are cigarettes

5. I have a car
6. I didn't speak to him
7. She hasn't seen that movie
8. You should study more

B. Answers will vary.

Examining Meaning and Use (p. 250)

Sentences a and c have the same meaning; sentences b and d have the same meaning.
All four sentences express a similarity between the two subjects.

D1: Listening for Meaning and Use (p. 251)

	SAME INFORMATION	DIFFERENT INFORMATION
2.	✓	
3.	✓	
4.		✓
5.		✓
6.	✓	

D2: Expressing Similarities and Differences (p. 251)

A. Answers will vary. Some answers are:
2. Chinese food
3. go to concerts
4. cook
5. go to the park with my friends
6. ate my vegetables

B. Answers will vary.

D3: Understanding Informal Speech (p. 252)

2. b
3. b
4. a
5. a
6. b
7. a
8. b
9. a

D4: Adding Information to Sentences (p. 253)

A.

Geography
2. Turkey isn't in Europe, but France is.
3. Guam is an island and so is Puerto Rico. OR Guam is an island, and Puerto Rico is too.
4. Austria isn't near the sea, and neither is Switzerland. OR Austria isn't near the sea, and Switzerland isn't either.

Food
1. Prunes are dried fruit, and so are raisins. OR Prunes are dried fruit, and raisins are too.
2. Strawberries are red, but bananas aren't.
3. Fish isn't fattening, but ice cream is.
4. Potatoes don't have seeds, and neither do carrots. OR Potatoes don't have seeds, and carrots don't either.

Animals
1. Chickens don't swim, and neither do turkeys. OR Chickens don't swim, and turkeys don't either.
2. Dogs can't communicate with sign language, but apes can.

3. Snails have shells, and so do turtles. OR Snails have shells, and turtles do too.
4. Elephants live in Africa, and lions do too. OR Elephants live in Africa, and so do lions.

B. Answers will vary.

D5: Comparing and Contrasting Information (p. 254)

Answers will vary. Some examples are:
Pedro Gonzalez has chosen a major, but Jenny Chang hasn't.
Jenny Chang was a member of a club, and so was Pedro Gonzalez.
Pedro Gonzalez didn't participate in sports, and neither did Jenny Chang.
Jenny Chang participated in student government, but Pedro Gonzalez didn't.
Jenny Chang didn't work on the school newspaper, and Pedro Gonzalez didn't either.
Jenny Chang has received an award, and so has Pedro Gonzalez.
Jenny Chang worked, and so did Pedro Gonzalez.

D6: Avoiding Repetition (p. 255)

The United States and the United Kingdom have many similarities and differences. One of the similarities is language. <u>People in the United States speak English. People in the United Kingdom speak English.</u> Some people say that Americans don't speak very clearly. Some people say that the British speak very clearly. American and British food is also similar in some ways. <u>Americans like to eat meat and potatoes. The British like to eat meat and potatoes.</u> The two countries also have similar holidays. Christmas is a very important holiday in both countries. <u>Most Americans don't work on Christmas. Most British people don't work on Christmas.</u> One big difference is the political system. The <u>United Kingdom has a queen. The United States doesn't have a king or a queen. In the United States, voters elect a president. In the United Kingdom, voters don't elect a president.</u>

Answers may vary. Here is an example of the rewritten paragraph:

The United States and the United Kingdom have many similarities and differences. One of the similarities is language. People in the United States speak English, and so do people in the United Kingdom. Some people say that Americans don't speak very clearly, but the British do. American and British food is also similar in some ways. Americans like to eat meat and potatoes, and the British do too. The two countries also have similar holidays. Christmas is a very important holiday in both countries. Most Americans don't work on Christmas, and most British

people don't either. One big difference is the political system. The United Kingdom has a queen, but the United States doesn't. In the United States, voters elect a president, but they don't in the United Kingdom. The elect a prime minister.

E1: Thinking About Meaning and Use (p. 256)

2. b   6. a
3. a   7. b
4. a   8. a
5. b

E2: Editing (p. 257)

2. They don't have enough money, but we do ~~too~~.
3. The books cost a lot of money, and the paper ~~was~~ *did* too.
4. She hasn't finished cleaning her room, and I ~~have~~ *haven't* either.
5. correct
6. We are going to go by plane, and so ~~they are~~ *are they*.
7. He is doing well in class, but she ~~is~~ *isn't*.
8. correct
9. He never gets a raise, and ~~I do too~~ *neither do I*.
10. Megan doesn't wear makeup, and neither ~~doesn't~~ *does* Donna.

CHAPTER 14

A3: After You Read (p. 262)

2. chamomile tea, mint
3. cayenne pepper
4. coffee
5. gingko biloba
6. honey

Examining Form (p. 264)

1. *Calorie* and *calories* are count nouns. *Milk* is a noncount noun.
2. The quantity expressions *several, many,* and *a few* go with count nouns. *A great deal of* and *a little* go with noncount nouns.
3. energy: little, a lot of, Ø
   prunes: *a few*, Ø
   protein: *a great deal of*
   people: *some*

B1: Listening for Form (p. 267)

A.

	COUNT	NONCOUNT
2.	✓	
3.		✓
4.	✓	
5.	✓	
6.		✓
7.	✓	
8.		✓

B.

Conversation 1
2. some

Conversation 2
1. many
2. a lot of

Conversation 3
1. a glass of
2. a cup of

Conversation 4
1. How much
2. a lot of
3. lots of

B2: Working on Form (p. 268)

2. b
3. a
4. a
5. b
6. b

B3: Asking Questions with *How Many . . . ?* and *How Much . . . ?* (p. 268)

Answers will vary. Some examples are:
How many eggs are in the recipe?
How many teaspoons of vanilla extract are in the recipe?
OR How much vanilla extract is in the recipe?
How many teaspoons of almond extract are in the recipe?
OR How much almond extract is in the recipe?
How many cups of sour cream are in the recipe? OR How much sour cream is in the recipe?
How many teaspoons of baking powder are in the recipe? OR How much baking powder is in the recipe?
How many teaspoons of salt are in the recipe? OR How much salt is in the recipe?
How many tablespoons of powdered cocoa are in the recipe? OR How much powdered cocoa is in the recipe?
How many cups of chocolate chips are in the recipe?
How many cups of milk are in the recipe? OR How much milk is in the recipe?
How many sticks of butter are in the recipe? OR How many tablespoons of butter are in the recipe? OR How much butter is in the recipe?
How many cups of flour are in the recipe? OR How much flour is in the recipe?

B4: Understanding Informal Speech (p. 269)

2. A few of
3. plenty of
4. a great deal of
5. a lot of
6. lots of
7. a lot of
8. plenty of

Examining Meaning and Use (p. 270)

1. Underline: many; few; lots of; a lot of
Ben, Josh, and Tony have a large number of friends.
Eva has a small number of friends.
2. Underline: little; a little
There is not enough time in 2a.

C1: Listening for Meaning and Use (p. 272)

		LARGE QUANTITY	SMALL QUANTITY	NONE
2.	milk		✓	
3.	cars			✓
4.	homework		✓	
5.	food	✓		
6.	books		✓	
7.	caffeine			✓
8.	tests	✓		
9.	money		✓	
10.	friends	✓		

C2: Understanding Quantity Expressions (p. 273)

2. b   3. a   4. a   5. a   6. a

C3: Talking About Small Quantities (p. 274)

2. a little
3. few
4. little
5. a few
6. a little

C4: Using Quantity Expressions (p. 274)

Answers will vary. Some examples are:
He bought a lot of hamburger buns, but he didn't buy a lot of hamburgers.
He bought plenty of potato chips but he didn't buy much salad.
He bought quite a lot of cake, but only a little pie.
OR He bought quite a few cakes but only one pie.
He bought a lot of coffee, but he didn't buy a lot of soda.
He bought a lot of plates but not a lot of napkins.

C5: Talking and Writing About Foods (p. 275)

A. Answers will vary. Some examples are:
A: How much fat does Healthy Grains have?
B: It has very little fat.
A: How much sodium does Chocolate Puffies have?
B: It has a lot of sodium.

B. Answers will vary.

Examining Meaning and Use (p. 276)

1. No, you can't make pancakes from this recipe. There is not enough specific information.
2. Specific quantity expressions that could be used include: *a cup of, a teaspoon of, a slice of,* or *a box of.*

D1: Listening for Meaning and Use (p. 277)

		SPECIFIC	GENERAL
2.	ground beef	✓	
3.	salt		✓
4.	onions		✓
5.	cream		✓
6.	spaghetti	✓	
7.	water	✓	
8.	bread		✓

D2: Choosing Specific Quantity Expressions (p. 278)

The following answers should be crossed out:
2. a pound of milk
3. a grain of bread
4. a bunch of rice
5. a gallon of fish
6. a slice of cereal
7. a bag of peanut butter
8. a yard of food
9. a quart of bananas
10. a drop of papers

D3: Using Specific Quantity Expressions (p. 278)

Answers will vary. Some examples are:
A: How much milk are you going to buy?
B: I'm going to buy a gallon of milk.
A: How much peanut butter are you going to buy?
B: I think I'll get two jars of peanut butter.

E1: Thinking About Meaning and Use (p. 279)

2. a
3. b
4. b
5. b
6. a

E2: Editing (p. 279)

2. We bought ~~many~~ *a lot of* food.

3. There isn't ~~many~~ *much* salt in the soup.

4. correct

5. I have *a* little money, so I guess we can go out to dinner

   tonight.

6. I bought a ~~grain~~ *carton* of eggs.

7. How ~~many~~ *much* does a pound of beef cost?

8. We had *a* foot of snow last night.

9. correct

10. She'll graduate soon. She only has a ~~little~~ *few* more

    courses to take.

CHAPTER 15

A3: After You Read (p. 282)

2. F
3. T
4. F
5. F
6. T

Examining Form (p. 284)

1. a. *A, the, a*
   b. the
   c. the
2. *fly*   count noun
   air   noncount noun
   plant count noun
   leaf   count noun
   parts count noun
   In these examples, *a* and *the* are used with singular count nouns, *the* is used with plural count nouns, and *the* is used with noncount nouns

B1: Listening for Form (p. 285)

		A	AN	THE	Ø (NO ARTICLE)
2.	botany				✓
3.	plants				✓
4.	hour		✓		
5.	books			✓	
6.	fork	✓			
7.	apple		✓		
8.	children			✓	
9.	pen	✓			
10.	flowers				✓

B2: Working on Form (p. 286)

2. Can you give me ~~a~~ *an* example?

3. I waited ~~an~~ *a* whole hour for you. Where were you?

4. If you're going to London, don't forget ~~a~~ *an* umbrella.

5. correct

6. You've met the Senator? What ~~a~~ *an* honor!

7. She's thinking about buying ~~an~~ *a* used car.

8. He isn't ~~a~~ *an* honest man.

9. correct

10. Cornell is ~~an~~ *a* university in New York state.

B3: Working on Singular and Plural Forms (p. 286)

2. Celia is taking classes now. OR Celia is taking some classes now.
3. The sandwiches are good.
4. We saw an interesting movie.

5. We've been here for an hour.
6. The new person at work is nice.
7. Mr. Smith has cows and a horse. OR Mr. Smith has some cows and a horse.
8. The girl needs a uniform for school.
9. There were insects in the bathroom. OR There were some insects in the bathroom.
10. A man was talking to my father.

Examining Meaning and Use (p. 287)

1. The speakers have a specific object or place in mind in 1b and 2b.
2. In 1a and 2a, the speakers have only a general idea of the object or place they mention.

C1: Listening for Meaning and Use (p. 289)

		INTRODUCING A NOUN	REFERRING TO A NOUN THAT THE LISTENER CAN IDENTIFY
2.	children		✓
3.	car	✓	
4.	teacher		✓
5.	restaurant		✓
6.	man	✓	
7.	bank		✓
8.	article	✓	
9.	car keys		✓
10.	meeting	✓	

C2: Choosing the Correct Article (p. 290)

2. The
3. Ø
4. the
5. The
6. a
7. the
8. the
9. some
10. Ø
11. an
12. the
13. the
14. the
15. the
16. Ø
17. Ø
18. an

C3: Using Definite and Indefinite Articles (p. 290)

2. the
3. a
4. the
5. the
6. the
7. a
8. the
9. Ø
10. the

C4: Guessing About Contexts (p. 291)

Answers will vary. Some examples are:
2a. The man is talking about a book that he has discussed with his wife before.
2b. The man is telling his wife about a book he has just bought. This is the first time he is telling her about it.
3a. The first man is telling the second man about a letter that they both have been expecting.
3b. The first man is telling the other man about a letter that arrived. It sounds like he wasn't expecting it, and the other man is hearing about it for the first time.
4a. The woman is asking her son if he bought a suit. She does not have a specific suit in mind.
4b. The woman is asking her son about a specific suit that they have already discussed.

C5: Using Nouns that Change Meaning (p. 292)

2. the
3. Ø
4. the
5. the
6. Ø
7. Ø
8. the

Examining Meaning and Use (p. 293)

1. 1a and 2a refer to a group of people or plants in general.
2. 1b and 2b refer to specific people or plants.

D1: Listening for Meaning and Use (p. 295)

		SPECIFIC PERSON, PLACE, OR THING	WHOLE CLASS OR GROUP
2.	a. kids	✓	
	b. dogs		✓
3.	a. girl	✓	
	b. information	✓	
4.	a. dolphin		✓
	b. animal		✓
5.	a. radio station		✓
	b. advertisements		✓
6.	a. doctor	✓	
	b. hospital	✓	

D2: Classifying and Defining Nouns (p. 295)

A. 2. insect
3. dog
4. flower
5. ape
6. fish

B. 2. A: What's a butterfly?
   B: A butterfly is an insect.
3. A: What's a poodle?
   B: A poodle is a dog.
4. A: What's a rose?
   B: A rose is a flower.

5. A: What's a chimpanzee?
   B: A chimpanzee is an ape.
6. B: What's a shark?
   A: A shark is a fish.

D3: Giving Your Opinion (p. 295)

Answers will vary.

D4: Using Articles in General Statements (p. 296)

A. 2. A
3. Ø
4. Ø
5. A

B. 2. A
3. The
4. Ø
5. The
6. Ø
7. Ø
8. A or The

E1: Thinking About Meaning and Use (p. 297)

Conversation 1
2. False

Conversation 2
1. It's not clear.
2. False

Conversation 3
1. False
2. True

Conversation 4
1. False
2. True

E2: Editing (p. 298)

The leaves of Venus flytraps are ~~the~~ clever traps. Each leaf
has ~~the~~ "trigger" hairs. When these hairs move, ~~a~~ the trap closes.
When ~~the~~ leaf is open, the trap is set, ready for ~~a~~ an insect to come.
The plant
~~Plant~~ attracts insects with ~~the~~ a sweet smell. When an insect
crawls across the leaf, it moves the trigger hairs. This is a signal
for ~~a~~ the trap to close. But the trap must receive two signals before
it closes. It will close only if one hair moves twice or if two hairs
move. This way, the plant makes sure that it has caught the ~~a~~ live
creature and not the ~~a~~ piece of grass or a leaf.

CHAPTER 16

A3: After You Read (p. 302)

2. a
3. b
4. c
5. a

Examining Form (p. 304)

1. Underline: fascinating; strong; gold
   Circle: clues; paper; tag
   The adjective come before the noun.
2. Title: Unusual Gifts
   Title: Unusual People
   line 1:   largest crossword puzzle
   line 3:   challenging crossword puzzle
   line 4:   91,000 squares
   line 5:   28, 000 words
   line 5:   100-page clue book
   line 5:   additional help
   line 7:   storage box
   line 9:   backpacker guitar
   line 10: light, compact guitar
   line 11: three pounds
   line 15: wooden body
   line 15: metal tuners
   line 16: soft, padded carrying case
   line 18: Galileo Liquid Thermometer
   line 21: unusual liquid thermometer
   line 22: clear glass tube
   line 24: handmade glass balls
   line 25: special liquid
   line 26: colored ball
   line 27: temperature changes
   line 28: lowest ball
   line 29: correct temperature
   line 32: large numbers
   line 34: Washable Leather Potholders
   line 35: strong, long-lasting potholders
   line 37: two soft, attractive leather pieces
3. The adjective is *washable*. It follows a stative verb and
   it describes *potholders*.

B1: Listening for Form (p. 306)

Conversation 1

		MOVIE	STARS	MAN
2.	same	✓		
3.	famous		✓	
4.	boring	✓		
5.	asleep			✓

Conversation 2

		KIDS	RIDES	ADULTS
1.	excited	✓		
2.	frightening		✓	
3.	fine	✓		
4.	tired			✓
5.	hungry			✓

B2: Identifying Adjectives (p. 306)

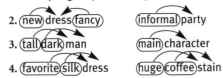

2. new dress fancy   informal party
3. tall dark man   main character
4. favorite silk dress huge coffee stain

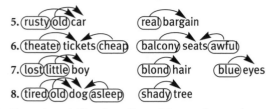

5. rusty old car   real bargain
6. theater tickets cheap   balcony seats awful
7. lost little boy   blond hair   blue eyes
8. tired old dog asleep   shady tree

B3: Forming Adjectives from Nouns (p. 307)

A. noun /ending
2. child / ish
3. help / ful
4. friend / less
5. home / less
6. dirt / y
7. hero / ic
8. success / ful
9. angel / ic
10. hair / y
11. curl / y
12. use / less

B. Answers will vary. Some examples are:
2. His behavior is like a child's.
3. This computer manual helps me a lot.
4. He did not have any friends when he arrived in the city.
5. In this city there are many people without a home.
6. The kitchen floor is full of dirt.
7. Everyone thought the policeman acted like a hero.
8. My parents are lawyers and they have both had a lot of success.
9. The little girl has a smile like an angel's.
10. He always wears shirts with long sleeves because his arms are full of hair.
11. She has beautiful hair with a lot of curls.
12. That guidebook is of no use (OR is not useful). It's over twenty years old.

B4: Forming Sentences with Adjectives (p. 308)

2. We want to go somewhere expensive and exotic.
   OR We want to go somewhere exotic and expensive.
3. They bought an old car.
4. I didn't see anything interesting.
5. The room was ten feet wide.
6. The sandy beach looked beautiful. OR The beautiful beach looked sandy.
7. I never do anything right.
8. Amy moved to a brick house.
9. My brother is asleep.
10. That was a delicious dinner.

Examining Meaning and Use (p. 309)

Underline: Italian leather; large blue riding; expensive European racing; favorite cotton
quality/opinion: expensive, favorite
size: large
color: blue
origin: Italian, European
material: leather, cotton
kind/purpose: riding, racing

C1: Listening for Meaning and Use (p. 310)

	CAUSES AN EMOTION	FEELS AN EMOTION
2.		✓
3.	✓	
4.		✓
5.		✓
6.		✓
7.	✓	
8.	✓	
9.		✓
10.	✓	

C2: Classifying and Ordering Adjectives (p. 311)

A.

QUALITY / OPINION	SIZE	AGE	SHAPE
lovely	huge	old	rectangular
honest	large	middle-aged	round
unusual	long	young	triangular
beautiful	miniature	antique	square
elegant	enormous	new	circular
fashionable	short	elderly	cylindrical
soft	tiny	modern	oval
hardworking	small		pear-shaped

COLOR	ORIGIN	MATERIAL	KIND / PURPOSE
brown	Greek	wooden	medical
pink	European	silk	toy
tan	French	glass	evening
yellow	Indian	suede	racing
gray	Japanese	leather	handmade
white		metal	decorative
purple		plastic	wedding
		wool	computer

B. Answers will vary. Some examples are:
2. We have an enormous round wooden dining-room table. It is Italian and very elegant.
3. Jane is a hardworking, modern young woman from England.
4. I saw an unusual new French movie last night. It was very romantic and funny.
5. I would like to own a fashionable European sports car. Perhaps it will be something powerful and fast, such as a Porsche.
6. My favorite childhood possession was a beautiful, antique wooden toy pyramid. It was small and each side was triangular.

C3: Choosing *-ed* or *-ing* Adjectives (p. 312)

Conversation 1
2. disgusted
3. disgusting
4. interesting

Conversation 2
1. exciting
2. excited
3. disappointed

Conversation 3
1. boring
2. bored
3. surprising

C4: Describing People, Places, and Things (p. 312)

Answers will vary. Some examples are:
My best friend is very smart and has a very friendly personality. She is short and thin.
I have a lovely, comfortable rectangular bedroom. It has two large square windows with a beautiful view of our colorful garden.
I have an exciting and challenging job with a German shipping company.
My teacher is friendly and very professional. She is a tall, middle-aged woman with short, curly brown hair.
My hometown is small and charming. It has warm and friendly people, and they are very helpful.
My neighbors are busy middle-aged people. They seem outgoing and friendly. They are going on a long European cruise next year.

C5: Writing Catalog Descriptions (p. 313)

Answers will vary. Some examples are:
2. This comfortable and stylish living-room couch is the perfect piece of furniture for a young family.
3. This lovely wooden decorative box is a perfect place to put your favorite jewelry.
4. This elegant rectangular evening purse has a lovely silver chain.
5. This colorful toy airplane will delight the young pilot in your family.
6. This fashionable yellow straw hat will go perfectly with your favorite summer dresses.

D1: Thinking About Meaning and Use (p. 314)

A.
2. b
3. a
4. b
5. b
6. a

B.
2. D
3. S
4. D
5. S

D2: Editing (p. 315)

I feel very ~~frustrating~~ *frustrated* because I never know what to buy for my father. Last year I bought him ~~a Swiss watch expensive~~ *an expensive Swiss watch* for

his birthday. He returned it and bought several pairs of ~~socks wool~~ *wool socks* and ~~snow new tires~~ *new snow tires* for his car. Last Christmas I bought him a ~~silk long beautiful robe~~ *beautiful long silk robe*. It was from France, and it wasn't cheap. He returned that too. He got a ~~cordless new lawnmower~~ *new cordless lawnmower* instead. This year for Christmas I've solved the problem. I'm going to give him ~~perfect something~~ *something perfect* – money! I'm sure he'll be ~~pleasing~~ *pleased* with that.

CHAPTER 17

A3: After You Read (p. 319)

Answers may vary. Some examples are:
1. project manager, lawyer
2. football player, construction worker
3. pilot, accountant
4. artist, architect

Examining Form (p. 320)

1. line 5: fortunately
   line 18: quickly
   line 30: carefully
   line 32: extremely
   line 41: enthusiastically, especially
   line 45: usually
2. quickly, carefully, enthusiastically
3. The adverbs of manner occur after the main verb in the magazine article.

B1: Listening for Form (p. 322)

2. carefully
3. careless
4. unexpected
5. slowly
6. angry
7. luckily
8. certainly

B2: Forming Adverbs of Manner (p. 323)

2. heavily
3. lightly
4. naturally
5. realistically
6. smoothly
7. —
8. simply

B3: Placing Adverbs in Sentences (p. 323)

2. Perhaps we'll see you at the soccer game.
3. We have probably met before. OR We probably have met before.
4. They greeted their guests enthusiastically. OR They enthusiastically greeted their guests.
5. He explained his ideas carefully. OR He carefully explained his ideas.
6. He has left the country unexpectedly. OR He has unexpectedly left the country.
7. Tomorrow I'm going to finish this project. OR I'm going to finish this project tomorrow.

8. We're going to be leaving soon. OR Soon we're going to be leaving.
9. She hasn't been around lately. OR Lately she hasn't been around.
10. Luckily, no one was hurt in the accident. OR No one was hurt in the accident, luckily.
11. Obviously, we'll need to change our plans. OR We'll obviously need to change our plans. OR We'll need to change our plans, obviously.
12. Surprisingly, she gave the right answer. OR She gave the right answer, surprisingly. OR She surprisingly gave the right answer.

B4: Identifying Adverbs and Adjectives (p. 324)

A. 2. adjective
3. adjective
4. adverb
5. adverb
6. adverb
7. adverb
8. adjective

B. 2. quietly
3. angry
4. terrible
5. happily
6. polite
7. bad
8. happy

C. Answers will vary. Some examples are:
2. I started college recently.
3. Maybe we'll go to the movies tonight.
4. He is a fast runner.
5. She worked very hard on her English essay.

Examining Meaning and Use (p. 325)

1. 1a. It rained <u>hard</u> last night.
   1b. <u>Unfortunately</u>, it rained while we were sleeping.
   Hard describes how the action happened.
   Unfortunately gives an opinion.
2. 2a. We have made our plans. We'll <u>definitely</u> leave at 7 A.M.
   2b. We haven't made plans. <u>Maybe</u> we'll leave at 7 A.M. The speaker is more certain about future plans in 2a.

C1: Listening for Meaning and Use (p. 326)

		SAME	DIFFERENT
2.	It snowed a lot last night.		✓
3.	He's been late for our meetings recently.		✓
4.	It's likely we'll go to Mexico this summer.	✓	
5.	I'm not studying very much this year.		✓
6.	Some buses are not arriving on time.	✓	

C2: Using Adverbs (p. 327)

Answers will vary. Bracketed answers show possible positions of adverbs.
1. I [recently] joined a gym. [Yesterday] I worked out in the weight room. My muscles are sore, but [tomorrow] I'm going to go back to the gym. [Soon] I'll be strong and healthy.
2. When Lee started taking my class, she didn't know English [well]. But she really studies [hard]. She'll [definitely] pass the class. [Maybe] she'll be ready for an advanced class next year.
3. Children [obviously] need to eat vegetables. [Unfortunately,] few children like them. [Luckily,] my children like vegetables. [Surprisingly,] they almost always ask for carrots instead of cookies.

C3: Identifying Adverbs with Different Forms (p. 327)

A. 2. hard
3. lately
4. high
5. hardly
6. late

B. Answers will vary.

Examining Form (p. 328)

1. In 1a the underlined word is an adverb. In 1b the underlined word is an adjective. Students should circle *pretty* in 1a and *very* in 1b.
2. In 2a *so* is followed by an adjective. In 2b *such* is followed by an article + adjective + noun.

D1: Listening for Form (p. 329)

2. very busy
3. such good friends
4. such a good time
5. so tired
6. such a hard test
7. so softly
8. really early

D2: Forming Sentences with Adverbs of Degree (p. 330)

2. They speak English quite fluently.
3. These instructions are somewhat confusing.
4. He types really quickly.
5. Those flowers smell so nice.
6. Jenny plays the piano very well.
7. We follow the news fairly closely.
8. It's not a very interesting book.

D3: Completing Conversations (p. 330)

2. so
3. such
4. so, such a
5. such an

Examining Meaning and Use (p. 331)

1. The person in 1a (Sara) plays tennis better.
2. The *that* clause in each sentence shows the result of the cold weather: *that the river froze* (2a) and *that I couldn't start my car* (2b). These clauses should be underlined.

E1: Listening for Meaning and Use (p. 332)

2. b
3. b
4. a
5. a
6. b

E2: Using Adverbs of Degree (p. 332)

2. fairly
3. really
4. really
5. somewhat

E3: Complaining (p. 333)

A. Answers will vary. Some examples are:
1. It was so awful that we got sick.
2. It's so noisy that it's hard to concentrate.
   The salary is so low that I can't pay my bills.
3. It's so expensive that I really can't afford it.
   He's so lazy that he never helps me clean.
4. They are so boring that I hardly pay attention to them.
   It's so big that it's hard to get from one class to another.

B.
1. It was such awful food that we got sick.
2. It's such a noisy office that it's hard to concentrate.
   It's such a low salary that I can't pay my bills.
3. It's such an expensive apartment that I really can't afford it.
   He's such a lazy person that he never helps me clean.
4. They are such boring professors that I hardly pay attention to them.
   It's such a big campus that it's hard to get from one class to another.

C. Answers will vary.

Examining Form (p. 335)

1. *Slowly* and *quickly* are adverbs; *good* and *tired* are adjectives. The adverbs modify verbs. The adjectives modify nouns. The adverbs come after the verb *be*. The adverbs come after action verbs.
2. *Too* comes before an adjective or adverb. *Enough* comes after an adjective or adverb.

F1: Listening for Form (p. 336)

2. too sweet
3. hard enough
4. too fast
5. too expensive
6. tall enough

F2: Forming Sentences with *Too* and *Enough* (p. 336)

2. That dress is too big to wear.
3. You're not driving slowly enough.
4. He looked too young to be her father.
5. Mark worked hard enough to get a raise.
6. Dan lives too far away to walk to school.
7. She wasn't in Spain long enough to learn Spanish well.
8. That movie wasn't good enough to win an award.

Examining Meaning and Use (p. 337)

Enough (in sentence a) has a positive meaning. *Too* (in sentence b) has a negative meaning.

G1: Listening for Meaning and Use (p. 338)

2. a
3. b
4. a

G2: Using *Too, Very*, and *So* (p. 339)

2. very
3. so
4. very
5. so
6. too

G3: Giving Reasons and Making Excuses (p. 339)

2. I'm too busy to go to the movies.
3. I wasn't early enough to catch the train.
4. I was too tired to finish painting the kitchen.
5. I didn't study hard enough to pass the final exam.
6. I couldn't swim fast enough to win the race.

H1: Thinking About Meaning and Use (p. 340)

2. b
3. a
4. a
5. b
6. a
7. b
8. a

H2: Editing (p. 341)

2. Andrea looks ~~beautifully~~ _beautiful_ in that dress.
3. He has _recently_ been ~~recently~~ in the hospital. OR _Recently_ he has been ~~recently~~ in the hospital. OR He's been ~~recently~~ in the hospital _recently_.
4. You are such _a_ kind woman.
5. He always works ~~hardly~~ _hard_.
6. She's ~~enough~~ _too_ shy to be a teacher.
7. correct
8. This ice cream tastes ~~deliciously~~ _delicious_.
9. He's such _a_ good ~~a~~ player that they made him captain of the team.
10. correct

CHAPTER 18

A3: After You Read (p. 347)

2. F
3. T
4. F
5. F
6. T

Examining Form (p. 348)

1. Comparative adjectives
   closer, more awake

   Comparative adverbs
   longer, more easily
   The two ways to form the comparative of adjectives and adverbs are: adjective/adverb + -er and more + adjective/adverb.

2. Comparative adjectives
   line 9:   less sleep, younger
   line 15: less attentive
   line 16: more difficult
   line 29: happier, nicer
   line 30: better
   line 35: lazier
   line 46: more alert

   Comparative adverbs
   line 11: earlier
   line 13: later
   line 26: more enthusiastically
   line 27: more smoothly

B1: Listening for Form (p. 350)

	-ER	MORE
2.	✓	
3.	✓	
4.		✓
5.		✓
6.	✓	

B2: Working on Comparative Adjectives and Adverbs (p. 350)

2. messier
3. more handsome
4. more happily
5. hotter
6. more expensive
7. more loudly
8. larger
9. more dangerously
10. more complicated
11. later
12. more polite

B3: Working on Comparatives in Sentences (p. 353)

Conversation 1
2. longer

Conversation 2
1. thicker
2. more advertisements

Conversation 3
1. better
2. harder
3. more quickly

Conversation 4
1. more difficult
2. more homework
3. worse

Conversation 5
1. taller
2. thinner
3. curlier
4. more freckles

Examining Meaning and Use (p. 352)

Example a talks about a larger amount. Example b talks about a smaller amount.

C1: Listening for Meaning and Use (p. 354)

2. a   3. b   4. a   5. b   6. b

C2: Expressing Differences (p. 354)

2. Cheetahs can run more quickly than greyhounds (can/do).
3. A meter is longer than a yard (is).
4. Earth travels more slowly around the sun than Mercury (travels/does).
5. A kilogram is heavier than a pound (is).
6. China has more people than India (has/does).

C3: Rephrasing Comparatives (p. 355)

2. I take more classes than him.
3. I've been waiting longer than they have.
4. Jack has more experience than me.
5. He worked harder than she.
6. He got more presents than I did/got.
7. They've lived here for more years than us.
8. She's friendlier than he.

C4: Talking About Changing Situations (p. 355)

Answers will vary. Some examples are:
The buses are becoming less and less reliable.
The economy is getting worse and worse.
The houses are getting more and more expensive.
My neighborhood is becoming more and more international.
The people are becoming more and more unfriendly.
The prices are getting higher and higher.
The schools are becoming more and more crowded.
The variety in the stores in our area is getting better and better.
The traffic is getting worse and worse.

Examining Form (p. 356)

1. Underline: new; young
   Circle: fast; loudly
2. Sentences b and d end with a verb or an auxiliary. Sentence a ends with a noun. Sentence c ends with an object pronoun.

D1: Listening for Form (p. 357)

2. as quickly as
3. as young as
4. as many problems as
5. as fast as

D2: Rephrasing Sentences with *As ... As* (p. 357)

2. We've spent as much money as they. We've spent as much money as they have. We've spent as much money as them.
3. Rita's son isn't as old as he. Rita's son isn't as old as he is. Rita's son isn't as old as him.

4. Rick didn't take as many classes as he. Rick didn't take as many classes as he did. Rick didn't take as many classes as him.
5. He doesn't have as many stamps as I. He doesn't have as many stamps as I have. He doesn't have as many stamps as me.
6. They played better than we did. They played better than we. They played better than us.

Examining Meaning and Use (p. 358)

1. In sentence a the boys are the same height.
2. In sentence b the boys are different heights.

E1: Listening for Meaning and Use (p. 359)

2. a
3. c
4. b
5. c
6. c
7. b
8. a

E2: Expressing Similarities and Differences (p. 360)

A. Answers will vary. Some examples are:
2. Koji doesn't clean as frequently as Derek.
3. Koji eats as much junk food as Derek
4. Koji has almost as many books as Derek.
5. Derek doesn't dress nearly as casually as Koji.
6. Derek isn't as interested in sports as Koji.

B. Answers will vary. Some examples include:
Derek isn't as athletic as Koji.
Koji doesn't like classical music as much as Derek.
Koji isn't as well organized as Derek.
Koji is nearly as tall as Derek.

E3: Using Descriptive Phrases with *As . . . As* (p. 361)

2. as gentle as a lamb
3. as light as a feather
4. as quiet as a mouse
5. as strong as an ox
6. as free as a bird
7. as hungry as a bear
8. as old as the hills
9. as tough as nails

F1: Thinking About Meaning and Use (p. 362)

2. b
3. a
4. a
5. b
6. a
7. a
8. b

F2: Editing (p. 363)

My new job is more good than my old one. I am
better
more happyer here. There are several reasons why. For one
happier
thing, we have flextime. That means that we can arrive at work
anytime between seven and ten and leave eight hours later. In
general, this company doesn't have as much rules as my old
many
company does. Also, the building is nicer of the old building,
than
and my office is biger than my old office. There are more
bigger
windows in this building than in my old building. The work is
more hard than the work at my old job, but I like the challenge
harder
of hard work. I like my new boss more than my old boss. She's
less bad tempered than he was, and she's helpfuler. Finally, I
more helpful
really like my co-workers. They are so much more nice than the
nicer
people I used to work with. We have a lot of fun together. The
day goes by more quicker. I'm glad I came here.
quickly

CHAPTER 19

A3: After You Read (p. 366)

2. f
3. e
4. d
5. a
6. b

Examining Form (p. 368)

1. the biggest, the strongest, the most valuable, the most expensive
2. The two ways to form the superlative are: *the* + adjective/adverb + *-est* and *the most* + adjective/adverb.

3. *the* + adjective + *est*:
line 3: the driest
line 5: the fastest
line 12: the fastest
line 13: the ugliest
line 14: the worst
line 15: the (world's) tallest
line 20: the fastest
line 43: the farthest

the most + adjective:
line 12: the most valuable
line 12: the most expensive
line 13: the most dangerous

B1: Listening for Form (p. 370)

	COMPARATIVE	SUPERLATIVE
2.		✓
3.	✓	
4.		✓
5.	✓	
6.		✓

B2: Forming Adjectives and Adverbs (p. 370)

	BASE FORM	COMPARATIVE FORM	SUPERLATIVE FORM
2.	high	higher	the highest
3.	badly	worse	the worst
4.	rapidly	more rapidly	the most rapidly
5.	sleepy	sleepier	the sleepiest
6.	famous	more famous	the most famous
7.	early	earlier	the earliest
8.	good	better	the best
9.	happy	happier	the happiest
10.	softly	more softly	the most softly
11.	wet	wetter	the wettest
12.	lovely	lovelier	the loveliest

B3: Working with Superlatives (p. 371)

2. the shortest
3. the brightest
4. the hottest
5. the densest
6. the most intense
7. the reddest
8. the most beautiful
9. the most massive
10. the bluest
11. the windiest
12. the strongest
13. the coldest
14. the tiniest

Examining Meaning and Use (p. 372)

Sentence b compares things in a group of three or more things. Sentence a compares only two things.

C1: Listening for Meaning and Use (p. 374)

Situation 1
2. Megan

Situation 2
1. Sun Palace
2. Seaview

Situation 3
1. Ed
2. Pete

C2: Asking for Opinions and Preferences (p. 374)

A. 2. What is the most interesting book you've ever read?
3. Who is the most unusual person you've ever known?
4. What is the prettiest place you've ever visited?
5. What is the worst movie you've ever seen?

B. Answers will vary.

C3: Weakening Superlatives (p. 375)

2. Basketball is one of the most popular sports (in the world).
3. Diamonds are one of the most valuable gems (in the world).
4. Death Valley is one of the hottest places (in the world/on earth).

C4: Making Recommendations (p. 375)

Answers will vary. Some examples are:
2. The best restaurant in town is Gigi's.
3. The nearest supermarket is on the corner of Maple Street and Third Avenue.
4. The nicest hotel in town is the Graymont Inn.
5. The most popular club in town is Tootsie's.
6. The biggest mall is the Galleria.
7. The cheapest movie theater is the Odeon.
8. The most interesting store is Reed Books.

C5: Expressing Thanks (p. 376)

A. 2. the latest
3. the weirdest
4. the most serious
5. the most enjoyable
6. the longest
7. the smelliest
8. the widest
9. the highest
10. the bloodiest
11. the greatest
12. the nicest

B. Answers will vary.

D1: Thinking About Meaning and Use (p. 377)

2. a
3. a
4. a
5. b
6. b

D2: Editing (p. 378)

I think that Paris is *the* most wonderful~~est~~ city in the world. It certainly is the ~~more~~ *most* romantic. It has some of the ~~most good~~ *best* art museums in the world. It also has some of the interesting~~est~~ *most* architecture, such as the Eiffel Tower. Then there is French food. I've been to many cities, and Paris has the best restaurants ~~than~~ *of* all. Of course, Paris is not the ~~most cheap~~ *cheapest* place to visit. In fact, it is one of the most expensive ~~place~~ *places* in the world, especially for hotels. But there are a few cheap hotels. Youth hostels cost the ~~less~~ *least* of all, so I stay in youth hostels.

CHAPTER 20

A3: After You Read (p. 383)

2. F
3. F
4. F
5. F
6. T
7. F
8. T

Examining Form (p. 384)

1. The underlined form in 1b is in the present continuous. We know this because the form follows the pattern *be*

(in present) + verb + -*ing*. The underlined form in 1a is a gerund. We know this because it has an -*ing* ending on the verb, but it does not have any form of *be* before it.

2. In sentence 2b the underlined phrase is the subject. In sentence 2a the underlined phrase is the object of the main verb.

3. Gerunds are singular. It is clear from the subject-verb agreement in sentences 1a and 2b; each of the gerund subjects is followed by the third-person singular form of the verb.

B1: Listening for Form (p. 385)

		GERUND	PRESENT CONTINUOUS
2.	saving	✓	
3.	working		✓
4.	eating	✓	
5.	buying	✓	
6.	taking		✓
7.	having	✓	
8.	spending		✓

B2: Working on Gerunds as Subjects (p. 386)

2. Taking classes
3. Not having money
4. Staying within a budget
5. Not carrying credit cards
6. Shopping on the Internet
7. Traveling
8. Saving a lot of money

B3: Working on Gerunds as Objects (p. 386)

2. discuss moving
3. start budgeting
4. consider not going
5. miss being
6. like watching

Examining Form (P. 387)

1. Underline: swimming; getting; lying; making
2. Circle: for; to; of; about
   These are prepositions.

C1: Listening for Form (p. 388)

2. instead of drinking
3. about quitting
4. forward to taking
5. tired of watching

C2: Working on Gerunds after Verb + Preposition (p. 388)

2. c
3. f
4. e
5. a
6. b

C3: Working on Gerunds After Adjective + Preposition (p. 388)

Answers will vary. Some examples are:
2. I'm good at making new friends.

3. I'm interested in making money.
4. I'm tired of studying all the time.
5. I'm fond of watching old movies.

Examining Meaning and Use (p. 389)

1. a
2. b
3. c

D1: Listening for Meaning and Use (p. 390)

	LIKE OR DISLIKE	POLITE REQUEST	HOW TO DO SOMETHING
2.			✓
3.		✓	
4.			✓
5.	✓		
6.			✓

D2: Making Polite Requests (p. 391)

Answers will vary. Some examples are:
2. A: Would you mind sitting down, please?
   B: Sure, no problem.
3. A: Would you mind opening the window?
   B: Sure. No problem.
4. A: Would you mind lending me a pen?
   B: Sure.
5. A: Would you mind holding the door for me?
   B: Of course.
6. A: Would you mind getting this down for me? I can't reach it.
   B: OK. No problem.

D3: Talking About How to Do Things (p. 392)

Answers will vary. Some examples are:
2. By putting it in a bank.
3. By eating less and exercising more.
4. By working hard and impressing your boss.
5. By looking in a dictionary.
6. By interviewing several people.

D4: Making Lists of Activities (p. 392)

Answers will vary. Some examples are:

Relaxing Activities
2. Going for a walk
3. Taking a hot bath
4. Reading a magazine

Stressful Activities
2. Writing a research paper
3. Going to a job interview
4. Taking an exam

Healthy Activities
2. Jogging
3. Playing tennis
4. Bicycle riding

Not Allowed in Class
2. Chewing gum
3. Speaking out of turn
4. Cheating on a test

E1: Thinking About Meaning and Use (p. 393)

2. a
3. b
4. a
5. a
6. b

E2: Editing (p. 393)

2. ~~Save~~ *Saving* money can be difficult.

3. Walking ~~are~~ *is* good exercise.

4. He got sick by ~~stand~~ *standing* out in the rain.

5. correct

6. ~~No~~ *Not* buying everything you want is a good way to save money.

CHAPTER 21

A3: After you Read (p. 397)

2. T
3. F
4. F
5. T
6. T

Examining Form (p. 398)

1. The underlined form in sentence 1a is in the simple present. The underlined form in sentence 1b is an infinitive.

2. The infinitive directly follows the verb in sentence 2a. The infinitive follows the object of the verb in sentence 2b.

   Verb + Infinitive (lines 31–40)
   line 31: started to get
   line 40: agreed to lose

   Verb + Object + Infinitive (lines 31–40)
   line 32: (not) to keep Stempel
   line 37: convinced Van Doren to cheat
   line 38: told Stempel to give

B1: Listening for Form (p. 400)

	INFINITIVE	NO INFINITIVE
2.	✓	
3.		✓
4.		✓
5.	✓	
6.		✓
7.	✓	
8.	✓	

B2: Working on Infinitives (p. 400)

2. a, b
3. b
4. a
5. a, b

6. b
7. a, b
8. a
9. b
10. a, b

B3: Working on *In Order* + Infinitive (p. 401)

2. We left early in order to get good seats. OR We left early to get good seats.

3. In order to stay awake, I drink coffee. OR I drink coffee in order to stay awake.

4. In order to get a scholarship, you need to do well in school. OR You need to do well in school to get a scholarship.

5. To get a better job, she's going to study English. OR She's going to study English in order to get a better job.

6. I didn't tell her about losing the money to avoid an argument. OR In order to avoid an argument, I didn't tell her about losing the money.

B4: Working on *It* Subject . . . + Infinitive (p. 401)

2. It takes time to learn a language well.
3. It is expensive to eat in restaurants.
4. It costs a lot to fly first class.
5. It is important not to tell lies.
6. It seems better to talk about your problems.
7. It is dangerous to drive on icy roads.
8. It is wise not to smoke.

Examining Meaning and Use (p. 402)

1. a. I left the house early in order <u>to arrive</u> on time.
   b. She hated <u>to eat</u> alone.
   c. It isn't easy <u>to leave</u> your family.

2. Sentences b and c express a feeling about an activity. The infinitive in sentence a expresses a reason for doing something.

C1: Listening for Meaning and Use (p. 403)

	TO EXPRESS A LIKE, DISLIKE, OR WANT	TO GIVE A REASON FOR DOING SOMETHING
2.		✓
3.	✓	
4.		✓
5.	✓	
6.	✓	
7.		✓
8.		✓

C2: Expressing Likes and Dislikes (p. 404)

Answers will vary. Some examples are:
2. to stay out late on Saturday night.
3. to vote in elections.
4. to eat fast food.
5. to go to the movies.
6. to get presents.

C3: Giving Reasons (p. 404)

Answers will vary. Some examples are:
2. (In order) to test their strength.

3. (In order) to relax.
4. (In order) to get a better job.
5. (In order) to borrow books.
6. (In order) to earn money.

C4: Rephrasing Gerunds and Infinitives (p. 404)

A. 2. It's not easy to learn to type.
3. Driving across the country will take several days.
4. It will be fun to go camping.
5. It isn't nice to ignore people.
6. Taking a vacation doesn't have to cost a lot.

B. Answers will vary.

Examining Meaning and Use (p. 405)

Sentences 2a and 2b have the same meaning. Sentences 1a and 1b have different meanings.

D1: Listening for Meaning and Use (p. 406)

2. same
3. different
4. same
5. different
6. same

D2: Contrasting Gerunds and Infinitives (p. 407)

2. to finish
3. seeing
4. getting
5. to make
6. to quit

D3: Rephrasing Gerunds and Infinitives (p. 407)

A. *Conversation 1*
3. no change possible

Conversation 2
1. like cooking
2. prefer eating out

B. *Conversation 1*
1. like to work
2. no change possible

Conversation 2
1. no change possible
2. began to write

D4: Making Suggestions (p. 408)

A. Answers will vary. Some examples are:
3. Remember to do stretching exercises before you do any activity.
4. Avoid eating fast food, smoking cigarettes, and drinking too much alcohol.
5. Try to keep to a regular exercise schedule.
6. Consider asking a friend to be your exercise partner.
7. Don't stop exercising if you can't get to the gym. Do something at home, like working out with an exercise video.
8. Finally, don't forget to drink plenty of water before, during, and after you exercise.

B. Answers will vary.

E1: Thinking About Meaning and Use (p. 409)

2. b
3. a
4. b

5. a
6. b

E2: Editing (p. 410)

2. It is useful ^to have an extra key for your house.
3. I was starting ~~saying~~ *to say* something when he interrupted.
4. correct
5. In order ^to get your driver's license, you have to take a test.
6. She stopped ~~to smoke~~ *smoking* a few years ago. She feels much better now.
7. I'm looking forward to ~~finish~~ *finishing* this report.
8. She needs to pass this course ~~for~~ *in order* to graduate.

CHAPTER 22

A3: After You Read (p. 412)

8
4
5
7
2
1
6
3

Examining Form (p. 414)

1. The phrasal verb has an object (*the stove*) in 1a.
Circle: the stove
The phrasal verb does not have an object in 1b.
2. Circle: *the stove*; the stove
The object comes after the phrasal verb in 2a. The object separates the phrasal verb in 2b.

B1: Listening for Form (p. 416)

2. up
3. out
4. up
5. up
6. out
7. off
8. along

B2: Working on Separable Phrasal Verbs (p. 416)

2. Fill the application out.
Fill it out.
3. He tried his new suit on.
He tried it on.
4. You should call Bill up after lunch.
You should call him up after lunch.
5. She dropped her daughter off.
She dropped her off.
6. I put my warm coat on.
I put it on.
7. Please take the garbage out.
Please take it out.
8. I can't figure this problem out.
I can't figure it out.

B3: Working on Inseparable Phrasal Verbs (p. 416)

2. 'll look after him
3. is coming by for me / is going to come by
4. looks up to her
5. to go over it
6. do without it
7. ran out of them
8. put up with it

B4: Working on Transitive and Intransitive Phrasal Verbs (p. 417)

A. 2. <u>came across</u>　transitive
3. <u>drop by</u>　intransitive
4. <u>pick up</u>　transitive
5. <u>called off</u>　transitive
6. <u>go over</u>　transitive
7. <u>left out</u>　transitive
8. <u>took off</u>　intransitive

B. 2. no change possible
4. We have to be there at 11, so I'll pick the boys up at 10.
5. The weather was terrible, so they called the race off.
6. no change possible
7. You might have left a word out here.

It is not possible to change some of the sentences because they contain inseparable phrasal verbs.

Examining Meaning and Use (p. 418)

1. c
2. a
3. b

C1: Listening for Meaning and Use (p. 419)

2. a
3. a
4. b
5. a
6. b
7. b
8. a
9. b
10. a
11. a
12. b

C2: Rephrasing Phrasal Verbs (p. 420)

2. Before you give me your test, you should <u>review</u> your work very carefully.
3. If you've finished your dinner, I'll <u>remove</u> your plates.
4. If some people can't come today, maybe we should <u>postpone</u> the meeting.
5. I need the dictionary for a minute; I'll <u>return</u> it to you right away.
6. Can you help me <u>choose</u> a dress for tonight?

C3: Understanding Phrasal Verbs (p. 420)

2. pick up
3. broke down
4. called up
5. turn up
6. got out
7. check out
8. catch up

D1: Thinking About Meaning and Use (p. 421)

2. a
3. b
4. a
5. a
6. b

D2: Editing (p. 422)

2. Tom is always on time; you can count ~~out~~ ^{on} him.
3. I haven't seen your book, but I'll tell you if I come across ^{it}.
4. The doctor told me to cut ~~salt~~ down on ^{salt}.
5. correct
6. It's not a very good paper; I might do ^{it} over ~~it~~.